DYNAMIC TEACHING
for DEEPER READING

DYNAMIC TEACHING
for DEEPER READING

Shifting to a Problem-Based Approach

Vicki Vinton

HEINEMANN
Portsmouth, NH

Heinemann
361 Hanover Street
Portsmouth, NH 03801–3912
www.heinemann.com

Offices and agents throughout the world

The author and publisher wish to thank those who have generously given permission to reprint borrowed material:

Figures 3.1 and 3.2: Adapted from *Unlocking Creativity: A Teacher's Guide to Creativity Across the Curriculum* by Robert Fisher and Mary Williams, Editors. Copyright © 2004 by Robert Fisher, Mary Williams, and the individual contributors. Published by Routledge, an imprint of the Taylor Francis Group. Reproduced by permission of Taylor & Francis Books UK.

Credits continue on p. vi

Cataloging-in-Publication Data is on file with the Library of Congress.
ISBN: 978-0-325-07792-5

Editor: Katie Wood Ray
Production editors: Sonja Chapman and Patty Adams
Typesetter: Valerie Levy, Drawing Board Studios
Cover photography and retouching: D. A. Wagner
Cover photo-illustration © D. A. Wagner
3D paper swarm: Robert Bowen
Cover design: Suzanne Heiser
Interior design: Susan Godel
Manufacturing: Steve Bernier

Printed in the United States of America on acid-free paper
21 20 19 18 17 RWP 1 2 3 4 5

To the readers of
To Make a Prairie,
who regularly renew my faith in the intelligence
and commitment of teachers

Contents

Acknowledgments

ERNEST HEMMINGWAY ONCE SUPPOSEDLY SAID, "There is nothing to writing. All you do is sit down at a typewriter and bleed." I didn't actually bleed for this book (nor did I use a typewriter), but writing is seldom easy for me. Rewarding, satisfying, invigorating, yes, but rarely simple or painless. And in addition to my passion for the work and ideas you'll find in this book, what kept me going when the going got tough was the support, inspiration, and feedback of the following people whom it's my honor to acknowledge here.

At the top of the list is my editor Katie Wood Ray, who read virtually every draft I wrote with a keen eye and the same piercing intelligence she brought to her own books about writing. Katie helped me find a structure for this book, which I find is often the most challenging part of writing, and her penetrating comments and questions helped push, clarify, and solidify my thinking at every step of the way. Endless thanks also goes to the many districts and schools that offered me invaluable opportunities to try out ideas in classrooms and workshops—and to the teachers, coaches, and administrators who pushed me to make the complex work of helping students become deep, insightful readers more actionable and concrete. In particular I want to thank Anthony Day, the Superintendent of the Sweet Home School District in upstate New York, and his amazing team of literacy coaches, Jacquie Stablewski, Mikal Brennan, Amy Zach, Holly Olmstead, and Heather Reichmuth; Anna Commitante, the Director of New York City's Department of Education's Office of Curriculum, Instruction, and Professional Development and Christine Cassidy and Eric Grow of the Los Angeles Unified School District, who, from opposite sides of the country, gave me the chance to work with stellar coaches and teachers; Charlotte Butler and her team of teacher leaders and district coaches in Aurora, Colorado; and the following schools in New York City where many of the classrooms examples took place: P.S. 105, P.S. 247, and M.S. 366 in Brooklyn, P.S. 51 in Manhattan, and P.S. 35, P.S. 45, P.S. 48, and P.S. 80 in Staten Island.

Additionally, I want to thank the dear friends and colleagues whose thinking directly contributed to this book: Terri Smith-Chavira, Fran McVeigh, Catherine Flynn, and Katherine Bomer, who each offered useful, timely, and deeply appreciated feedback on individual chapters; Steve Peterson, who, in addition to sharing the story about the students reading *The Blue Ghost*, helped me see the power of "What if?" questions; Mary

Lee Hahn, who helped me see the possibility of playoff game brackets to support thinking; Collette Bennett, who introduced me to the seventeen-page Screenwriters' Rule; Lucy West and my colleagues at Metamorphosis, who introduced me to the concept of rich tasks and the rapid (versus gradual) release of responsibility; and Renee Dinnerstein and Matt Glover, who invited me to join a study group going to Reggio Emilia, Italy, to consider the implications of their socioconstructivist approach to teaching on literacy instruction here at home, which profoundly impacted my thinking.

I'd also like to thank Lisa Fowler and the wonderful production and design team at Heinemann for collaborating with my partner David Wagner to first envision and then create the stunning image for the cover. David also believed in my ability to write this book, even when my own faith faltered—and were it not for his endless patience and support, this book might still be unfinished.

Foreword

ARE THERE ANY ORIGINAL IDEAS LEFT? If you google that question, you get about 175,000,000 hits in less than a second. It seems I'm not the only one to wonder. Though I didn't read 175,000,000 responses, the answer seems to be yes . . . and no. So let's slim down the question a bit. Are there any original ideas left in education? That takes us to about 140,000,000 responses. Let's try, "Are there any ideas left in teaching reading?" This time we're down to about 125,000,000. And the answer still seems to be yes . . . and no.

I'm going to take the liberty of answering the question in the context of the book you're about to read, *Dynamic Teaching for Deeper Reading: Shifting to a Problem-Based Approach*. Using a problem-based approach to teach reading will be, to many, an original idea. There. I've answered it. In this book, Vicki Vinton develops what will be, to many, a wholly original approach to teaching reading. To those readers who may find themselves skeptical at the thought of a truly original idea in the teaching of reading, I acknowledge that Vicki builds on some truly important ideas from other writers and practitioners as well as lots of her own experiences, but she weaves these concepts together in a way that is, to me, something quite original. And something original in our field is too rare and very exciting.

In *Dynamic Teaching for Deeper Reading*, Vicki asks her readers to consider turning much of what we have learned about reading instruction upside-down. I must confess, I love being told to turn something upside-down! It sparks my sense of adventure and keeps me intellectually engaged. She suggests that we view students as insatiable problem solvers in reading. She invites us to *compose opportunities* for children to discover meaning independently and then to notice and name what they have done rather than always telling them what they're about to do, modeling, and sending them off to do it. She invites us to ask children, "What did you think?" and "How did you figure that out?" after puzzling through a text together. She acknowledges the critical role of the teacher, but, wait for it . . . trusts kids to figure things out. And they do.

This isn't an unfamiliar experience in my own professional life. In my work as a consultant, I'm often asked and always honored to conduct a demonstration lesson in a teacher's classroom while others observe. It's a daunting prospect because I don't know the children. Every lesson is, for me, the first day of school.

But there is a distinct advantage to my work and that is, strangely enough, that I don't know the children! I don't know the labels they've been given; I haven't heard about their behavior last year; I don't know the "home situation;" I don't know their test scores, and I don't know what they supposedly *can't* do. I get to dip them into new learning experiences and stand back to observe what happens. I trust that students can and will rise to the occasion, solve their own problems as readers, think at high levels, and work with a sense of purpose and agency. And they do.

My ignorance is often bliss. There is nothing I love more than seeing a child surprise him or herself by thinking deeply or solving a tricky portion of text by talking it through with another reader. But that's not the way we've typically done things. I wish we could all erase our memories about the way we were taught to read. For so many years teachers, doing the best with what they knew at the time, sat us in our desks and taught us what we needed to know to sound out a word, read a sentence, then a paragraph, then a story, and so on. We sat. We listened. We did what we were told. We tried to copy what the teacher had done, if we were even lucky enough to have a teacher who modeled for us. We answered questions at the end of the stories and nonfiction chapters and somehow some of us were lucky enough to become voracious readers anyway. I cannot recall a single example before college in which I was asked to share an opinion or interpret a text for myself.

Vicki wants children to have the thinking experiences many of us waited decades for—now! She argues that we need to create opportunities with increasingly complex thinking challenges to help students discover multiple meanings in text, providing appropriate levels of scaffolding along the way. She says, "To me, that means seeing teaching as being less about explaining or showing students how to do things and more about creating and facilitating opportunities for them to learn through exploration, problem-solving, and discovery." She includes invaluable information about helping children with book selection, and suggests that we shift our focus from complex texts to complex thinking about texts. She argues that book selection isn't as much about level or lexile; in fact, she points out a number of examples where the stated level or lexile is ridiculously out of synch when comparing books or considering our background knowledge about the books.

What we're talking about here is the difference between a deductive and an *inductive* approach. In a deductive approach, the teacher begins with a general statement, gives examples, possibly models and then asks students do to the same work independently. In an inductive approach, we turn the process upside-down. We watch children create approximations and examples in their work and then notice and name what they have done. We then tell them what other readers do in order to comprehend and what they can do, not just in the book they're reading now, but in virtually any book. In small groups, children problem solve their way, through dynamic interchanges, into unearthing the meaning, exchanging ideas to persuade their peers, coming to common conclusions (sometimes!).

As Vicki says, "Once I set students up to *problem solve* by articulating an initial teaching point, I shifted into the role of facilitator. You may also have noticed that, as a facilitator, I used a combination of open-ended and text-dependent questions to elicit the students' thinking, and I regularly paused to notice and name both *what* and *how* they were thinking and making meaning." Vicki uses a series of "Core Practices" with real books and actual conversations with kids to show exactly how this can work in the classroom.

I particularly loved the chapter on pursuing an inductive approach when children are reading independently. Her approach to conferring when the teacher is unfamiliar with the text is just plain useful. She shows us how children reading books they have chosen can still engage in problem solving in the quiet of their minds and hearts.

This is also a provocative book—in the best way. When I read about ideas that I have toyed with but never considered as an approach as I have in this book, that book is original to me. It lays out a more comprehensive structure to approaches I've been toying with in the classroom. I deeply appreciate it when an author pulls it all together like that.

And, there are ideas about which I have nagging questions in this book. I don't find myself wholly affirmed or agreeing with every premise in *Dynamic Teaching for Deeper Reading*. I disagree outright now and then; I'm provoked into merging some of my existing ideas with those Vicki presents; I whole-heartedly embrace most.

This is exactly what I think we should experience in reading a professional text. It should challenge some of our long-held ideas about practice. It should cause us to think about our craft in new ways—and we should feel ourselves pushing back in others. When you sit down to discuss the ideas in this book, I wish nothing more than that those discussions are dynamic (see title of the book!!) and argumentative (in a civil way, of course!) and provocative. I hope you and your colleagues are stirred and inspired and that you experience a great deal of cognitive dissonance. Are we really a profession if we don't spar a bit? Are we engaging in spirited and informed discourse if we don't?

Ken Robinson says "Creativity is the process of having original ideas that have value." *Dynamic Teaching for Deeper Reading* differentiates between critical thinking and creative thinking, by the way, which is an original and exciting notion in and of itself! Dig in—the book you're about to read is both creative and original.

—Ellin Oliver Keene
October, 2016

INTRODUCTION
Plunging into *Dynamic Teaching* for Deeper Reading

The only way to make sense of change is to plunge
into it, move with it, and join the dance.
—Alan Watts

Many years ago, before my grandmother died, she marveled at how the world had changed during her lifetime. Having grown up with a horse and wagon in the farmland that's now the New York borough of Queens, she lived to see a man walk on the moon on her own color TV. That breadth of change—from horses to rockets and from hand-cranked Victrolas to color TVs—seems incredible. But while I've often thought that I wouldn't see such sweeping change in my own lifetime, I've increasingly found myself almost dizzy from the speed with which the world of education has changed since Dorothy Barnhouse and I first started writing *What Readers Really Do* (2012). At that point, the Common Core State Standards (CCSS) were still being drafted, so terms like *close reading*, *performance-based tasks*, and *text-dependent questions* had not yet entered the average teacher's lexicon—let alone stirred up the kind of controversy that led *The Atlantic* writer John Tierney to predict a coming revolution in public education and *Education Week*'s Michele McNeil to report, "Not since the battles over school desegregation has the debate about public education been so intense and polarized" (2013). Other terms such as *grit*, *productive struggle*, and *mindsets* hadn't yet become buzzwords, nor had technology-inspired practices, such as flipped classrooms and maker-movement projects, come on the scene.

Friends and colleagues who've worked in education for longer than even I have say they've seen this before. A pendulum is swinging, they say, and it will swing back again. But I wonder if there's something more to these changes than pendulum swings and trends—something, in fact, as life changing as my grandmother's journey from horses to spaceships. Consider for a moment these mind-reeling facts from a fascinating—and slightly scary—video called "Did You Know? Shift Happens":

- There are about 540,000 words in the English language; about 5× as many as during Shakespeare's time.

- It is estimated that a week's worth of *The Times* contains more information than a person was likely to come across in a lifetime in the 18th century.

- In 1900, human knowledge doubled every 100 years. In 2014, [it] doubled every thirteen months. By 2020, [it] will double every twelve hours.

- Researchers predict that 65% of today's grade schoolers will hold jobs that don't yet exist . . . using technologies that haven't been invented in order to solve problems we don't even know are problems yet. (Fisch, McLeod, and Brenman 2014)

These facts all speak to the unprecedented speed at which the world is changing and to the exponentially growing amount of information in it. And I think they have serious implications for what needs to happen in schools in general and in the teaching of reading in particular.

 ## IMPLICATIONS FOR TEACHING READING IN A COMPLEX, CHANGING WORLD

It's quite possible that the Common Core State Standards will be one of the casualties of all of this rapid change, as more families opt their children out of Common Core standardized tests and more states withdraw their support. It's worth noting, however, that many of the states that have abandoned the CCSS have simply rebranded them as their state standards, with only minimal changes—and even those who've made more sweeping revisions have preserved key elements. So throughout this book I'll use the Common Core State Standards as a benchmark or reference through which I'll explore and question assumptions, practices, and beliefs.

For instance, the Common Core creators believe we best prepare students for that future by throwing them into complex texts that are often way beyond their ability to navigate and by building their vocabulary and content knowledge through the reading of complex nonfiction. But that's not quite how I see it. That's not to say we shouldn't help students build robust vocabularies and become more informed about the world. But given the ever-increasing volume of both information and words, we simply can't teach the background behind every cultural, historical, scientific, or geographic reference or allusion an author might make or every word students might encounter in every text they read.

Additionally, with all the human knowledge that's being generated at such mind-boggling speed, what we teach as fact today might not be so tomorrow. Pluto, for instance, is no longer a planet. New evidence has shown that people were living in North and South America much earlier than was thought—and they may not have crossed the Bering land bridge to get here. And who can keep up with the thinking about dinosaurs? First we learn brontosauruses never existed and now comes the startling news that many were covered with feathers or fluff, even those who didn't fly. The bottom line is that if building content knowledge is the end goal, Google is there, ever at the ready, to give us whatever information we may need faster than it takes us to type a few words or questions into its search engine. But if we are not teaching content knowledge and vocabulary, then what?

For me the answer is *thinking*, specifically the kind of thinking we're asking students to engage in as they read. Is it the kind that fosters the habits and dispositions of critical *and* creative problem solvers and thinkers, which Tony Wagner and Ted Dintersmith, the authors of *Most Likely to Succeed: Preparing Our Kids for the Innovation Era* (2015), say will be needed in our rapidly changing and complex world as much as, if not more than, vocabulary and content knowledge? Or do we save that for science, math, or a one-period-a-week Genius Hour? And what kind of thinking are we, as teachers, engaged in when we plan and implement reading instruction? Are we being critical and creative problem solvers as well? And are we using those capacities not just to find resources or engaging lesson hooks, but to nurture independent thinking as students are actually reading?

From my own work and professional reading, I know many teachers are actively engaged in trying to solve the problems their students face. But I also know that, in the current culture of mandates, accountability, and "fidelity" to programs, the answer is often no. Recently, for instance, the Education Trust, a nonprofit advocacy group dedicated to educational equity, published a study that looked at the kinds of reading assignments and tasks students were being asked to do in the age of the Common Core (Santelises and Dabrowski 2015). One of the group's major findings was that "many—if not most—assignments were over-scaffolded . . . [with] much of the work actually done for the students rather than by them" (4). And the researchers took particular aim at close-reading and text-annotation assignments, which they said "were so tightly scripted they actually appeared to interfere with the deep understanding of complex text" (4).

To be fair to teachers everywhere, many of the Education Trust's findings are directly related to one of the Common Core State Standards' ELA Shifts, which call for teachers to "provide appropriate and necessary scaffolding and supports so that it is possible for students reading below grade level" to make "the require[d] 'step' of growth" up what they call the "staircase of complexity" (Achieve et al. 2013, 6). This do-whatever-it-takes approach to getting students through complex texts, however, often results in teachers crossing the boundary between scaffolding and rescuing, which Terry Thompson calls "scaffolding's evil twin brother" (2010). Rescuing occurs whenever we're more concerned with reaching the objective of a lesson or finishing a task than with building students' agency as thinkers and learners. And that line gets crossed the moment a teacher is doing more work than the students.

Unfortunately, rescuing can happen not only with Common Core–style close-reading lessons but with strategy instruction as well, where scaffolding—be it through modeling, prompting, or the use of graphic organizers—is often offered as a matter of course, whether students need it or not. Additionally, as strategy instruction advocate P. David Pearson notes in *Comprehension Going Forward*, too often comprehension strategies are being taught in isolation, severed from "the goal of acquiring knowledge and insight" (2011, 251). In fact, the combination of overscaffolding and the tendency to teach strategies as ends unto themselves, rather than as means to arrive at deeper meaning, led him and the book's other contributors to conclude that strategy instruction "stands in need of reform" (250).

What's interesting here is that from two different camps, both the Education Trust and the contributors to *Comprehension Going Forward* think it's time to reimagine how we teach students to read and think deeply. And they both believe this reimagining is needed because, as The Education Trust puts it, some of "the implementation approaches we have chosen are overly mechanical, denying the dynamic nature of teaching needed for strategic thinking" (Santelises and Dabrowski 2015, 18).

And here's where *Dynamic Teaching for Deeper Reading* comes in.

 ## WHAT THIS BOOK OFFERS

This book offers an answer to the "What next?" question both *Comprehension Going Forward* and the Education Trust raise. I'll show you how students can become the insightful and passionate readers and learners we all want them to be—*and* the critical and creative problem solvers and thinkers they'll need to be in our increasingly complex world. The book builds on the process of meaning making that *What Readers Really Do* explored, though if I've done my job well enough, it can be read as a stand-alone text. Unlike that earlier book, however, this one looks at both fiction and nonfiction as well as explicitly connects the work to all of the shifts, concepts, and terms that have cropped up over the last four years, from *close reading* to *mindsets* and from *grit* to *complex texts*. It will also more explicitly help you build your own capacities as a problem solver and thinker as well as develop a repertoire of dynamic teaching moves. And it will deepen your understanding of what it means to read closely and deeply so that you can, in the words of Lucy Calkins, "outgrow yourself" as a reader in order to both meet the higher demands the Common Core has set and enjoy what you read even more.

To accomplish this, the book is divided into two main sections: "On Beliefs and Big Ideas" and "On Problems and Practice." The first section consists of four chapters, each of which establishes a theoretical foundation and framework for the chapters on practice that follow. I've chosen this structure for the same reason Katie Wood Ray chose it for her book *Study Driven*: "because it represents one of my most fundamental beliefs about teaching: that best practice is always *informed* practice" (2006, xii). Here, this means the practices I share in this book all grow out of the big ideas and beliefs you'll see in Section 1, where you'll find the following:

- Chapter 1 offers a vision of what complexity really means and how to tackle it by shifting from a skills-based to a meaning-based focus in curriculum, and from a direct instruction to an inquiry or problem-based approach in teaching

- Chapter 2 examines a more holistic approach to preparing students for college and careers by shifting the emphasis from complex texts to complex thinking

- Chapter 3 explores thinking: what it means to think critically, where and how creative thinking fits in, and what it really means to read closely and deeply

- Chapter 4 looks at the complex relationship between teaching and learning

If you're the kind of reader, however, who likes to see what things look like in action before considering the bigger ideas, feel free to jump into Section Two first and use the cross-reference notes you'll find there to dip back into Section One as needed. The chapters in Section Two focus on how to create and implement dynamic learning opportunities that set students up to solve the kinds of problems texts pose at the literal, inferential, and thematic levels. Each of those chapters will

- explore a specific problem texts pose for readers;
- share a classroom example of students wrestling with that problem, with me facilitating their thinking process through responsive feedback versus scaffolding;
- explain a handful of core planning and facilitating practices;
- include an "Understanding a Problem-Based Approach" section, which explores a particular aspect of problem-based teaching, such as the role of questioning and the nature of the task;
- offer a "Steering the Ship" chart that summarizes the teaching moves from the classroom; and
- close with a "Why This Work Matters" section, which connects the chapter's work to larger issues and questions in the field of education—and life.

Additionally, between these chapters, you'll find "Considering Complexity" interludes, which detail other problems texts can pose for readers and offer resources, strategies, and tips for how to help students navigate them. Together, all these pieces form a whole that can support you in applying and transferring the thinking to your own grade, classroom, or school. And in the very next chapter, you'll begin to see why thinking about the whole, instead of pieces, is important. But before you dive in, let me acknowledge the following.

I recognize that what I'm proposing in this book may seem like one more hoop someone's asking you to jump through, one more shift you're being told to make. On the heels of all the change and upheaval that has come with the CCSS—and all the blaming and belittling of teachers that has been unleashed as well—you have reason to feel that way. All I ask is that you read forward, as the philosopher Francis Bacon says, "not to contradict and confute; nor to believe and take for granted; . . . but to weigh and consider" (Bacon {1625} 1986, 209). Just consider, as change swirls all around us, and then see what you think.

SECTION
ONE

On Beliefs and Big Ideas

To believe in something, and not to live it, is dishonest.
—Mahatma Gandhi

WHETHER WE'RE FULLY AWARE OF IT OR NOT, every single one of us comes with a set of beliefs and assumptions about children, learning, and teaching that affect the actions and decisions we make in classrooms each day. In each of these chapters, I share my own beliefs about the purpose of education, what children need from us, and why reading is so important, and along with those beliefs, I explore some big ideas, from "What does it mean to be college and career ready in a world that's rapidly changing?" to "What does it really mean to think critically, read closely, and learn?"

I offer these in the hope they can become shared beliefs. But I also hope they inspire you to question, reflect on, and clarify your own beliefs and assumptions. For I believe that it's only when we're aware of what we believe and assume that we can look squarely at our own teaching practices to assess their effectiveness and impact—and be the teachers our students need us to be.

The Necessity of a Problem-Based Approach to Teaching Reading

If we teach today as we taught yesterday,
we rob our children of tomorrow.
—John Dewey

In January 2000, at the start of the new millennium, the great physicist Stephen Hawking made the prediction that this would be "the century of complexity." Given that the word *complexity* comes up in almost any discussion of literacy these days (especially when it comes to texts), his comment seems almost prescient. But what, exactly, did he mean by the word? Surely not Lexile levels. So I typed the words "complexity Hawking" into Google and ran one of the 3.5 billion searches Google responds to each day. In less than half a second, Google brought me about 383,000 results, the second of which was a link to an article titled "What Is Complexity?" from the Washington Center for Complexity and Public Policy (Sanders 2003). Clicking on the link, I discovered this useful definition: "Simply stated, complexity arises in situations where an increasing number of independent variables begin interacting in interdependent and unpredictable ways."

If you take in the news at any hour of any day on any kind of device, you'll see all sorts of situations that meet this definition, whether they're in the Middle East, the rain forest, or the far reaches of the galaxy. In fact, complexity can occur almost everywhere you look. The Washington Center for Complexity notes, for instance, that traffic is a complex system, as is the weather, the immune system, and the stock market. And by this definition, I'd say classrooms are complex, if for no other reason than they're filled with twenty or more unique individuals, each full of surprises and contradictions, different histories, personalities, and moods, all interacting in interdependent and often unpredictable ways.

Reading is also highly complex because it involves a slew of cognitive, linguistic, and sociocultural processes that all must somehow work together, often simultaneously, in order for words and texts to have meaning. And reading is even more complex if we see it not just as the ability to decode words or even to comprehend what those words mean literally (which is sometimes challenging enough), but also as the ability to interpret and consider what the author might be trying to say about the human condition. Texts, of course, can also be complex—not only in the way the Common Core authors define them. And when you add the complexity of teaching to the complexity of reading and texts all happening in the complex world of a classroom, you've got, in the words of Jerry Lee Lewis, a whole lotta complexity goin' on.

 # TACKLING COMPLEXITY

For many of us, the word *complexity* connotes something hard and possibly unpleasant, with the idea of tackling it conjuring up images of hugging a cactus or wrestling with a bear. The good news, though, is that while the Washington Center for Complexity and Policy doesn't focus on education per se, it offers a few more useful ideas not only about *what* complexity is but *how* to tackle it. According to T. Irene Sanders (n.d.), the center's executive director, complex situations require a particular kind of thinking that takes into account how multiple variables interact. That thinking involves "putting the pieces together, rather than taking them apart, [which] allows you to see connections, relationships and patterns of interactions" (3). It also "requires a big picture view of situations and a synthetic approach," and that's quite different from how people have traditionally addressed complex systems, by employing "the typical analytic mindset, which . . . stud[ies] smaller and smaller pieces of a big question" (3).

The Problem: A Focus on Pieces

Unfortunately, that analytic mindset permeates the Common Core reading standards and the programs and approaches they've spawned. Students are repeatedly asked to analyze particular aspects of a text—the development of a character, a text's structure, an author's choice of words—rather than to think more deeply about how those pieces all work together in complex and meaningful ways. And the key shifts the standards require in literacy deal with the complexity of reading by putting a heavy focus on two separate pieces: vocabulary and content knowledge.

In his latest book, *Making Learning Whole*, David Perkins (2009) of Harvard's Project Zero calls this focus on pieces an "Elements First" approach to teaching. This approach, he explains, aims to help students "ramp into complexity gradually by learning elements now and putting them together later" (3). Too often, however, students never get the chance to put all the elements or pieces together, and he finds this so problematic and troubling that he's dubbed this approach "elementitis," as if it were a disease (4).

When it comes to the teaching of reading, elementitis is at play when we break down the complex process of reading into discrete, separate pieces. We teach strategies, for instance, one at a time, despite the fact that reading for meaning requires using a whole suite of them. We teach literary elements and text structures separately, spending anywhere from a day to a week on, say, character, setting, and problem and solution before moving on to the next. And we create lesson plans addressing individual standards despite the fact that many are involved if we're reading for meaning.

To make matters worse, we also offer students scaffolds that act as shortcuts for more complex work. We provide them with a crib sheet of words, for instance, that signal particular text structures—*although* and *whereas* for compare and contrast, *consequently* for cause and effect. And we teach them that the main idea is often found in the first or last sentence, or can somehow be magically cobbled by stringing key words together. These shortcuts may help students in the short term, but I have to wonder if, by focusing on what's easy and expedient rather than on what's complex, we don't shortchange them in the long run. Those text structure crib sheets, for instance, may help students identify the structure of a nonfiction text. But they may discourage students from attending to how nonfiction writers often explore causes and effects, problems and solutions *and* multiple perspectives in a single text in order to capture the complexity of a topic or issue. And when we give students shortcuts for finding the main idea, we discourage them from engaging in the more complex work of synthesizing the whole, through which main ideas would emerge.

For better or worse, this "skillification" of reading focused on teaching pieces is so ingrained in so many schools that it's hard to imagine what reading with the whole in mind might actually look like. So to make all these complex ideas more concrete—and get a clearer vision of the difference between teaching focused on pieces and teaching focused on the whole—let's read a short excerpt from a text and consider two different ways to approach it.

READING FOR THE WHOLE VERSUS PIECES

Following is the opening of Lois Lowry's *Number the Stars*, a work of historical fiction written for upper-grade students. Try to read it, imagining you have no background knowledge about the time period and history to draw on, and see how much you can figure out just by putting pieces of the text together in order to see connections, relationships, and patterns of interactions—that is, by considering the whole.

> *"I'll race you to the corner, Ellen!" Annemarie adjusted the thick leather pack on her back so that her schoolbooks balanced evenly. "Ready?" She looked at her best friend.*
>
> *Ellen made a face. "No," she said, laughing. "You know I can't beat you. Can't we just walk, like civilized people?"*
>
> *"We have to practice for the athletic meet on Friday. . . . Come on, Ellen," Annemarie pleaded, eyeing the distance to the next corner of the Copenhagen street. "Please?"*
>
> *Ellen hesitated, then nodded. "Oh, all right. Ready," she said.*
>
> *"Go!" shouted Annemarie, and the two girls were off, racing along the sidewalk. . . .*
>
> *Annemarie outdistanced her friend quickly as she sped along, past the small shops and cafés of her neighborhood in northeast Copenhagen. Laughing, she skirted an elderly lady in black. . . . The corner was just ahead.*
>
> *Annemarie looked up, panting, just as she reached the corner. Her laughter stopped. Her heart seemed to skip a beat.*
>
> *"Halte!" the soldier ordered in a stern voice.*
>
> *The German word was as familiar as it was frightening. Annemarie had heard it often enough before, but it had never been directed at her until now.*
>
> *Behind her, Ellen also slowed and stopped. . . .*
>
> *Annemarie stared up. There were two of them. That meant two helmets, two sets of cold eyes glaring at her, and four tall shiny boots planted firmly on the sidewalk, blocking her path to home.*
>
> *And it meant two rifles, gripped in the hands of the soldiers. She stared at the rifles first. Then, finally, she looked into the face of the soldier who had ordered her to halt.*
>
> *"Why are you running?" the harsh voice asked. His Danish was very poor. Three years, Annemarie thought with contempt. Three years they've been in our country, and still they can't speak our language. (1–3)*

If you were able to set your background knowledge aside (which, granted, can be hard), you may have figured out what many of the fourth through sixth graders I've shared this passage with have. The characters are in a place called Copenhagen and, at least in the first half of the passage, it seems like a friendly place where schoolgirls laugh and race down streets lined with shops and cafés. But then something happens and the whole mood changes as the girls encounter two soldiers with rifles, tall boots, and cold eyes who speak a different language. You don't need to know what a Nazi is to grasp that the girls are afraid of them. And if you pretended you didn't know the words *halte*, *Danish*, and *contempt*, you might have done what many students have: wondered if Danish is the language spoken in Copenhagen, if *halte* could mean *stop* in the soldiers' language, and if *contempt* expresses something Annemarie feels toward the soldiers who don't speak her language despite having been in her country for three years.

Of course, not every fourth through sixth grader is able to figure all of that out. But every student I've used this excerpt with has been able to construct what Dorothy Barnhouse and I called in *What Readers Really Do* a "first-draft" understanding of what the whole passage meant, using conditional language, like "might be" or "could mean." And that's very different from what students do when we implement practices focused on teaching pieces.

TEACHING READING WITH A FOCUS ON PIECES

To compare the two approaches, let's look at how you might teach the same passage with a focus on pieces instead of the whole. You might, for instance, begin with what Doug Lemov, the author of the hugely popular *Teach Like a Champion*, says is one of the techniques effective teachers use: preteaching background material before reading, which is designed to "prevent misunderstandings before they crop up rather than remediating them afterward" (2010, 285). In this case that would mean teaching the students about the setting by providing some background information on World War II and, perhaps, a quick look at a map to see where Denmark and Germany are.

After that, you might preteach vocabulary, which, depending on your students, might include the words *adjusted*, *pleaded*, *outdistanced*, *helmet*, *halt*, and *contempt*. Or you might ask students to read the passage and circle the words they don't know and then try to figure out their meaning using context clues—which wouldn't necessarily mean thinking about the whole, only about a sentence or two before and after the word. Once that was done, you would move on to the heart of your lesson, which would focus on more pieces. With a workshop approach, for example, you might offer a minilesson on genre, a literary element, or a strategy or skill and then ask students to do one of the following, after modeling the teaching point through a think-aloud:

- fill out a T-chart to distinguish between factual and fictional details
- identify the characters, setting, and/or point of view on a worksheet
- infer a character trait for each of the girls based on what they do, think, and say
- practice an individual comprehension strategy, such as questioning, predicting, or envisioning
- practice a skill, such as annotating or summarizing

On the other hand, if you use text-dependent questions to support close reading of texts, you'd ask students to answer questions aligned to particular standards, such as "Why did Annemarie's heart skip a beat?" which would involve students in the work of the first CCSS anchor reading standard: to "read closely to determine what the text says explicitly and to make logical inference." Questions like these are yet another way of focusing on pieces of a text, and instead of having students use conditional language, you'd probably ask them to use the assertive language of claims and evidence in their responses. And if a poor student were perplexed—or thought Annemarie's heart skipped a beat because she'd lost her breath running—you might once again offer a think-aloud to "help" the student "get" it. Then you'd move on to another piece by asking another text-dependent question.

A More Meaningful Way Forward: A Focus on the Whole

It's possible that by combining several of the pieces-focused activities above, a reader might arrive at an understanding of the whole, but that's not really their purpose. They're meant to build genre knowledge or skills, teach strategies, or meet individual standards, rather than construct meaning, which was the purpose behind what I had you do. As a proficient reader—with background knowledge you might not have been able to ignore— I'm sure you read the *Number the Stars* excerpt with relative ease. But if you could have peered inside your brain as you made sense of the passage, you'd have seen that you were engaged in the same kind of thinking process you'd employ if you were reading a fantasy, science fiction, or a dystopian novel, where you'd have no background knowledge because the setting wouldn't be real.

To see that for yourself, try reading the opening of Suzanne Collins' *The Hunger Games*, imagining this time that you're a reader who has managed not to see the movie or read the book, and see how much you can figure out here.

> *When I wake up, the other side of the bed is cold. My fingers stretch out, seeking Prim's warmth but finding only the rough canvas cover of the mattress. She must have had bad dreams and climbed in with our mother. Of course, she did. This is the day of the reaping.*
>
> *I prop myself up on one elbow. There's enough light in the bedroom to see them. My little sister, Prim, curled up on her side, cocooned in my mother's body, their cheeks pressed together. . . .*
>
> *Sitting at Prim's knees, guarding her, is the world's ugliest cat. . . . Prim named him Buttercup, insisting that his muddy yellow coat matched the bright flower. He hates me. Or at least distrusts me. Even though it was years ago, I think he still remembers how I tried to drown him in a bucket when Prim brought him home. . . . The last thing I needed was another mouth to feed. But Prim begged so hard, cried even, I had to let him stay. . . .*
>
> *I swing my legs off the bed and slide into my hunting boots. . . . I pull on trousers, a shirt, tuck my long dark braid up into a cap, and grab my forage bag. On the table, under a wooden bowl sits a perfect little goat cheese wrapped in basil leaves. Prim's gift to me on reaping day. I put the cheese carefully in my pocket as I slip outside.*
>
> *Our part of District 12 is usually crawling with coal miners heading out to the morning shift at this hour. Men and women with hunched shoulders, swollen knuckles. . . . But today the black cinder streets are empty. Shutters on the squat gray houses are closed. The reaping isn't until two. May as well sleep in. If you can.* (3–4)

Just as many students are able to figure out that Copenhagen is a place where Annemarie and Ellen live and form a first impression of it, you probably figured out that in *The Hunger Games*, the narrator (whose name and gender you actually don't know yet) lives in a place called District 12. You probably thought District 12 seemed bleak because you noticed details about people sleeping on rough canvas sheets, walking down black streets with hunched shoulders, and thinking twice about keeping a cat because of the paucity of food. You might also have figured out that whatever the reaping was, it didn't sound like fun, just as you could figure out that the soldiers in *Number the Stars* were scary without having to know about Nazis.

Academically speaking, readers do this by inferring, though not quite in the way we typically teach and model it, which, if written as an equation, would look like this:

text detail + background knowledge/schema = inference

If you happened to live in a farming community, however, knew the word *reap*, and followed that formula, you might think the reaping was a time to gather crops. But if you were a city kid, you'd be out of luck. If you tried to figure out what the reaping was, though, not by leaving the text to access your schema, but by connecting and fitting details together, you could develop a first-draft understanding of the reaping, which might look like this:

Prim had bad dreams the day of the reaping + the black cinder streets are empty + the shutters on the houses are closed + you might not be able to sleep = the reaping doesn't sound like fun

To be clear, I'm not suggesting that text-to-self, text-to-text, or text-to-world connections have no place in reading. There may, in fact, be some of those hidden in this equation. But the work of making sense of the whole is based more on reasoning and logic than on accessing schema. Additionally, because it involves putting pieces together to see the relationships between and the patterns within them, thinking about the whole is also more complex. And while readers might not have the full picture for either *Number the Stars* or *The Hunger Games* yet, they'll eventually get there as they continue to read and connect and synthesize new details.

Of course, unlike with *The Hunger Games*, the experience of reading *Number the Stars* would definitely be enriched if students learned something about the history as well. But delaying that until students were really engaged with the book—and curious about what was going on—would let them experience the characters' feelings as Annemarie does herself, with the full horror of the situation dawning on her slowly. This is, after all, both the power and the gift of historical fiction: to make us feel, not just know, the weight of history. When we focus on pieces or scaffolds too much, we rob students of fully experiencing that power and gift. We also rob them of the opportunity to figure things out for themselves, an ability they'll need in their complex, unpredictable future—where teachers won't be there to frontload information or vocabulary for whatever they encounter.

LETTING THE TEXT SET THE AGENDA

But how, you might be wondering, do you teach students to think complexly to consider the whole as they read? After all, I simply asked you to read it, without setting any purpose beyond trying to figure out what was going on. I didn't provide any further instruction—or instructions, as in steps or procedures. Nor did I offer an example or a model. I did, however, heed a plea made by David Coleman, one of the chief architects of the Common Core State Standards. He's someone I don't often agree with, but in a speech he gave during the Common Core's rollout, he too argued against the "skillification" of reading, which he called "strategy-of-the-week" instruction, saying:

> Nothing could be more lethal to paying attention to the text in front of you
> than such a hunt and seek mission. Why not instead let the text set the
> agenda? . . . Why not let those strategies emerge to solve real problems rather
> than constantly interrupting us or setting an agenda? . . . [After all,] when
> have you read a difficult text ever in your life and said, "I've got it now. It's a
> cause and effect text not a problem and solution text. Now, I got it." We lavish
> so much attention on these strategies in the place of reading, I would urge us
> to instead read. (2011)

For Coleman, letting the text set the agenda has come to mean having teachers and/or curriculum publishers develop and ask students text-dependent questions, which seems like just another way of imposing an agenda on a text. Here, though, I let the text set the agenda by putting you in a problem-solving stance where you read not to practice a strategy or skill or to answer a text-dependent question, but to wrestle with the "real problems" these texts posed, which in both cases entailed figuring out what kind of world you were in as a reader and why the characters were doing and feeling what they were. And by fitting pieces of the text together and using whatever strategies you had up your sleeve, you developed a first-draft understanding of the big-picture whole.

USING A PROBLEM-BASED APPROACH TO READING

Pedagogically speaking, you could say I used a problem-based approach to teaching reading. I presented you with a text containing problems and set you up to solve them in order to figure out what the text meant, which is, in fact, what authentic readers do with any text they encounter (Barnhouse, Vinton 2012). They have some reason to be reading, and they read to find meaning in the text they've selected. Had we been together in a classroom or a conference or interacting in a webinar, I would have "taught" you by notic-ing and naming what you'd done to solve the problems the text posed in order to make the thinking visible and transferrable to other texts. And if this text were too difficult for you, rather than provide more scaffolding, I would have offered a more accessible one that posed similar problems because, in a problem-based approach, my aim as a teacher is to help you develop your problem-solving capacities as a reader, not to get a particular text.

As a teaching practice, problem-based teaching and learning took off in medical schools in the 1980s as professors shifted from teaching their students through lectures and textbooks to setting them up to solve the kind of complex diagnostic problems they'd experience in the field. Its roots, however, go all the way back to John Dewey, whose words seem as needed today as they were a century ago. Dewey thought learn-ing required thinking, not "a diet of predigested materials" (1938, 46). And believing that "we only think when confronted with a problem," he felt teachers should "give the pupils something to do, not something to learn" (as in strategies or elements). Then "if the doing [were] of such a nature to demand thinking" (as wrestling with a problem is), "learning would naturally result." (1916, 181).

These ideas are back in play now in some math, science, and social studies rooms, where in addition to inquiry- and problem-based learning, you often see students engaged in project-based and maker-movement work. A problem-based approach also takes a prominent place in Elizabeth Green's recent book *Building a Better Teacher* (2014), where she highlights the work of Magdalene Lampert. As a lower-school teacher and then as a professor of education at the University of Michigan, Lampert has helped scores of math teachers shift from teaching procedures and strategies (for what Lampert calls "answer-getting") to letting students wrestle with problems. This wrestling, or what's frequently called productive struggle, helps students not just do the math but also understand the underlying concepts. And that, in turn, promotes the transfer and application of thinking from one problem to another.

Problem-based teaching and learning, however, hasn't gotten much traction in read-ing, where we tend to think that problem solving is needed only at the word level. I'd argue, though, that every text worth its salt begs its readers to consider the questions "What is this text really about?" and "What might the author be trying to show us about what it means to be human in this complex world of ours?" To figure that out, as you'll see throughout the book, readers often have to solve a slew of smaller problems, from figuring out the antecedent of a pronoun to considering why a character might have changed or why a nonfiction writer chose a certain word. And all of that can entail productive strug-gle, which also hasn't taken hold in reading—at least not in the full meaning of the term.

According to Kay Merseth, the director of the Harvard Graduate School of Education's Teacher Education Program, productive struggle is "not about guessing what the teacher wants to hear or about finding a particular answer. It's about the *process of thinking,* making sense and persevering in the face of not knowing exactly how to proceed" (Clyburn 2012). Too often, though, what passes as productive struggle in reading is asking students to persevere through an exceedingly hard text to find a particular answer or to give the teacher what she—or the program she's using—is looking for, which only captures one piece, not the more complex whole, of what's meant by true productive struggle.

My hunch is that a problem-based approach and real productive struggle haven't caught on more in reading because they can't be easily packaged. Additionally, both require lots of active thinking from students and teachers alike. Consider, for instance, TV shows like *House*, where a doctor must somehow figure out what's behind a perplexing array of symptoms, interacting in interdependent and unpredictable ways, before a patient dies—or mankind is wiped out through some horrible pandemic. Usually there are several possible diagnoses and cures that must each be tested, with new complications that spring up unexpectedly, and plenty of detours, wrong turns, and dead ends before the final solution emerges moments before the show ends.

Of course, no one will die during a problem-based reading session, but readers will need to experiment, explore, and test out a variety of ideas, not all of which will pan out, and your challenge will be to figure out how to gently steer the class while preserving the agency of all of your students as readers, which initially can feel daunting. As you'll see, though, in Section Two, there are specific teaching moves you can make with students at any grade with any text—and with practice, these moves can be mastered by any teacher. You will, however, need to consider Magic School Bus driver and teacher extraordinaire Miss Frizzle's advice "to take a risk, make mistakes and get messy" as well as M. Scott Peck's impassioned plea to

> abandon the urge to simplify everything, to look for formulas and easy
> answers, and to begin to think multi-dimensionally, to glory in the mystery
> and paradoxes of life, not to be dismayed by the multitude of causes and
> consequences that are inherent in each experience—to appreciate the fact that
> life is complex. (1993, 14)

And if we believe that life *is* messy and complex, then we need to bring some of that messiness and complexity into our classrooms.

Shifting the Focus from Complex Texts to Complex Thinking

When you want to teach children to think, you begin by treating them seriously when they are little, giving them responsibilities, talking to them candidly . . . and making them readers and thinkers of significant thoughts from the beginning. That's if you want to teach them to think.

—Bertrand Russell

Let me begin by introducing Takayaki. He's a third grader who, perhaps, like some of your students, is a quiet but hard-working English language learner who struggles in the current climate of acceleration and high-stakes testing but still has much to teach us. I met him during an independent reading conference, when he was halfway through Mary Pope Osborne's *Season of the Sandstorms*, a level M book in the Magic Tree House series. According to his teacher, he'd recently moved from level L to level M and was quite proud of that, but when I asked him how the book was going, he lowered his head and confided in a whisper I almost couldn't hear, "It's hard."

I suggested we take a look at the book to see how I could help him, and agreeing, he turned to the page he was on and haltingly read the following passage, stopping often to try to sound out words I doubted he knew the meaning of.

> *Jack tried to open the lid of the box, but he couldn't. In the dark, his finger pressed against a keyhole. "Forget it," he said. "It's locked."*
> *"Shh! Listen!" said Annie.*

> Jack listened. He heard a high-pitched moaning sound. It sounded like music from a violin. Wafting through the dry sand dunes, the haunting music grew louder.
>
> "What is it?" said Jack.
>
> "Uh-oh," said Annie. "Now I hear something else."
>
> Jack held his breath. He heard hooves galloping over the desert. "The bandits!" he said. (44)

When Takayaki finished this section, I asked him what he thought was happening, and having spent so much mental energy on decoding, all he could say was, "They have a box." And when I asked if he had any idea about what was in the box, he answered by lowering his head again—this time without saying a word.

THE CHALLENGES OF COMPLEX TEXTS

Seeing the book through Takayaki's eyes, I, too, thought it was hard—so much so that his teacher and I wondered if it had been mislabeled or misshelved (it hadn't). But *Season of the Sandstorms* is nowhere near as hard as many of the books found in Common Core–aligned reading programs for third grade. One popular program, for instance, has third graders read Seymour Reit's *Behind Rebel Lines,* which tells the real-life story of Emma Edmonds, a young Canadian woman who disguised herself as a man in order to join the Union Army during the Civil War. According to Scholastic's Book Wizard, the book comes with a Lexile level of 830, a Fountas and Pinnell level of T, a grade-level equivalent of 7.2, and an interest level of grades 6–8. To give you a feel for the difficulty of this text, here's an excerpt from Chapter 1, in which Emma Edmonds, dressed in men's clothing, attempts to join the Union Army:

> The line inched slowly along step by step, carrying Emma past a billboard covered with recruiting posters. The words leaped out at her: VOLUNTEERS TO THE RESCUE! . . . PATRIOTISM AND LOVE OF COUNTRY! . . . RUTHLESS TREACHERY! . . . DEFEND OUR NOBLE UNION! . . . VINDICATE THE HONOR OF OUR GLORIOUS FLAG!

> *She frowned at the fancy wording—all that fuss and bombast. Still*
> *she had to admit that was how she really felt—she and thousands of others.*
> *Bother the fancy speeches and flag-waving politicians—the fact was that*
> *alarm bells were ringing everywhere. The country was in peril and had to*
> *be saved.* (3)

Clearly, the gap between where Takayaki is as reader and what *Behind Rebel Lines* demands of its readers is huge. In fact, it's precisely gaps like these that impelled the authors of the CCSS to focus on the reading of complex texts. This focus, however, has risked turning third grade into the new middle school, middle school into the new high school, and high school into the new college, regardless of where students actually are. Insisting that students like Takayaki read a text like *Behind Rebel Lines* seems like the educational equivalent of throwing a child who can barely dog paddle into the deep end of a pool. Some children, of course, do learn to swim that way, though others can develop a fear of water that can last a lifetime. And given how difficult Takayaki found *Season of the Sandstorms*, it's hard to imagine him not feeling frustrated, if not downright defeated, by a text like *Behind Rebel Lines*. We could, of course, follow the do-whatever-it-takes scaffolding approach the Common Core standards and other programs prescribe to get him through it and answer text-dependent questions, like "Why did Emma say the billboard had 'fancy wording'?" and "Which words might be considered 'fancy' and why?" But what would Takayaki learn from all that—beyond, perhaps, that *treachery* is a fancy word? That figuring out a single word is more important than getting the overall meaning? That it's OK if nothing really makes sense as long as you somehow get through it?

One thing seems fairly certain: He'd learn the lesson E. M. Forster warned of when he said that "spoon feeding in the long run teaches us nothing but the shape of the spoon" (2008, 412). And is that what any of us really want for the readers in our rooms?

 ## DIFFERENT VIEWS ABOUT WHAT IT MEANS TO READ

How we choose to address the gap between where readers like Takayaki are and where they need to be to succeed depends on our vision of college and career readiness and of reading itself. As Tom Newkirk wrote in "The Text Itself" (2012), the authors of the CCSS conceive of the act of reading as one of "extraction"—of knowledge, insight, information, and evidence—with the text viewed as a "repository" of those riches. Readers, thus, are like miners in an underground mine, digging out nuggets of ore with pickaxes. And the ultimate point of this extraction is to analyze, gather evidence for claims, and answer text-dependent questions.

This is a dramatically different view of reading than what's envisioned by many others who see reading as an act of *transaction*, not *extraction*. Here, for instance, is how writer Rebecca Solnit described a transactional concept of reading:

> *The object we call a book is not the real book, but its potential, like a musical*
> *score or seed. It exists fully only in the act of being read; and its real home*
> *is inside the head of the reader, where the symphony resounds, the seed*
> *germinates (2013, 63).*

This vision of reading requires readers to bring their whole selves to a text—their feelings, experiences, observations, and thoughts. The authors of the standards, however, want students to stay "within the four corners of the text," which, as Newkirk says, "den[ies] (or compartmentalize[s]) the rich recursive interplay of the personal, generational, cultural, and textual dimensions of reading" (2012).

Like Newkirk, I believe that making students stay within the four corners of a text gives them a sterile and narrow view of reading, which may not be even doable. After all, it seems as impossible to me to leave our lived lives behind when we read as it would be to leave our eyes or our ears. And even if it were possible, is it really desirable? Not, I think, if you believe that reading is a skill needed not only for academic and professional success, but, as Susan Sontag says, also "an education of the heart [that] enlarges your sense of human possibility, of what human nature is, of what happens in the world" (1995).

Clearly, we all want our students to have the opportunity to go to college and/or land a respectable and satisfying job that pays a living wage, and we're keenly aware that an inability to read complex texts can impact their chance to succeed at both. My hunch, though, is that most of us want more for our students than academic and professional success. We want readers who are ready for all sorts of meaningful relationships and the kind of active, engaged civic life that President Obama (2015) spoke of in an interview with writer Marilynne Robinson:

> *When I think about how I understand my role as citizen, setting aside being*
> *president, the most important set of understandings that I bring to that position*
> *of citizen, the most important stuff I've learned I think I've learned from*
> *novels. It has to do with empathy. It has to do with being comfortable with the*
> *notion that the world is complicated and full of grays, but there's still truth*

there to be found, and that you have to strive for that and work for that. And the notion that it's possible to connect with someone else even though they're very different from you.

This kind of learning only happens if readers bring their minds *and* their hearts to a text, and as a teacher of reading, that means I want students to be able to analyze *and* interpret, reason *and* imagine, critique texts objectively *and* respond to them personally. And I want them to do this with real independence and a strong sense of agency and identity as readers, in ways that support academic success *and* a love of reading. This doesn't mean, however, that addressing the gap between where many students are as readers and what they'll be faced with in college and careers isn't a worthy goal. It is. What I'm questioning is how we go about addressing it. In particular, what kinds of texts should we put in students' hands and what should we ask them to do with those?

 ## TOWARD AN ALTERNATIVE APPROACH TO TEXT COMPLEXITY

The Current Thinking on Text Complexity

In Appendix A of the CCSS document, the authors present a text complexity model that has since become the de facto tool for measuring the complexity of texts across the country and in many American schools abroad. This model consists of three factors that teachers and curriculum publishers are asked to consider when choosing texts for whole-class instruction:

1. a text's *quantitative* dimension as determined by Lexile levels, which use a computer algorithm to give a numeric score to a text based on its word frequency and average sentence length

2. a text's *qualitative* dimension, which looks at the complexity of a text's structure, meaning, language features, and knowledge demands, as determined by an individual or team, often using a rubric

3. *the reader and the task*, which includes often unpredictable variables such as the experience and motivation of the reader and the complexity of the task itself

Each of these factors is supposed to be given equal weight and consideration, but if you look at the kinds of texts that appear in both curriculum material and standardized tests, you'll see several patterns emerge: First, students are being asked to read texts with very high Lexile levels—often, as with *Behind Rebel Lines*, higher than what the standards have set as the range for a grade band to read. Second, when it comes to the qualitative dimension, you'll find a preponderance of texts like *Behind Rebel Lines* that come with particularly challenging vocabulary and lots of knowledge demands, which reflects the standards' overall emphasis on vocabulary and content knowledge, versus meaning and structure.

Then there's the reader and the task, about which the Common Core has little to say. The teaching material that comes with *Behind Rebel Lines*, for instance, suggests that teachers "remind students they may need to adjust their reading rate as they encounter unfamiliar words" and prompt them "to look for context clues that can help with understanding" (2013, 23). It does not, however, suggest that teachers should choose a different text, only that they continue to scaffold until the students get it. This means that too often teachers are doing the heavy lifting, nudging and prodding students toward whatever it is they're supposed to get—and if that fails, simply telling them.

Looking at this model through the lens of complexity, you could say the standards writers haven't attended to how these three factors interact in interdependent and unpredictable ways. Instead they've employed that old analytic mindset. And they've done so to the detriment not only of students like Takayaki, but of everyone who'll inherit an even more complex world than we can imagine.

A New Way to Think About Text Complexity

For all these reasons, I believe we need a more complex approach to both measuring and reading complex texts. Bringing readers more fully into the picture would, by itself, do much to meet that goal, but I think we need to also reconsider the quantitative and qualitative dimensions as the CCSS define them. Lexile levels, for instance, can be problematic because they don't take into account reader-based factors like age appropriateness. Ernest Hemingway's classic *The Sun Also Rises*, about a group of dissolute and war-damaged expatriots living in Spain after World War I, has the same Lexile level as *Clifford Loves Me!*, one of the Clifford, the Big Red Dog picture books—and I'm sure none of us would think Hemingway was appropriate for a Clifford lover.

On the other hand, Fountas and Pinnell reading levels do take into account the age appropriateness of a book. But there's often a spectrum within a given level, with some books being much harder than others—so much so that sometimes the level designations don't make sense. Consider, for instance, the level N book *The Empty Envelope,* by Ron Roy (an A–Z Mysteries book), which Takayaki's classmate Alyssa was reading. I conferred with her right before I sat down with Takayaki, and I found her two-thirds of the way through the book, just about to read this passage:

> *Dink's eyes got big, then he grinned. "It's perfect! If it works, the stamp goes back where it belongs and those two crooks go to jail!"*
>
> *Ruth Rose's first call was to Officer Fallon.*
>
> *The boys listened as she explained about the letters, the stolen stamp, and her plan.*
>
> *Ruth Rose listened, then started nodding. "Uh-huh. Got it. Right. Okay, bye!"*
>
> *"What'd he say?" Dink asked.*
>
> *Ruth Rose gave Dink a thumbs-up. Then she called information and got the number for the Shangri-La Hotel.*
>
> *She dialed, then asked, "Is Doris Duncan there, please?"*
>
> *Ruth Rose grinned at Dink and Josh. She mouthed the words, "They just walked in!"* (60)

If you think this seems much easier than *Season of the Sandstorms,* you're not alone. The vocabulary seems more accessible, the setting is more familiar, and the plot doesn't involve magic or time travel, which can add another layer of challenge for readers. In the Common Core's vision of text complexity, these factors are part of a text's qualitative dimensions, which are supposed to be considered in tandem with a text's quantitative levels. The problem here is that assessing the qualitative features can be time-consuming and challenging—so much so that many states and organizations have developed qualitative-text-complexity rubrics to help assess this dimension. Unfortunately, though, the descriptors in these rubrics are often abstract or vague, or they involve what feels like circular logic—such as saying that a text is highly complex if its meaning is highly complex, which isn't terribly useful. So I propose that we shift from the current vision of text complexity to one that fully acknowledges the role of the most unpredictable piece, the students, by recalibrating the balance between the dimensions in order to ensure that it's students, not teachers, who are doing the thinking (see Figure 2.1).

READING COMPLEX TEXTS WITH LOTS OF TEACHER SCAFFOLDING	READING MORE ACCESSIBLE TEXTS WITH LOTS OF STUDENT THINKING
A high Lexile level	A more reasonable Lexile level
+ some qualitative features (especially around language and knowledge demands)	+ some qualitative features (especially around meaning)
+ lots of scaffolding and support to complete a task focused on a single standard, strategy, or skill	+ minimal scaffolding and support to consider the meaning of a whole text
= students reading complex texts simply	= students reading more accessible texts more complexly

FIGURE 2.1 *Alternative Approaches to Text Complexity*

SET THE TASK ON MEANING

If we let the text set the agenda, the task naturally becomes figuring out what the text means—and I believe that considering and constructing an understanding of a text's meaning should be the purpose of reading, rather than practicing strategies or skills or meeting a particular standard. The late, great Grant Wiggins said this as well when he wrote, "The goal is NOT skill or strategy mastery, but text understanding" (2015). And former ILA president Timothy Shanahan shared some research on his blog that shows that "if you set a specific purpose for reading"—such as practicing a skill or extracting information—"students will do a better job of accomplishing that purpose" but their overall comprehension will suffer. That's because, as Shanahan writes, "when you focus so specifically on a particular idea you are likely to get it, but that leads you to ignore the rest of the text message" (2016).

Of course, making meaning to consider a text's message is not a simple thing. As Dorothy Barnhouse and I wrote in *What Readers Really Do*, comprehension is

> *the floor, not the ceiling, of meaning making. Readers take what they comprehend line-by-line and use that to construct an understanding of the bigger messages, concerns or themes of the text, . . . by connect[ing] the dots of their line-by-line, page-by-page comprehension in order to see a bigger picture that may not have been apparent before. (2012, 42–43)*

This deeper understanding is what I believe we, as teachers, need to aim for, since it's only when we read at this depth that our sense of human possibility is enlarged, we educate our hearts as well as our minds, and we are ready not only for college and careers but for whatever life might bring us.

CONSIDER HOW MUCH A READER HAS TO FIGURE OUT

Because the Common Core State Standards and the curriculum they've spawned have placed such a premium on the acquisition of vocabulary and content knowledge, much reading instruction is focused on texts that put lots of demands on readers at the word and knowledge levels. If, however, you believe that the ability to innovatively solve problems by putting pieces together in order to see connections, relationships, and patterns— that is, by thinking complexly—is equally or even more important, you'll want to choose different kinds of texts. And that's especially the case if you also believe that we need to bring readers more fully into the equation and set the task on meaning.

For this alternate approach to text complexity, you'll want to use texts that are relatively accessible at the word and knowledge levels but offer readers lots of problems to solve at the level of meaning. To be sure, a reader's ability to make meaning can be impacted by words and content knowledge, but problems also occur every time a writer conveys information implicitly instead of stating it directly. Think back, for instance, to the opening of *The Hunger Games;* Suzanne Collins didn't explicitly tell you what the reaping was, but by connecting details, you could figure out it was an event that inspired dread and fear. And if you take another look at *The Empty Envelope*, you'll see that the writer conveys something implicitly there, as well: He doesn't state what Officer Fallon said to Ruth Rose on the phone. But by fitting pieces together and using some logic, you could figure out that he probably told her that the crooks were at the Shangri-La Hotel, which is exactly what Alyssa thought when she read the passage.

SHIFT THE FOCUS FROM TEXTS TO THINKING

Students' ability to solve problems like these affects how much meaning they're able to make, and solving such problems allows them to ultimately wrestle with a text's messages, ideas, or themes, which, once students move beyond fables and simple fact books, are conveyed indirectly. So I propose that rather than using problematic Lexiles and vague rubrics that contain circular reasoning, we assess a text's complexity by how much a reader has to figure out that the writer has conveyed indirectly. In effect, this shifts the focus from the complexity of a text to the complexity of thinking a reader must engage in in order to understand it, and this is critical for several reasons.

If our ultimate goal is truly independence, we need students to do much more thinking than highly scaffolded approaches ask of them—and students simply can't take on more complex thinking if the text is too difficult at the word and knowledge levels. Also, students build their identity and sense of agency as readers when they're the ones doing the work, and as students have more positive and agentive reading experiences, they become more competent and confident. That, in turn, can increase their motivation as thinkers and readers, and as their experiences and motivation change, they'll be far more ready to take on increasingly challenging texts without us having to scaffold so much. That's because this alternate approach can actually change the way the variables of the text complexity model interact, by trading in some of the complexity of texts for the complexity of thinking. And this can happen in a way that doesn't risk destroying a student's interest in reading.

 ## PLANNING FOCUSED ON READERS, NOT TEXTS

When the goal of teaching is for students to read increasingly complex texts, planning is focused on *texts* and the scaffolds students need to get them through those texts. In contrast, when the goal of teaching is for students to engage in more complex thinking, planning is focused on *readers* and what they need to engage in that thinking. It's a shift that requires a more complex approach to planning, but I think the payoffs are huge as students get so much more from their reading than answers to a string of text-dependent questions.

Taking a More Complex Approach to Balanced Literacy

For planning instruction focused on readers, you'll want to use variations of the components of balanced literacy: read-aloud, shared reading, small-group work, and independent reading, plus word study. These components were designed to work together to help students become independent readers through a gradual release of responsibility, where the level of teacher support eases as students move from read-aloud, where the teacher offers maximum support, to independent reading, where support is minimal. By considering how the components interact to support a big-picture goal, balanced literacy takes a complex approach to teaching reading. What it sometimes lacks, though, is a deeper vision of the work of reading that students are being released to do, as well as a more dynamic implementation. So you'll want to adapt and repurpose the components to meet these more complex means and ends by following these five steps:

1. Combine read-aloud and shared reading into a shared interactive read-aloud that gives students access to the text by distributing copies or projecting it. Seeing the author's words this way will support more text-based thinking and talk while you read the text aloud.

2. Hand over the responsibility of making meaning in that read-aloud directly to students, by setting them up to problem solve rather than watch you solve problems. This way they can experience for themselves the whole range of problems readers must deal with to deeply understand a text, while developing a vision of what that thinking looks, sounds, and feels like.

3. Instead of launching independent reading with a minilesson where you demonstrate a strategy or skill, remind students of what they've already done and experienced in the read-aloud and invite them to deliberately try to do that same work in their independent books. This acknowledges that it's far easier to transfer and apply something you've already done than something you've just watched and heard.

4. Based on how individual students handle (or don't) the problems they face in the read-aloud and their independent books, form flexible, needs-based small groups that offer students more time to practice solving particular kinds of problems in accessible texts that pose those problems.

5. During independent reading conferences, observe and listen carefully to students to get a sense of how deeply they're reading and how much they're taking away from the read-aloud and small-group work. Then offer a teaching point based on what you've observed and heard, rather than impose a predetermined agenda.

Designing a Complex Plan of Action

To understand this more complex approach to balanced literacy and how it can support individual readers, let's think again about Takayaki. His teacher and I want for him what we want for every student as a reader: to be academically successful, enjoy what he reads, *and* reap the deep personal and societal benefits that reading offers. But when I sat down to confer with him, he was barely able to do the baseline comprehension work needed to meet the first CCSS anchor reading standard: "Read closely to determine what the text says explicitly and to make logical inferences from it." And with so little comprehension in place, he couldn't really enjoy the book, let alone begin to consider what *Season of the Sandstorms* might have to say to him about teamwork, siblings, courage, or any other themes the book explores.

Our job, thus, was to come up with a plan of action, using the repurposed components of balanced literacy, to help Takayaki build his identity and sense of agency as a reader so that, over time, he'd be ready to tackle more complex thinking in more complex texts. And to do that we considered these three questions:

1. What kind of problems is this reader facing?

2. What kind of text does this reader need?

3. How can we help this reader develop a more complex vision of reading?

NAMING THE PROBLEMS READERS FACE

According to John Dewey, "a problem well put is half-solved" (1938b). That is, the more precisely you can articulate the problems a reader faces, the more likely you'll be able to come up with precisely targeted solutions. So you'll want to think about that first question, taking into account both the challenges students face as readers and their socio-emotional needs, then name those problems as specifically as possible. With Takayaki, for instance, his teacher and I thought that several factors impacted his ability to grow and thrive as a reader: His vocabulary was limited, he didn't know how to deal with the problems unknown words posed beyond painstakingly trying to sound them out, his confidence as a reader was low, and the text he was reading wasn't a good match for him. And with this articulated, we designed the following action plan.

USING SMALL GROUPS TO FOCUS ON SPECIFIC PROBLEMS

As you confer with students, you'll undoubtedly see that different readers face different challenges. Some struggle with figurative language, for instance, while others have trouble with pronouns—and some can navigate those problems with ease but still aren't sure how to engage with the deeper work of interpretation. Small groups composed of students who all share the same challenges are incredibly useful, as they offer students time to grapple with the very problems that impede them, in a supportive setting. So, in addition to using word study to help Takayaki build his vocabulary, his teacher and I decided to gather a group of students who all needed to learn some additional ways to deal with unknown vocabulary. Specifically, we wanted Takayaki to see and experience how much he could figure out if he read around the words he didn't know or, in some cases, assigned placeholders. (See "Considering Complexity: The Problem of Vocabulary," on page 57). This two-pronged approach would help him build his word bank *and* his ability to work around unknown words—which, given the volume of words in the world, he'd inevitably need. It would also help him become a more resourceful and resilient reader, which would help address another problem he faced: his lack of confidence.

USING INDEPENDENT READING TO DEVELOP STUDENT AGENCY AND IDENTITY

As you can see with Takayaki, helping students make good book choices involves more than just matching them with a right-level book. But what kind of book did Takayaki need? The simple solution would be to say he needed a book at a lower level, which would mean sending him back to the classroom library to choose something from the level L bin. A more complex approach, however, recognizes that students are far more than levels, and that while an easier book might offer Takayaki more opportunity to get the gist, demoting him would do nothing to strengthen his already fragile identity as a reader. And as for persevering through *Season of the Sandstorms* in order to develop grit, I believe the Takayakis in our rooms display enough grit every day in school and don't really need us to demand even more of them.

Fortunately, however, his teacher and I remembered *The Empty Envelope*, the book his classmate Alyssa was reading, and we wondered if Takayaki might be interested in trading *Season of the Sandstorms* for that. *The Empty Envelope* potentially offered a more enjoyable reading experience without any level stigma attached, and it came with the added bonus of having a classmate he could talk to about it, which could be beneficial, as well, since many students who struggle gain much when reading becomes more social. And all of that could impact his experience and motivation as a reader.

What we didn't know, though, was how much meaning he could make in a text that had more accessible vocabulary but did pose other problems. Without the burden of so many hard words, for instance, could he figure out implicitly conveyed information, as Alyssa had with the phone call, or would he simply read right past that, unaware there was something to figure out? And was he even aware there were deeper levels in books and ways for readers to access and consider them? All of that remained to be seen. But Takayaki was thrilled with the idea of setting the Magic Tree House book aside and reading *The*

Empty Envelope instead. For him, this was a great solution that directly addressed all of the immediate problems he faced. And so we turned to that final question: How could we help him and others like him develop a more complex vision of reading?

USING READ-ALOUD TO HELP STUDENTS DEVELOP A MORE COMPLEX VISION OF READING

Shared interactive read-alouds are perfect vehicles for letting students see and experience what reading for deeper meaning looks, sounds, and feels like. But to fully experience the thinking for themselves, with a minimum of scaffolding, students need texts that are complex at the level of meaning but that don't pose too many problems at the word and knowledge levels. So with this in mind for Takayaki's class, we decided to use Patricia Polacco's picture book *Pink and Say* instead of *Behind Rebel Lines*, which would put excessive vocabulary demands on even the most proficient readers.

Pink and Say tells the story of two young Union soldiers, one black and the other white, who forge a powerful but heartbreaking friendship during the Civil War—and with a Lexile level of 590 and a grade-level equivalent of 4.9, it seemed a much more suitable choice for a third-grade Civil War book (though, for inexplicable reasons, its Fountas and Pinnell level was higher than *Behind Rebel Lines*). Polacco's book was much more accessible at the word level, and the illustrations offered some support. But perhaps most importantly, like *Number the Stars*, *Pink and Say* was full of clues that offered active, attentive readers multiple opportunities to figure out and develop a first-draft understanding of the historical period and setting, while also having much to say about friendship, war, injustice, and bigotry. Here, too, we weren't sure how much Takayaki would be able to make of it, but the read-aloud would give him access to a more sophisticated text than he could read on his own, and he'd be exposed to and supported by all the thinking of his classmates, which would also help him see different ways of thinking about texts.

MOVING UP TO A MORE COMPLEX TEXT

Choosing a book to help students develop a vision of both the deep thinking work of reading and how texts operate is important. But during the read-aloud, it's equally important to pay attention to students' thinking as they turn and talk about the text. What you hear will give you even more insight into the kinds of problems different students might need practice solving, which, in turn, can inform your next steps in conferences and small groups. Listening carefully also helps you see how much students are strengthening their identities and sense of agency as readers and thinkers, and that can help you decide if and when the whole class or a small group of students is ready to move to a more complex text. And as you design a dynamic plan of action, it's worth exploring that possible next step by having a more complex text in mind.

With Takayaki's class, we thought we could use the following excerpt from Paul Fleischmann's *Bull Run*, which consists of short monologues from a wide cast of characters whose lives are all connected and impacted by the Civil War's battle of Bull Run. I invite you to read it now, thinking about what a reader like Takayaki might make of it if he'd both learned *and* felt something troublesome *and* moving about the Civil War from *Pink and Say* and had had some small-group practice in navigating unknown vocabulary by using context clues, assigning placeholders, or simply reading around them, in order to get the gist.

> Though my skin is quite light, I'm a Negro, I'm proud of it, and I wept with joy along with my brethren at President Lincoln's call for men. How we yearned to strike a blow in the battle! Though the state of Ohio refused us the vote and discouraged us from settling, we rose to her aid just the same. . . . All recognized that Cincinnati was vulnerable to capture. We therefore proposed to ready a company of Home Guards, its numbers, training, and equipment to be provided by the black citizens of the city and its services offered to her defense. At last the nation's eyes would behold the Negro's energy and courage.
>
> We set up two recruiting stations. They were filled at once with scores of volunteers. Cheered by this magnificent response, we planned a second meeting at a schoolhouse. Arriving, I found the building all but ringed by a crowd of clamoring whites. Many had clubs. Several were drunk. "It's a white man's war!" one addressed me point blank. "You'll do no damn parading about with guns!" I've tried to forget the coarser things said. I inserted the key in the door's padlock, but a police captain roughly drew it out. He announced that our meeting was canceled and our entire enterprise with it, on the grounds of inviting mob violence. "Go back to your miserable homes!" he ordered us, rather than the whites, "And stay there!"
>
> I vowed that I would do otherwise. (7–8)

While Takayaki might still struggle with this, there's a good chance he'd be able to recognize the lack of respect and bigotry the character faces here. That is, this kind of complex action plan could help him get the meaning of the text, despite its many challenges. Of course, planning this way requires some problem solving on your part as well, as you grapple with which texts to choose and what kind of small-group work different students might need. But the fact is we cannot help students become problem solvers if we're not problem solvers ourselves. And along with that, here are a few other things to remember when planning for complex reading and thinking:

- Reading is far more than an academic skill; it's also an education of the heart, so let students transact with, not extract from, what they read.

- Set the purpose of reading on considering and understanding a text's meaning, versus practicing a single standard, strategy, or skill or answering text-dependent questions.

- When assessing a text's complexity for meaning, consider how much the author hasn't said explicitly that a reader has to figure out.

- Focus on helping students build their identities and sense of agency as readers—rather than on getting them through a text—knowing that as their experience and motivation change, they'll be ready to tackle harder texts.

- Every student is more than a reading level, so in addition to considering readers' academic needs, think about their socio-emotional needs whenever you choose or suggest a text.

- Levels can be useful, but they're only rough guides. Nothing replaces your professional judgment—and the students' needs and interests.

Toward More Complex Views of Thinking, Close Reading, and the Reading Process

The essence of the independent mind lies not in what it thinks, but in how it thinks.

—Christopher Hitchens, *Letters to a Young Contrarian*

Awhile ago a story about a first-grade teacher who had to give her class a practice computerized test made the rounds of my corner of Facebook. One of the questions showed a man sitting at a table with a cup of tea and asked the students what, from the following choices, he should put in the tea:

    A. Gum

    B. Milk

    C. Mud

    D. Cake

As the teacher circulated around the room, she paused behind one of her students just as he clicked on answer C, and her already heavy heart filled with even more worry over how her class would do. Did this poor child even know what tea was? Had he understood the question? Did he really know how to use the computer or was he just playing around? But then, sensing her behind him, he turned in his chair, and with a chuckle whispered, "I just put mud in that man's tea."

Clearly this child knew what he was doing, and what he revealed was a sly sense of humor, a mischievous streak, and some out-of-the-box, divergent thinking. But none of that would be recognized because in the binary world of standardized tests, his answer was wrong—and only answers, not thinking, count.

I doubt I need to convince you of the limits of standardized tests to assess students' capabilities—especially the current crop of tests, which too often focus on picayune questions about exceedingly hard texts that are phrased in highly convoluted ways. Instead, I offer this story as a reminder that thinking comes in many shapes and sizes and that to thrive in our complex world, we need multiple ways to think. And this chapter will explore different kinds of thinking, all of which I believe students need to engage in as they read, interpret, and analyze texts *and* consider whatever light they might shine on who we are and what we may become.

 ## CRITICAL THINKING:
What It Is and What It Isn't

Like the word *complexity, critical thinking* is a term we don't always define for ourselves, let alone our students, though it appears in most discussions about standards, tests, and what should happen in classrooms. In the context of standardized testing, you might think critical thinking means using reasoning and logic to identify a correct answer on a multiple-choice question or support a predetermined idea with evidence. But as many philosophers, scientists, and writers have said, critical thinking is more complex than that, involving a range of dispositions and habits of mind that must all be present and working together for the thinking to truly be critical.

Cognitive scientist Daniel Willingham (2007), for instance, says that critical thinking involves three types of thinking that most of us associate with thinking critically: reasoning, making judgments, and problem solving. But for the thinking to be truly critical, he says, it also must have these "three key features: effectiveness, novelty, and self-direction," which he explains as follows:

- Critical thinking is effective because "it avoids common pitfalls, such as seeing only one side of an issue, discounting new evidence that disconfirms your ideas, reasoning from passion rather than logic, [and] supporting your ideas with evidence" (11).

- It's novel because "you don't simply remember a solution or a situation that is similar enough to guide you" (11).

- And it's self-directed in the sense that "the thinker must be calling the shots: We wouldn't give a student much credit for critical thinking if the teacher were prompting each step he took" (11).

This three-pronged definition of critical thinking doesn't really match the thinking required for tests or many classroom practices. For instance, to prepare for tests that purport to measure critical thinking, we often teach students to use a process of elimination to increase their chances of getting a right answer, which encourages them to use a similar solution to guide their thinking. And every time we offer prompts to help students complete a task, the thinking no longer is truly critical because it's not self-directed.

We do, however, frequently ask students to support ideas with evidence, which as Willingham notes is part of critical thinking, but we don't always ask them to revise their ideas if they encounter new information that conflicts with what they've been thinking, nor to consider multiple sides of a topic or issue before asserting a claim. In fact, in our rush to get answers or have students make claims, we rarely give them enough time to truly engage in critical thinking.

In the classroom work in Section Two, you'll see students engaged in this more complex vision of critical thinking, as they reason and test out ideas and employ unique ways to solve problems with minimal input or scaffolding, which ensures that the thinking is self-directed. But you'll also see them engaged in a kind of thinking that rarely, if ever, comes up in conversations about the English language arts standards: *creative* thinking.

CREATIVE THINKING:
It's More than Mud in the Tea

According to Daniel Pink, best-selling author of *A Whole New Mind: Why Right-Brainers Will Rule the Future*:

> *The last few decades have belonged to a certain kind of person with a certain kind of mind—computer programmers who could crank code, lawyers who could craft contracts, MBAs who could crunch numbers. But the keys to the kingdom are changing hands. The future belongs to a very different kind of person with a very different kind of mind—creators and empathizers, pattern recognizers and meaning makers. These people—artists, inventors, designers, storytellers, caregivers, consolers, big picture thinkers—will now reap society's richest rewards and share its greatest joys. (2006, 1)*

I think we'll need both kinds of people and minds in our complex world, and the best way to ensure that is to give students plenty of opportunities to think both critically and creatively. By this, however, I don't mean offering creative options for projects or coursework (though I think that's nice). No, I'm talking about inviting students to think creatively as they're actually reading—and for that we need a more complex understanding of creative thinking.

As it is, many people associate creative thinking with the ability to draw, dance, compose music, or write fiction or poetry—that is, the thinking involved in artistic creation. Or they see it as the kind of divergent, out-of-the box thinking our first grader engaged in as he clicked the word *Mud* on the test. But many in the fields of education, psychology, and cognitive science tend to think of creative thinking more broadly as the ability "to imagine, explore, synthesize, connect, discover, invent and adapt" (Sternberg and Williams 1996, 3). This kind of thinking is urgently needed in our rapidly changing world, and I believe it also has a place in the process of reading to make meaning.

Let's begin to explore that by taking a look at a chart adapted from Robert Fisher's "Creative Minds: Building a Community of Learning for the Creative Age" (2007, which compares critical and creative thinking (see Figure 3.1).

CRITICAL THINKING	CREATIVE THINKING
Analytic	Generative
Probability	Possibility
Judgment	Suspended judgment
Hypothesis testing	Hypothesis forming
Objective	Subjective
The answer	An answer
Left brain	Right brain
Closed	Open-ended
Reasoning	Speculating
Logic	Intuition
"Yes, but . . ."	"Yes, and . . ."

FIGURE 3.1 *Critical Versus Creative Thinking*

On the one hand, these two types of thinking can seem like complete opposites: One's objective; the other is subjective. One's closed; the other open-ended. However, I believe that creative thinking is actually the invisible and often unrecognized thinking that helps readers eventually make more nuanced and insightful judgments and claims. Or put another way, thinking creatively is the behind-the-scenes work that's needed for students to more thoughtfully complete many of the Common Core–style tasks they're being asked to do.

Creative and Critical Thinking in Action

To illustrate how both kinds of thinking are needed, let's consider the role of critical and creative thinking in understanding a passage from Patricia Reilly Giff's *Fish Face,* a Polk Street School book. The book has a Fountas and Pinnell level of M and a 310 Lexile level, but it's surprisingly complex in terms of meaning because of the amount of information that's conveyed indirectly. As you read it, imagine what your students might say if asked to make a claim about the characters or to identify their traits after reading this passage:

> *Just then the classroom door opened. It was the principal. There was a girl with him.*
>
> *She had curly brown hair and little red ladybug earrings.*
>
> *Emily pushed at her own straight-as-a-stick hair. She flicked at her ears.*
>
> *No earrings.*
>
> *Plain.*
>
> *Her mother said she couldn't have her ears pierced until she was ten. At least.*
>
> *Maybe she should ask again. Beg.*
>
> *"We have a new girl," the principal said, "here from Florida. . . . This is Dawn Bosco."*
>
> *Ms. Rooney said, "Let's find a seat for you, Dawn."*
>
> *Emily raised her hand. . . .*
>
> *Ms. Rooney looked at Emily and nodded. "Sit next to Emily," she told Dawn.*
>
> *Emily looked up at Ms. Rooney.*
>
> *She was the best teacher in the whole school. . . .*
>
> *She was probably the best teacher in the whole world.*

Dawn came down the aisle. She slid into the desk next to Emily.

While Ms. Rooney talked with the principal, Dawn began to unpack her schoolbag. She pushed Emily's notebook a little so it wasn't on her desk.

"You have a pretty name," Emily whispered.

Dawn didn't say anything. She took a notebook out of her schoolbag. It was pink with flowers on it.

Then she unpacked her pencil box. It was the kind with drawers. Inside were paper clips. And erasers. And little round things to stick on looseleaf.

It had everything. Even a blue pencil with a pink tassel.

At last Dawn looked at her. "What's your name again?"

"Emily."

"Oh," Dawn said.

Emily waited for Dawn to say she had a pretty name too.

Instead, Dawn said. "My middle name is Tiffanie."

Lucky.

"That's nice," Emily said. . . .

"What's your middle name?" Dawn asked.

Emily didn't answer at first. She didn't have a middle name.

Dawn began again. "What's—"

"Theresa," Emily said. "Emily Theresa Arrow." (10–14)

Many students, including those reading books at higher levels, if asked to provide answers or make claims without first engaging in some creative thinking, might read this passage and conclude that Emily is nice, kind, or friendly and that Dawn is shy. In each case, they could support those conclusions with evidence from the text: Emily is nice because she wants the new girl to sit next to her and says friendly things, like "You have a pretty name"; Dawn is shy because she's a new girl and she didn't reply to Emily. Students who drew these conclusions would be engaged in the reasoning and making-judgments components of critical thinking, but they'd also be missing an enormous amount that the writer conveys less directly. In fact, they might have read right over those details without giving them much thought because they were reading to complete a task, not to understand the text more deeply.

On the other hand, students who were invited to read closely and connect, explore, and speculate before making final judgments, as creative thinkers do, would stay open to multiple possibilities. They might think that Emily could be nice, kind, and friendly *and* also envious, while Dawn might be shy *and* also mean. These hypotheses are more complex and insightful than seeing the characters as friendly or shy, and they can ultimately help students create richer, more complex claims and analyses, simply because they incorporate so much more of the text. They're also a great demonstration of what Ron Ritchhart, Mark Church, and Karin Morrison discuss in their book *Making Thinking Visible* about levels within types of thinking:

> *Rather than concerning ourselves with levels among different types of thinking,*
> *we would do better to focus our attention on the levels or quality within a*
> *single type of thinking. For instance, one can describe at a very high and*
> *detailed level or at a superficial level. Likewise . . . analysis can be deep and*
> *penetrating or deal with only a few readily apparent features. (2011, 7)*

Here we've envisioned two groups of students, one that has thought about the characters at a superficial level and another that's done more penetrating work. We could explain this by seeing the first group as literal thinkers and the second as more perceptive ones. But by doing that, we'd fall into the trap of fixed mind-set thinking. Instead, we could view this as a teaching issue, where some students benefited from instruction on considering possibilities *and* forming claims—with creative thinking presented as equally important to reading as critical thinking work is—while others missed out on that learning. Robert Fisher explains this equal importance thus:

> *We need both critical and creative thinking, both analysis and synthesis, both*
> *the parts and the whole to be effective in our thinking. We need reason and*
> *intuition, order and adventure in our thinking. We need creative thinking to*
> *generate the new, but critical thinking to judge it. (2007)*

Of course, critical and creative thinking—let alone the recursive intertwining of the two—aren't so easy to teach. And it's especially challenging if we use that old analytic mind-set and break this complex mix of thinking into parts by planning a series of activities designed to meet a goal written up on the whiteboard, like "Students will be able to come up with novel ways to reason their way to a claim," or "I can suspend judgment when I read." With a problem-based approach to teaching reading, however, we can create situations that position and invite students to think both creatively *and* critically in ways that will also prepare them to deal with the problems in our complex world.

A MORE COMPLEX AND MEANINGFUL VISION OF CLOSE READING

Close reading is yet another term ushered in by the Common Core standards, where it quickly devolved into a set practice where students are required to read a text three times: the first to get the gist, the second to consider its structure and craft, and the third to evaluate and consider its significance—or as some put it, to determine what it says, how it says that, and what it means. Students arrive at these three different understandings by answering a series of text-dependent questions aligned with the purpose of each read, with teachers invited to offer scaffolds, such as think-alouds or prompts, if students don't get the answers.

But here's the problem: Because the questions themselves are so text-specific, the thinking isn't always transferrable from one text to another, which means they're not designed to support independence. And like *Notice & Note* authors Kylene Beers and Robert Probst, I fear "that a focus on text-dependent questions may create a nation of teacher-dependent kids" (2012, 43). Also, it's unlikely that students will transfer this process to other texts on their own because reading a text three times is simply an unsustainable expectation. So here you'll find two shifts you can make to hold onto the goal of reading deeply for meaning while still teaching for independence.

Close Reading as an Outcome, Not a Procedure

On his blog, Timothy Shanahan suggests that we should see close reading not as a teaching technique or reading procedure, but "as an outcome to be strived for" (2013). That is, close reading shouldn't be about how many times students read a text, whether they annotate or not, or whether they can answer a specific number of text-dependent questions. What's important is how deeply they come to understand and consider what the author might be trying to show them—in other words, what they think the text means at the literal, figurative, inferential, and thematic levels.

Of course, the question then becomes *how* to achieve this outcome without all those prescribed steps and scaffolding. I believe the answer is to bring that complex mix of creative and critical thinking into classrooms by setting students up to wonder, generate questions, and form hypotheses, then to test out those hypotheses, using reasoning and logic, to arrive at a final judgment or claim. (See Figure 3.2.) By doing this, students will also be engaged in an age-appropriate version of Harvard's "How to Do a Close Reading" guide (Kain 1998).

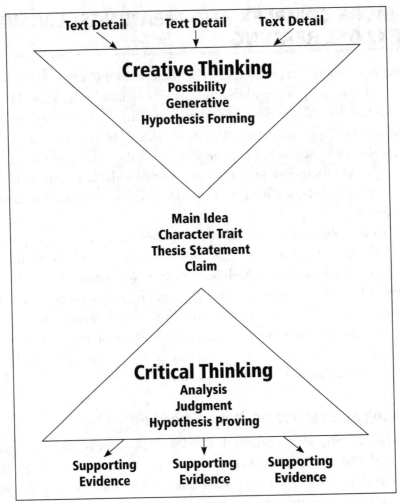

Text Detail   Text Detail   Text Detail

Creative Thinking
Possibility
Generative
Hypothesis Forming

Main Idea
Character Trait
Thesis Statement
Claim

Critical Thinking
Analysis
Judgment
Hypothesis Proving

Supporting   Supporting   Supporting
Evidence   Evidence   Evidence

FIGURE 3.2 *Creative Thinking + Critical Thinking = Close Reading*

According to Harvard, close reading is a two-step (versus three-read) process. The first is to observe and note "anything that strikes you as surprising or significant, or that raises questions," while the second step is to interpret your observations by first "look[ing] for patterns in the things you've noticed" and then "ask[ing] questions about the patterns—especially how and why." This second step inevitably entails returning to the text to consider how other parts and details support or challenge your thinking—thereby ensuring that the critical thinking is effective. And "in this way," Harvard's guide states, "we engage in a process that is central to . . . the whole academic enterprise: we reason toward our own ideas."

Reading Closely Versus Close Reading: More than Just Semantics

Harvard's vision of close reading and the one I'm proposing bring the reader's agency into the process in a way that teacher-driven practices don't. But this vision of close reading seems so far from the highly prescriptive and overly scaffolded versions found in many classrooms that I tend to talk about students "reading closely" rather than doing a "close reading." "Read closely," after all, are the very first words of the CCSS anchor standards for reading, while the term *close reading* doesn't actually appear in the standards at all. And while this might seem like a matter of semantics, I think there's a real difference.

Close reading is a noun, while *reading closely* is a verb; one's a thing and the other's an action—or as Dewey might say, one is something to learn and the other, something to do. And according to Henry Hitchings, the author of the *New York Times* article "Those Irritating Verbs-as-Nouns" (2013), several things happen when we turn verbs into nouns. The noun version, he says, "is not so dynamic" as the verb, and it "can have a distancing effect" because it's "less personal." He does note, however, that "that form of words may improve our chances of eliciting a more objective response," which is what the CCSS seem to value when they ask students to stay within the four corners of the text.

In the end, though, it doesn't matter what you call it. Once again what's important is what you're aiming for: depth of student thinking, text understanding, independence, and a love of reading. And if close reading, as a noun, fades away as the Common Core initiative splinters, I believe this is a vision of reading that can last and transcend any set of standards.

BEYOND BEFORE, DURING, AND AFTER: Re-envisioning the Reading Process

Teachers of writing often have a chart displayed somewhere in their rooms that shows students the stages of the writing process so they have a vision of how writers manage to go from a blank page to a finished piece. Teachers also keep that process in mind when they make decisions about what to teach when to a whole class or in a conference. For example, if students were in the collecting-ideas stage, they'd offer a strategy or two for brainstorming, not for revising. But is there an equivalent process in reading, something that describes the stages readers go through as they move from knowing nothing about a text (the equivalent of a writer's blank page) to a deep understanding of it (i.e., a finished piece)?

If you ask Google, you'll find variations on a three-stage reading process, which lists what readers should do before, during, and after they read. Before reading, for instance, students should set a purpose for reading, activate prior knowledge, and preview the text. During reading, they should remember their purpose, check for understanding, make connections, and, in a few—but far from all—iterations, think about what they're reading and use fix-up strategies if they're confused. Then once they've finished, they should recall what they read, reflect on what they learned, and reread if they think they missed something.

The Reading Process for Narratives

With all this talk of complexity, you may already be thinking that this three-stage process seems too simple. Nor does it acknowledge that we read different kinds of texts differently, even if our purpose is always set on meaning. With both fiction and nonfiction narratives, for instance, readers engage in specific kinds of thinking as they make their way from the beginning to the middle to the end of a text. Beginnings are where writers introduce characters and their problems (often indirectly) and plant some tantalizing seeds and clues about what might happen and why. So when they start a narrative, readers need to read closely and fit pieces together to draft a first impression of the characters and how they're dealing with whatever situation the writer has put them in, while also holding on to whatever questions those tantalizing details might raise (Barnhouse and Vinton 2012).

Middles, on the other hand, are when things get messy. New complications and disruptions appear, characters have setbacks, they push and they're tested, and nothing is as it first seemed. And readers deal with this messiness by paying close attention to how what was introduced in the beginning is changing and developing. They also start thinking about what the writer might be trying to show them about people and life in the middle, by continually revising their first-draft understandings and forming hypotheses about why what's happening is happening as they encounter new twists and turns.

Endings, however, are like final reckonings, where characters are either rewarded or punished, get what they wanted, or solve their problems (or not). They're also the place where readers get the clearest glimpse of what the writer might be trying to show them. To do that, though, readers need to think about *how* the problem or situation did or didn't get solved. Think, for instance, of the classic storyline about a boy who wants a girl who doesn't want him. On the one hand, you could say that the story is about love. But whatever the writer might be exploring or trying to say about love depends on how the story is resolved. A story where the boy gets the girl by luck, for example, suggests something different about love and relationships than one where the boy gets the girl through ingenuity or candor. And a boy who doesn't get the girl but winds up falling in love with someone he'd originally discounted as too quiet or plain says something else entirely. As readers read closely to consider the *how* in the ending, they revise their hypotheses into interpretations (Barnhouse and Vinton 2012). And all of this can be envisioned as a circular process (see Figure 3.3).

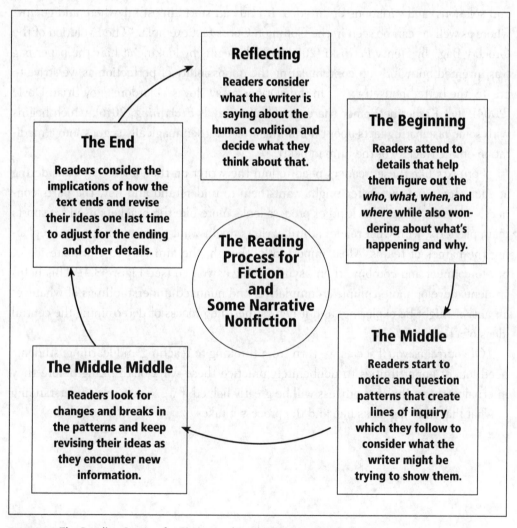

Reflecting

Readers consider what the writer is saying about the human condition and decide what they think about that.

The Beginning

Readers attend to details that help them figure out the *who*, *what*, *when*, and *where* while also wondering about what's happening and why.

The End

Readers consider the implications of how the text ends and revise their ideas one last time to adjust for the ending and other details.

The Reading Process for Fiction and Some Narrative Nonfiction

The Middle

Readers start to notice and question patterns that create lines of inquiry which they follow to consider what the writer might be trying to show them.

The Middle Middle

Readers look for changes and breaks in the patterns and keep revising their ideas as they encounter new information.

FIGURE 3.3 *The Reading Process for Fiction and Some Narrative Nonfiction*

The Reading Process for Expository Nonfiction

Expository nonfiction, however, doesn't have the same structure narratives have, with a beginning, middle, and end that moves through time as the plot unfolds. Instead, once you move beyond basic all-about books, nonfiction writers tend to take their readers on a journey of thought about a particular topic, event, or phenomenon, exploring different aspects of it across a text. Depending on the text, that journey could explore any or all of the following: causes and effects, pros and cons, different perspectives, problems and solutions, and variations on an idea. It also can start almost anywhere and go anywhere as well, as can be seen in the Common Core's text exemplar "The Evolution of the Grocery Bag," by Henry Petroski (2003), which begins by looking at how the paper bag was invented but winds up contemplating the impossibility of perfection as we strive to create "the better mousetrap," or in the glorious essay "Joyas Volardores," by Brian Doyle (2004), that Katherine Bomer shares in *The Journey Is Everything* (2016), which begins with some fascinating facts about hummingbirds but then magically segues into a meditation on the fragility of the human heart.

For texts like these, readers need to join the writer on the journey, by considering at each step what the writer might want them to understand and how the parts connect with each other. This kind of process looks more like the brackets used for sports team play-offs, with what readers think writers might want them to understand replacing the names of teams. Most importantly, though, the aim isn't to eliminate ideas, but to connect and combine them, synthesizing as you go (see Figure 3.4). This helps students develop more complex, cumulative, and nuanced understandings of whatever an author might be exploring, and it demystifies the process of determining the central ideas of a text.

Of course, as you'll see as we turn from thinking to teaching and learning, students need lots of opportunities to deliberately practice these ways of thinking before they internalize them. But that process will be greatly helped if we have a real understanding of what that thinking looks like and the process it takes.

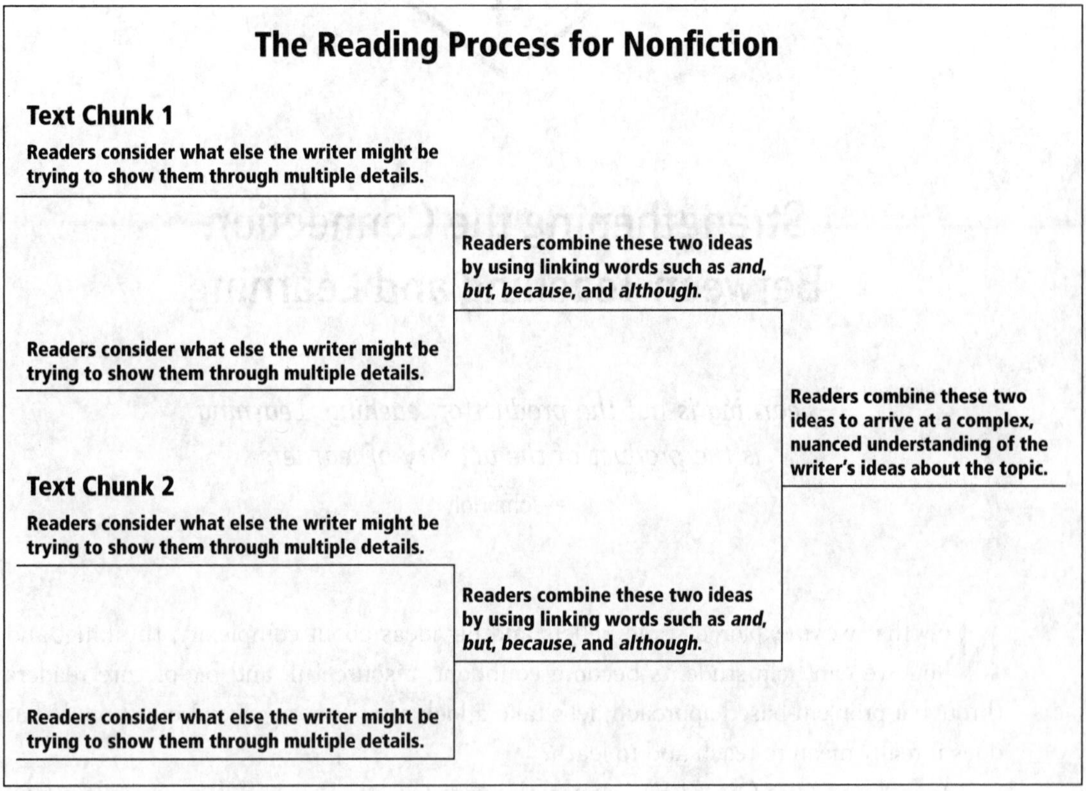

The Reading Process for Nonfiction

Text Chunk 1

Readers consider what else the writer might be trying to show them through multiple details.

Readers combine these two ideas by using linking words such as *and*, *but*, *because*, and *although*.

Readers consider what else the writer might be trying to show them through multiple details.

Readers combine these two ideas to arrive at a complex, nuanced understanding of the writer's ideas about the topic.

Text Chunk 2

Readers consider what else the writer might be trying to show them through multiple details.

Readers combine these two ideas by using linking words such as *and*, *but*, *because*, and *although*.

Readers consider what else the writer might be trying to show them through multiple details.

FIGURE 3.4 *The Reading Process for Nonfiction: Combining Versus Eliminating Ideas*

Strengthening the Connection
Between Teaching and Learning

*Learning is not the product of teaching. Learning
is the product of the activity of learners.*

—John Holt

Now that we've explored some beliefs and big ideas about complexity, thinking, and how we can help students become confident, resourceful, and big-picture readers through a problem-based approach, let's take a look at one more crucial question: What does it really mean to teach and to learn?

According to the Oxford Dictionary, the verb *teach* means to "show or explain how to do something" or to "give information about or instruction in a subject or skill." But if you've ever wondered why students *still* don't understand something you know they've been taught—be it the capitalization of proper nouns or how to write a summary—you know there's something missing from these definitions: *learning*. Most of us expect that teaching should result in learning—with the progressive educator Paulo Freire believing "there is, in fact, no teaching without learning" (1998, 31). But learning is yet another complex process, involving all sorts of unpredictable variables that can impede or interfere with the process. Students may not fully comprehend what was taught or find it meaningful enough to remember. They may not have had enough time or exposure to practice the concepts or thinking or may have been too exhausted, hungry, or anxious for learning to really take hold. As teachers, of course, we can't overcome all of these factors, especially those students bring with them from outside the classroom, but we should expect that teaching will ultimately lead to learning. And if learning is the ultimate goal, we need to be sure that our teaching methods support how students learn.

A CLOSE LOOK AT LEARNING

Just as with other types of thinking, learning can happen at a superficial level or a deep and penetrating one. Students, for instance, can remember something long enough to pass a quiz or complete an assignment, only to forget it afterward. Or they can learn how to follow a procedure, such as writing a five-paragraph essay or annotating a text using symbols, without necessarily understanding the deeper purpose of essays or annotation.

Deep and penetrating learning, on the other hand, is characterized by the learner's ability not just to remember what was learned, but to transfer and apply it from one setting, situation, or text to another. And this kind of learning is much harder to achieve. In fact, in a series of literacy blog posts, Grant Wiggins (2015) also wrote that not only is transfer of learning poor, but many students don't seem to understand that "the long-term and bottom-line goal of education is transfer of learning." This lack of transfer, he writes, is demonstrated every time a student says, "That's unfair! You asked us questions different from the ones we went over in class!" or "If you wanted us to use some prior learning, why didn't you just ask us to use it?" Additionally, he shares that on a major state assessment in Massachusetts, a significant number of high school students failed to identify a seventeen-paragraph piece on colorblindness as an essay because it had more than five paragraphs, which suggests they hadn't learned a more deep and penetrating understanding of the genre.

Wiggins suggests we need to make sure students understand that transfer is the goal by explicitly saying so. But beyond that, what else can we do? Fortunately, there's a whole new field of science, called educational neuroscience, that's devoted to studying the interactions between the brain and learning. Researchers in this exciting new field have shed much light on how people learn at those deeper, more penetrating levels, and their findings have implications for how we might teach to maximize learning. And interestingly enough, educational neuroscience offers evidence that supports some of the current trends in education, while raising questions about others.

The Power of Growth Mindsets

If you walk into many schools these days, you're likely to see bulletin boards or classroom charts touting the benefits of growth mindsets. The concept grew out of decades of research undertaken by the psychologist Carol Dweck, but educational neuroscience has now also shown that particular kinds of experiences can literally make our brains grow. One recent study from England, for instance, showed that the more time London cab drivers spent "navigating the twists and turns of the city streets," the larger the part of their brains associated with spatial learning grew (Hinton, Fischer, and Glennon, 2012). Applied to reading, this research suggests that the more time students spend navigating and making sense of the twists and turns of texts, the more their neural capacity to do that will grow. And this is why David A. Sousa, the author of *How the Brain Learns*, says that teaching is "the only profession whose job is to change the human brain every day" (2011, 10).

The Impact of Stress

On the flip side, many educational neuroscientists' findings raise questions about some teaching practices. Brain scans, for example, have shown that learning is minimized when students experience stress—and in our current climate of high-stakes testing, classroom stress and the anxiety that comes with it have never been higher. Stress, however, also includes experiencing bouts of frustration and boredom, which, like anxiety, have been scientifically proven to cause our brains to literally shut down, preventing new learning from taking hold. Yet we're often encouraged to instructionally address this by helping students develop more grit so they can forge on regardless of how they feel, which simply doesn't jive with the brain research findings. In fact, neurologist, educator, and *Edutopia* blogger Judy Willis says that virtually the opposite is true: "When teachers use strategies to reduce stress and build a positive emotional environment, students gain emotional resilience and learn more efficiently and at higher levels of cognition" (2014). This stands in stark contrast to the hard-knocks school of teaching, which tends to see practices that consider students' feelings as unneeded, even harmful, coddling.

The Necessity of Time and Repetition

In many schools across the country, teachers are required to identify and write learning outcomes on the board for the lessons they teach—often prefacing them with the words "I can" or "Students will be able to" (SWBAT), followed by the standard or skill they're expected to master by the end of the lesson. Research from educational neuroscience, however, has shown that the brain needs repeated encounters with concepts and ideas as well as lots of opportunities to actively engage with them in order to truly learn them. So while students may be able to meet a specified objective by the end of a period, that doesn't necessarily mean they've learned it well enough to transfer and apply the learning. For transfer, learning must move from our short-term memory banks to our working memory, and that requires much more time and practice—and involves a far more complex process—than "I can" practices suggest.

According to Atul Gawande, for instance, mastering anything involves learners "going from unconscious incompetence to conscious incompetence to conscious competence and finally to unconscious competency" (2011). This means students often start out unaware there's something they can't do—or even something *to* do—and the first step in the process is to become aware of that. Once they're aware, students begin to understand that they can, indeed, do something if they put their mind to it and deliberately practice, which involves consciously engaging in and reflecting on a process of thinking or actions to improve. Over time, all that practice helps students internalize the thinking so they can automatically engage in it when it's needed. And none of that can actually happen in a single class period or literacy block.

The Importance of Pleasure

Finally, there's what I'll call the pleasure factor, a word that rarely, if ever, appears in discussions about education these days. Yet just as educational neuroscience has shown that reducing stress increases learning and memory, making learning pleasurable apparently does that, too, by releasing the brain chemical dopamine, which supports the retention of learning. And what beyond recess, pizza parties, and field trips do students find pleasurable at school? Research has an answer for that, too: Students find pleasure in activities where they have some choice and opportunity to explore and discover for themselves. Activities like this allow students to experience what educator and psychologist Jerome Bruner asserted was "one of the few untarnishable joys of life": "being able to 'go beyond the information' given to 'figure things out'" (1996, 129). And they're also the exact kind of activities that John Holt says produce true learning (see epigraph).

THE SOUND OF READERS LEARNING

Now let's apply all this science of learning to reading to hear what it sounds like when students are figuring out all the twists and turns of a text in order to discover what an author is conveying *and* some key concepts of reading in general. The following short piece, called "Louisa's Liberation," is from Jean Little's gem of a book *Hey World,*

Here I Am!, a collection of vignettes, poems, and fictional journal entries written by a character named Kate. A good example of the kind of text you'll want to use with a problem-based approach to reading complex texts, it's relatively accessible at the word level, but quite complex in terms of meaning. I invite you to read the piece to consider what Little might be trying to show her readers through it—then listen in as a group of fifth graders try to figure that out, too.

"LOUISA'S LIBERATION"

Emily and I got talking and we decided

It was up to us to make sure Louisa grew up liberated.

"They start teaching them sex stereotypes

in Nursery School, my mother read," I said.

"Well, there's no time like the present," said Emily.

"Let's find her and do something."

We went in search of Louisa.

She was in the backyard with all her toys laid out in a row.

She was trundling around, as busy as a bee,

    so involved she didn't even notice us arriving.

"Louisa, what are you doing?" Emily asked.

Louisa, still preoccupied, answered, "This is my hospital.

These need operations. Those are dying."

Emily and I exchanged looks as Louisa went back to work.

"Isn't that great!" murmured Emily.

"She's not stuck in a kitchen, playing house; she's a nurse!"

Louisa glanced up.

"No, I'm not," she said. "I'm a doctor." (59)

As a proficient reader, you probably thought Jean Little was saying something about gender stereotypes in this vignette—and you may have even found yourself laughing as you realized she was playing a joke on Kate and Emily, who seem in need of liberation themselves. If you pushed yourself further to consider more specifically what Little might be saying about stereotypes, you might have concluded that she was trying to show us that even people who think they're enlightened can fall into stereotyping. You might also have found yourself thinking your students wouldn't get that for any number of reasons. They might lack background knowledge about the women's rights movement or not know words like *liberation, trundling,* and *preoccupied.* Or you might have wondered if they have the maturity to reach a similar conclusion. And you'd be right—at least about what students don't know.

This particular group of fifth graders, for instance, didn't know the word *liberation.* One of the students thought it could be connected to the word *library* because of what seemed like a common root, but that idea didn't quite work when they tried it out in the second line ("It was up to us to make sure Louisa grew up liberated."). Noticing the details about teaching and school, however, two others wondered if *liberation* might mean "education," and because this word worked in both the noun and the verb form, they used it as a placeholder as they kept reading. That helped them figure out the next problem they faced: Why did Kate and Emily want to find Louisa and what was it they were going to do?

They all thought the two girls wanted to teach Louisa something, with a few also thinking it might have to do with the words "sex stereotypes" (which they pointed to, rather than spoke). And with all this thinking on the table, they were ready to wrestle with the rest of the piece, including what the significance might be of playing house versus nurse and doctor and how all that connected to Emily and Kate trying to educate Louisa. Here's a taste of their conversation:

> Ava: *I think it's important she's pretending to be a doctor, not a nurse, because doctors help people and nurses just help the doctor.*

> Luce: *Yeah, and one of my aunts is a nurse and she told me doctors get paid a lot of money. So they're sort of more important than a nurse.*

> Antonio: *And Louisa thinks she can be anything she wants to be, not just a nurse but a doctor.*

Ava: But Kate and Emily thought she was playing nurse, so maybe they didn't think she could be a doctor.

Luce: And maybe they thought that because lots of women are nurses but only some are doctors.

Antonio: But she didn't need them to teach her anything. She already thought she could be anything she wanted. And they were just happy she wasn't in the kitchen.

Nick (who'd been quiet till then): Oh! I think I just figured out what liberation means. It's like the Statue of Liberty. Louisa's free to be anything she wants to be because liberty is like freedom.

Ava: Yeah, she's not in a box, but Kate and Emily sort of are because they only expected her to be a nurse.

Antonio: It's like she's more liberated and mature than they are. But maybe Louisa can liberate them.

Given the time to question and ponder, these students arrived at the same implicit and complex idea you, yourself, may have reached. And as they began to talk about what they learned through the story about people and life, some said they thought Jean Little had taught them that it's not necessarily age that determines maturity. Others thought they learned that sometimes you might be in a box even if you think you're not. When I asked if they thought they'd learned anything as readers from this experience as well, here's what they had to say:

Ava: "Yeah, it's like there was an inside story and we figured it out."

Nick: "It's really important to figure out words, especially if they're in the title."

Antonio: "We also had to think about what we didn't know, not just what we did."

Luce: "That was really hard, but fun!"

Luce's comment seems like a testament to the "untarnishable joy" of figuring things out for yourself—and the fact that rigor doesn't have to be the opposite of pleasure. And the whole experience allowed these students to realize something they never had before: that there could be a story inside the story. Having now seen that, their next step would be to bring that awareness to other texts they read and to deliberately try to figure out what the writer might be showing them. Of course, these students would need lots of practice before they internalized this learning and thinking, and teaching would play a vital role in this process.

FROM THE SCIENCE OF LEARNING TO THE ART OF TEACHING

If we believe there's no teaching without learning *and* that learning stems from the activity of learners, then we need a vision of teaching that supports these beliefs. To me, that means seeing teaching as being less about explaining or showing students how to do things and more about creating and facilitating opportunities for them to learn through exploration, problem solving, and discovery. This vision of teaching is a real shift from what many have considered to be the gold standard in literacy practices for some time: explicit instruction accompanied by teacher modeling, with responsibility released to students over time. It's worth noting, however, that P. David Pearson, who, with Margaret Gallagher, first articulated the gradual release of responsibility model, has said, "There is no inherent virtue in explicit instruction and modeling. . . . We could begin a sequence by asking students to 'try it on their own,' offering feedback and assistance as students demonstrate the need for it." And when asked how much explicit instruction a teacher should provide, his answer was, "As little as possible" (2011, 248).

This doesn't mean embracing the hands-off vision of teaching put forth by some proponents of grit, who advise teachers to refuse to answer students' question and instead make them look answers up at least once each period in order to develop grit (Maats and O'Brien 2015). As you'll soon see, a problem-based approach to teaching is anything but hands-off. There's lots and lots of teaching to do, including some explicit instruction and, if needed, teacher modeling. What's different, though, is when, how, and why to offer this teaching, and while I'll explore that in depth starting in the next chapter, here are a few basic principles.

The Power of Feedback

Feedback has long been seen as a powerful form of teaching, though increasingly researchers are recognizing that certain types of feedback are more effective than others. It turns out, for instance, that grades and written comments on student assignments, which are the most common form of feedback, are the least effective. That's because, as Dylan Wiliam writes in *Embedded Formative Assessment,* "in such situations, feedback is rather like the scene in the rearview mirror rather than through the windshield. Or as Douglas Reeves once memorably observed, it's like the difference between having a medical [checkup] and a postmortem" (2011, 120).

Impactful feedback, on the other hand, is characterized by several features. It's descriptive versus evaluative and occurs in real time as students are actually grappling with problems, instead of once the work's done. Or as John Hattie puts it, from the students' perspective, it should feel "just in time, just for me, just for where I am in the learning process and just what I need to help me move forward" (2012, 123). Much of the teaching in a problem-based approach happens through this kind of feedback. In fact, it's precisely this use of timely, responsive, and ongoing feedback that makes this approach to teaching reading more dynamic than other methods.

The Power of Language to Position

Dylan Wiliam has also written that, when all is said and done, "the thing that really matters in feedback is the relationship between the student and the teacher" (2014), and this belief correlates with neuroscience findings that students learn best when teachers create positive emotional environments. Of course, many factors contribute to those environments and relationships, but in closing I'd like to consider just one: the power of our words to position and empower students to learn.

As Peter Johnston writes in *Choice Words,* language "actually creates realities and invites identities," and our words "can position students differently in relation to what they are doing, learning or studying" (2004, 9). Consider, for instance, the language used in the hands-off teaching suggestion that teachers *refuse* to answer students' questions and instead *make* them look the answers up. That language positions the teacher as the authority figure in the room, who not only dictates the students' activities but holds (and can withhold) the answers. But what if, instead, teachers expressed uncertainty in response to students' questions and then asked how they might figure something out?

That language sends a very different message about who students are and what they're capable of doing. It positions students to see themselves as people who are capable of figuring things out—and given the negative impact stress has on learning, who do you think will learn more here, students who are invited to figure things out or those who are chastised by the teacher and told what to do?

That language also invites students to see us not as authority figures who hold all the answers and power, but as learners who are sometimes unsure and must figure things out as well. This stance carries its own kind of power and, in fact, is another way of modeling. Rather than explicitly showing students how to *do* a strategy or skill, we're implicitly modeling how to *be* something. Specifically, we're modeling the dispositions and habits of mind of complex thinkers, readers, and learners who are comfortable with uncertainty and know that stumbling is simply a part of the process.

This means letting students see us as excited, passionate, curious, and sometimes confused learners who wonder, ponder, and ask questions we don't always know the answers to. In his book *Creating Cultures of Thinking*, Ron Ritchhart (2015) suggests that this kind of modeling can be even more powerful than instructional demonstrations, but for some of us, this is hard. We may question how deeply we think, and lacking that confidence, we may also be wary of revealing what we don't know. But in his article "Looking for Trouble: A Way to Unmask Our Readings," Tom Newkirk shares how much can be gained by getting past those perceived failings:

> *Opening up the discourse to allow for the expression of confusion and difficulty . . . allows us all, teachers and students, to drop the masks that can inhibit learning. We can all act as the fallible, sometimes confused, sometimes puzzled readers that we are. We can reveal ourselves as learners, not always the most graceful of positions.* (1984, 765)

But, perhaps, it's the stance our students most need to see us take.

SECTION TWO

On Problems and Practice

Practices are our beliefs in action.
—Regie Routman, *Read, Write, Lead*

AS YOU'LL SEE IN THE FOLLOWING TABLE, we've already begun to explore how beliefs can inform and shape actions, but in this section, we'll look at the specific teaching practices that come with a problem-based approach, all of which are aligned with the beliefs and ideas you saw in Section One. Each chapter will focus on a particular problem texts pose for readers, and each will share some core practices that can position your students to grapple with those problems in order to deeply understand what the writer might be conveying about people, the world, and life. And to kick off this section, we'll begin with a "Considering Complexity" interlude that looks at the problems posed by vocabulary.

BIG IDEAS AND BELIEFS IN ACTION

IF WE BELIEVE THIS . . .	WE MUST DO THIS . . .
Our students face an increasingly complex world where they'll need to solve problems we haven't yet imagined, using knowledge that is exponentially growing	Help students become resourceful and innovative problem solvers who can think both creatively and critically
Reading is a complex process that requires the coordinated use of multiple strategies, skills, and mindsets in the service of meaning making	Set students up to read strategically, drawing on and developing a range of strategies to figure out what the writer might be trying to show them about the world and the human condition
Learners need lots of time to practice the thinking of reading and feel the joy of figuring things out	Create pleasurable learning opportunities for students that position them to figure out the problems a text poses in order to deeply understand it

FIGURE I.1 *Big Ideas and Beliefs in Action*

Considering Complexity:
The Problem of Vocabulary

The Common Core State Standards put a premium on vocabulary acquisition, and while you'll certainly want to help students build a wider vocabulary, you'll also want them to learn other ways to deal with the problems unknown words pose so they can become more resilient and resourceful readers and have a strong bank of words. One way to do this is to ask students to highlight or underline the words they *do* know in a text, rather than the ones they *don't*, in order to see how much they can grasp despite the vocabulary challenges. Here, for instance, is the beginning of a Time magazine article by Eugene Linden called "Can Animals Think?", which many sixth graders in New York City were asked to read a few years ago.

Can Animals Think?

After years of debate, ingenious new studies of dolphins, apes and other brainy beasts are convincing many scientists that the answer is yes.

In a sun-dappled pool not far from the clamor of Waikiki Beach, two female dolphins poke their heads out of the water, waiting for a command. "O.K.," says Louis Herman, founder and director of the Kewalo Basin Marine Mammal Laboratory, "now let's try a tandem creative." Two graduate students, positioned at opposite ends of the 50-ft. tank, throw full body and soul into communicating this message to the animals, Phoenix and Akeakamai. First the humans ask the dolphins to pay attention by holding a finger high in the air. Then they tap the index fingers of each hand together, forming the gesture that has been taught to mean tandem. Next they throw their arms up in an expansive gesture that signifies creative. The dolphins have just been told, "Do something creative together." (54)

Now read the words two sixth-grade English language learners highlighted (shown here in bold).

> **After years of** *debate,* *ingenious* **new studies of dolphins, apes and other brainy beasts are convincing many scientists that the answer is yes.**
>
> **In a** *sun-dappled* **pool not far from the** *clamor of Waikiki* **Beach, two female dolphins** *poke* **their heads out of the water, waiting for a command. "O.K.," says Louis Herman,** *founder and director* **of the** *Kewalo Basin Marine* **Mammal Laboratory, "now let's try a** *tandem creative."* **Two graduate students,** *positioned* **at opposite ends of the 50-ft. tank, throw full body and soul into communicating this message to the animals,** *Phoenix and Akeakamai.* **First the humans ask the dolphins to pay attention by holding a finger high in the air. Then they tap the** *index* **fingers of each hand together, forming the** *gesture* **that has been taught to mean** *tandem.* **Next they throw their arms up in** *an expansive gesture that signifies* **creative. The dolphins have just been told, "Do something creative together."** *(54)*

By highlighting and focusing on what they can read, rather than what they can't, students like these can often get the gist of a passage in a way that also builds their confidence, sense of agency, and identity as readers. And from there you can invite them to see if they can figure out other words by drawing on their background knowledge of things like proper nouns (e.g., realizing that *Waikiki* could be the name of the beach) or by assigning a placeholder like the word *something* (as in "now let's try a *something*" that's called a "tandem creative").

You may, of course, want to return to words that students don't know after reading the article—especially Tier 2 words, like *debate*, *positioned*, and *gesture*. But beginning with what students know rather than what they don't can increase their curiosity about the text and individual words, which in turn increases their engagement and motivation.

But best of all, this strategy can be used with any text that puts vocabulary demands on readers of any age, grade, or level. And when combined with other vocabulary strategies and tools, like those found in Janet Allen's book *Inside Words* (2007) and Isabel Beck, Margaret McKeown, and Linda Kucan's *Bringing Words to Life* (2013), along with work on using advanced context clues, you'll be able to offer students a powerful, multifaceted, *complex* approach to dealing with vocabulary words.

Creating Opportunities for Readers
to Figure Out the Basics

*Never tell people how to do something, tell them what
to do and let them surprise you with their ingenuity.*
—General George S. Patton, *War As I Knew It*

Consider for a moment the following students, who all were reading supposedly just-right books during independent reading time:

- a fourth grader two-thirds of the way through one of the Katie Kazoo, Switcheroo books who somehow missed the fact that Katie's not called "Switcheroo" for nothing: She switches into other people whenever she wishes for something

- a fifth grader nearing the end of the Time Warp Trio book *Hey Kid, Want to Buy a Bridge?* who wasn't quite sure if a character named Mug was one of the Time Warp Trio boys or the villain of this installment

- an eighth grader several chapters into *Jumping Off Swings* who thought that a boy character was pregnant because he hadn't figured out that each chapter in this YA novel was told from a different character's perspective

In addition to reading books they had chosen themselves at their assessed level, all of these students had received instruction—sometimes over years—on comprehension strategies such as monitoring comprehension and envisioning. Yet none of them could consider the deeper layers of meaning in their chosen books because they hadn't figured out the basic who, what, when, and where of the story line. And none had any idea that they were, in fact, completely lost.

EXPLORING THE PROBLEM: Figuring Out the Basics

As you've seen, writers often convey basic information indirectly rather than directly, and this can present a problem for readers at any grade or level. It's a problem that can also crop up on any page of a book, but it's especially tricky at the beginning, where writers often throw readers into a scene without so much as a proper introduction to the who, what, when, and where of the story (Barnhouse and Vinton 2012). In fact, this technique is so common it even has a name—*in media res*, which in Latin means "in the midst of things." Many writers, in effect, hit the ground running, tossing names and information at readers like balls in a batting cage, alluding to events that have already happened and relationships that may come with baggage, trusting their readers to field those balls and somehow make sense of it all. And that makes *in media res* beginnings particularly useful to share with students who you know or suspect may struggle at making basic inferences.

To see what I mean, let's look at the beginning of Patricia MacLachlan's Newbery Medal-winning book *Sarah, Plain and Tall*, a perennial favorite that has a Lexile level of 560, which puts it near the low end of the grades 2–3 complexity band despite the complexity of the writing. As you read it, try to pay attention to how much information is conveyed indirectly and what, as a reader, you have to do to figure out what hasn't been said.

> *"Did Mama sing every day?" asked Caleb. "Every-single-day?" He sat close to the fire, his chin in his hand. It was dusk, and the dogs lay beside him on the warm hearthstones.*
>
> *"Every-single-day," I told him for the second time this week. For the twentieth time this month. The hundredth time this year? And the past few years?*
>
> *"And did Papa sing, too?"*
>
> *"Yes. Papa sang, too. Don't get so close, Caleb. You'll heat up."*
>
> *He pushed his chair back. It made a hollow scraping sound on the hearthstones, and the dogs stirred. Lottie, small and black, wagged her tail and lifted her head. Nick slept on.*
>
> *I turned the bread dough over and over on the marble slab on the kitchen table.*

"Well, Papa doesn't sing anymore," said Caleb very softly. A log broke apart and crackled in the fireplace. He looked up at me. "What did I look like when I was born?"

"You didn't have any clothes on," I told him.

"I know that," he said.

"You looked like this." I held the bread dough up in a round pale ball.

"I had hair," said Caleb seriously.

"Not enough to talk about," I said.

"And she named me Caleb," he went on, filling in the old familiar story.

"I would have named you Troublesome," I said, making Caleb smile.

"And Mama handed me to you in the yellow blanket and said . . ." He waited for me to finish the story. "And said . . . ?"

I sighed. "And Mama said, 'Isn't he beautiful, Anna?'" (3–4)

As a proficient reader, you may have figured out the problems the text posed so automatically you weren't even aware of all the thinking work you were doing (see Figure 5.1). But students often read this passage not even knowing what they don't know. Many, for instance, don't catch the narrator's name in the last line, and they turn the page without understanding how Caleb and Anna are related or that something has happened to Mama. Additionally, some think Papa's there in the room because he's referred to in the dialogue, and others believe Nick is a person because they've missed that the word *dog* is plural.

Fiction writers often reveal more explicitly what they've alluded to indirectly as a story unfolds, so readers usually have other opportunities to catch what hasn't been stated directly if they just keep reading. The thing, though, is this: Readers have to *know* they're confused or don't know something, and students who continue reading without actively connecting details or being aware of what they don't know often wind up lost in books that are supposedly just right for them. So for students who struggle with making basic inferences, you'll want to design opportunities for them to figure out the basics in a text that conveys information indirectly.

HOW READERS FIGURE OUT THE BASICS

WHAT THE WRITER CONVEYS INDIRECTLY	WHAT A READER THEREFORE HAS TO DO
The narrator's name	Recognize the first-person point of view and look for clues in dialogue
The narrator's gender	Pay attention to pronouns and their antecedents
The narrator's relationship to the other characters	Pay attention to dialogue and/or actions that suggest a particular relationship
Where and when the scene is taking place	Pay attention to small details that offer clues about place and time
Who's saying what to whom	Track exchanges of untagged dialogue and/or attend to pronouns
Who's doing what to whom	Pay attention to pronouns and their antecedents
An event that happened in the past	Connect details that refer to something that's happened and/or pay attention to verb tense
What the characters might be feeling and why	Pay attention to what characters think, do, and say

FIGURE 5.1 *How Readers Figure Out the Basics*

LOOKING CLOSELY AT A PROBLEM-SOLVING SESSION

In the small-group session that follows, you'll see me work with five second graders whose teacher worries that they aren't progressing the way she'd hoped. On reading assessments, each child has been stuck at level J for a while, which, according to Fountas and Pinnell (2015), indicates readers in "need of intensive intervention." None of them participate much in whole-class read-alouds, and each comes with a history often associated with students who struggle: Anya and Sylvie are both English language learners, Monique is dyslexic, William (who fidgets with a pencil throughout) has been diagnosed with ADHD, and Bobby . . . well, Bobby is one of those children who, for no diagnosable reason, simply seems unmotivated.

Planning for the Session

What none of these children needs is a text with a high Lexile level and lots of challenging vocabulary, so I select something at their level that requires the kind of thinking they'll need in order to transition to books with less picture support and more implicitly conveyed information: *No More Monsters for Me!* by Peggy Parish. Despite a Lexile level of 70, Parish's text poses many of the same problems you saw in *Sarah, Plain and Tall*: It opens in the middle of a situation that began before the book started, and it has a first-person narrator whose name isn't directly stated. Also, to figure out who's telling the story and what's going on, students have to read actively and connect details together, all of which makes it a good choice for these readers.

In addition to the Core Practice on choosing a text below, I employ several other core practices you can read about in this chapter. I begin the session with an explicit teaching point (see "Crafting a Teaching Point," on page 67), give the students a choice for how to read the text (see "Offering Choice," on page 70), and decide what, if any, scaffolds to offer (see "Considering Scaffolds: To Model or Not," on page 72). You can look at these practices before or after the session, but as you read the session, try to attend to the teaching moves I make and to what the students reveal about themselves as readers as they wrestle with the problems this text poses.

CORE PRACTICE: **Choosing a Text**

Many of you are undoubtedly adept at choosing texts for specific teaching purposes. You select mentor texts for writing workshop because they contain great examples of craft moves you want to share with your students. You pick a text for reading because it lends itself well to teaching a particular strategy or skill, or because its content or theme is something you think your students will enjoy or benefit from considering. You also know your students as readers. You know who zooms through books, hooked on plot, and who skims to find fun facts. You know who your literal thinkers are, your book abandoners, your series addicts. And you also know which students claim to hate reading and which don't seem to be growing as readers—even if the reasons are unclear.

For a problem-based approach whose end goal is meaning, you'll want to choose a text based on two criteria: Look for a text that's relatively accessible at the word level but is complex because the writer conveys information and meaning indirectly *and* that presents the specific kinds of problems your students

Implementing and Facilitating the Session

In my lap sits Peggy Parish's book *No More Monsters for Me!* while in front of me sit Anya, Sylvie, Monique, William, and Bobby, with looks that run the gambit from mildly curious to wary. I begin the session by telling them that we've come together to practice something readers need to do, especially as they read harder texts, and I name that "something" specifically with a teaching point: *Sometimes writers don't come right out and tell us exactly what's happening, so readers need to be aware of what they don't know and then try to figure out what hasn't been said by paying close attention to the details the writer gives them.*

CORE PRACTICE: **Choosing a Text** (Continued)

could use practice grappling with. Given how often we've simplified or offered students shortcuts for the deepest and most meaningful work in reading, virtually every student needs lots of practice in figuring out a text's big ideas or themes. But some students can't begin to do that big-picture work because smaller problems trip them up.

Some students, for instance, struggle to figure out which words are essential in a text and which they could read over, and for those, you'd choose a text that offered opportunities to wrestle with that problem. For the types of students I noted earlier, you could set those literal thinkers up to consider more than one level of meaning in a text that conveys information indirectly through figurative language (See "Considering Complexity: The Problem of Figurative Language," on page 109), and you could help those fun-fact collectors experience what happens when you consider the connections and patterns between facts to begin to see the ideas that hold the facts together, in a text in which that happens. And while any number of factors might be involved in a student's lack of progress or professed hatred of reading, it's often because students are struggling to transition to texts that put more demands on them just to figure out the basic who, what, when, and where.

You'll find suggestions for texts that pose particular problems in the "Considering Complexity" interludes, but as you become more aware of the kinds of problems texts pose and students struggle with, you'll inevitably begin noticing those problems in lots of different books.

Next I share that we'll try this out with *No Monsters for Me!* and I explain exactly how we'll do that. We'll read several pages of the text together, and we'll pause after each one to share what we think is happening and why. And since I want us to focus on thinking, not decoding, I offer to help out with any unknown words. I then pass out photocopied pages to each child and give them a choice: Would they like to read it silently, take turns, or have me read it out loud?

Monique says she'd like to take turns, and since everyone seems amenable to that, I ask her to start us off on the first page, which she reads out loud, with me helping her pronounce "Minneapolis Simpkin." (See Figure 5.2.)

"Not even a tadpole, Minneapolis Simpkin," yelled Mom.
"And I mean it!"
"Okay, okay," I yelled back.

5

FIGURE 5.2 *First Page from* No More Monsters for Me!

Once Monique is finished, I ask the students what they think is happening. William says he thinks the mom and the little girl are fighting, and when I ask him how he figured that out, he says, "Because it says they yelled."

I acknowledge how he has gone back to the text, but then I ask if anyone knows why they're fighting, at which point Bobby, who hasn't seemed to be paying attention, speaks up and says the girl's a troublemaker. When I ask him why he said that, he looks at me like I'm from Mars and explains what he thinks should be obvious: "Because she's yelling back at her mom and she shouldn't do that."

"OK," I say, "they could, indeed, be fighting because she's a troublemaker. But does anyone have any other ideas?"

"Maybe because of this," Anya says, pointing to the words *Minneapolis Simpkin.*

Understanding a Problem-Based Approach: *"Questions That Shift the Focus from Answers to Thinking,"* page 75

"Hmm," I say, "*Minneapolis Simpkin*. Do we have any idea what those words mean?" Monique suggests that perhaps it's what the mom is cooking and she doesn't want to give the girl any yet, while Sylvie thinks it could be the little girl's name. I ask each child to explain her thinking, and Monique points to the picture while Sylvie says, "Well, the mom's talking to her, so that could be her name."

At that point Bobby blurts out, "That's just too weird."

CORE PRACTICE: Crafting a Teaching Point

At the beginning of a problem-solving session, you'll want to offer an initial teaching point that sets students up for the thinking work you'll be inviting them to do. These teaching points are similar to the kind you may already offer students, but whether you craft your own or adapt them from another source, here are a few guidelines to keep in mind.

First, try to connect what you're asking students to do to some understanding about how texts and writers work. In this session, for example, you'll see me telling students something writers do: "Sometimes they don't come right out and tell us exactly what's happening." Then I share what readers, therefore, need to do and how: "They need to be aware of what they don't know and then try to figure out what hasn't been said by paying close attention to the details the writer gives them." Framing a teaching point this way gives students a reason to do what you're asking them to do, and it helps them learn the thinking work of reading *and* how texts operate, both of which can help them transfer the learning from one text to another.

Second, be mindful of the language you use. I steer clear of the kind of figurative language that's common in minilessons, such as "Good readers hunt for treasure as they read." Language like this often baffles students and makes the already abstract thinking work of reading even more abstract. Academic terminology can have the same effect, especially when it's used before students have experienced the thinking for themselves.

Also try to avoid qualifiers like *good*, as in "*Good* readers figure out what's going on by paying close attention to the details." In *Choice Words: How Our Language Affects Children's Learning* (2004), Peter Johnston explains that words like this can create a binary or fixed mind-set, where, despite our best intentions, students start to see themselves as either good or bad readers. When "we *unwittingly* use language to position [students]," he says, "we provide them with the means

I ask Anya and William what they think of Sylvie's idea, but they shrug their shoulders noncommittally, so I suggest we keep reading and see if we get any more clues about why they're fighting and what *Minneapolis Simpkin* might mean. (See Figure 5.3.)

Mom and I always yell a lot.
But this time,
she was really mad.
And so was I.
I stamped out of the house.
I did not care
what Mom said.
I was going to have a pet.
I would take a long walk
and think about this.
So I walked
down the road.

6

Suddenly I heard
a funny noise.
The noise came
from the bushes.
I stopped and listened.

7

FIGURE 5.3 *Second Page from* No More Monsters for Me!

CORE PRACTICE: **Crafting a Teaching Point** (Continued)

to name and maim *themselves*" (79). Rather, he urges us to "*wittingly* use [language] to do the reverse—provide children with the means and the desire to construct themselves as responsibly literate democratic citizens" (80).

Finally, don't worry about offering a new teaching point each day. You can stick to a handful of basic ones that get at the core concepts of what readers need to do based on how writers and texts work. Limiting the number of things you teach will not only make your work easier but also give students more time to practice the thinking work of reading in order to ultimately internalize both the concepts and the thinking—or as Atul Gawande put it, to move from conscious to unconscious competence (see "The Necessity of Time and Repetition," on page 46, in Chapter Four).

William reads the next page, and as soon as he's finished, Bobby is off and running again. "See," he says, "she's a trouble-maker. I think she wanted to go outside after dark and her mother said no. And now she's really gonna get into trouble because there might be some older kids hiding in the bushes who aren't nice. Or maybe she'll be stopped by a policeman and she's, like, only seven years old!"

Understanding a Problem-Based Approach: *"Questions That Help Student Stay in the Text," page 77*

I notice and name what Bobby has done: He has thought about what he knows can happen to children who go out by themselves after dark and used that to come up with an idea about why the characters are fighting. Then I steer the group back to the text by asking if there's anything in the words that give us more clues to either Bobby's idea or to anyone else's.

At this point, Anya points to the word pet and says that she thinks the girl might want a pet and her mom has said no. This sparks an aha moment for Sylvie, who sees a connection between Anya's idea and the reference to a tadpole in the first line of the book, which makes her think this is part of an ongoing discussion about the girl wanting a pet. Monique likes this idea as well, but William is sticking with Bobby. So I suggest we read forward with these ideas in mind, and Anya reads the next spread (see Figure 5.4).

"Something is crying,
Minneapolis Simpkin,"
I said to myself.
"I will find out

8

what it is."
I looked in the bushes.
Was I surprised!

9

FIGURE 5.4 *Pages from* No More Monsters for Me!

"There are those words again," I comment before recapping our thoughts so far: that Minneapolis Simpkin could be what's in the soup pot or the little girl's name. Then I ask the group what they're thinking now.

Understanding a
Problem-Based Approach:
*"Deciding Not to Ask
Questions,"* page 78

Monique says she no longer thinks it's what the mom was cooking. But it could be an expression, she says, like "Oh, my gosh," which Bobby and William also think is possible. And so after noting how they've revised their thinking, just as readers do, we turn to the final page spread for the day, which Sylvie reads aloud. (See Figure 5.5.)

CORE PRACTICE: Offering Choice

If you cherish independent reading, you understand the importance of choice and its connection to engagement, motivation, and sense of ownership. Choice, however, is important beyond independent reading, and there are several ways you might offer choice in a problem-solving session. You might select more than one text that poses the same problem and let students choose which one to read. You can let students choose how they'd like to read—either silently, taking turns, or listening to you. And if they choose to take turns reading, you can let them choose how they want to handle unknown words, either by trying to sound them out or asking for help from you or a classmate.

All of these are *procedural choices*, and giving students any one or more of them contributes to the dynamic of the group or class in several significant ways. In effect it says, "I trust you to make your own decisions," which helps students build a more positive, responsible identity as readers. It also says, "There's no one right way to do things," which can encourage students to share ideas and take risks, which is critical to the problem-solving stage, where things can get a bit messy. And when you let students decide how to deal with tricky words, you send out another message: that how you think about the words is as important, if not more so, than how you read them.

Of course, there are times when it doesn't make sense to offer these kinds of procedural choices—especially when you're working with a whole class of students. But a problem-based approach, by its very nature, gives students much cognitive choice. That is, while students may not have a choice in what they read or how they read it, they have an enormous amount of choice in how and what to think as they develop and share ideas and theories. This is critical because researchers believe that even more than procedural choices, giving students lots of opportunities to make cognitive choices "may be the essential ingredient without which motivation and engagement may not be maximized" (Stefanou et al. 2004, 109).

"Wow! A baby monster!"
I yelled.
I looked at the monster.
It looked at me.
Then it ran to me.
I put my arms around it.
"Don't cry," I said.
"Minneapolis Simpkin
will help you."
The monster stopped crying.
We stood there
hugging each other.
"A monster for a pet?"

10

I asked.
Mom never said no
to a monster.
But I never asked her that.
Will she say yes?
I needed time
to think about this.
But there was no time.
It started raining.

11

FIGURE 5.5 *Pages from No More Monsters for Me!*

Several students let out an "ah" as Sylvie reads the line about the mom never saying no to a monster. When I ask them what's behind their "ahs," William jumps in, points to that line, and says, "They *were* fighting about a pet!"

I then ask Bobby what he thinks, and in typical Bobby fashion, he says, "Yeah, but she still shouldn't go outside at night by herself. And that's her name, Minneapolis Simpkin." When I ask him how he figured that out, he says it's because it wouldn't have made sense if the girl said, "Don't cry . . . *oh, my gosh* will help you." "But," he adds, "it's still a weird name. And it's weird that she talks to herself like that."

Understanding a Problem-Based Approach: *"Questions That Probe Student Thinking," page 76*

With the problems these pages posed now resolved, I wrap up the session by noticing and naming the reading work the students have done. First, I acknowledge that Bobby was right: the girl does have a very different sort of name, which is what confused us at first. I point out, though, what we all could learn from Sylvie: Sometimes writers don't come right out and tell us a character's name; instead they slip it into a line of dialogue and leave it to us to figure that out. I also applaud them for how they read closely, looking for clues to answer their questions and revising their thinking when they read something new. "That's exactly what readers need to do. No one knows everything right from the start; we just have to pay attention and keep thinking." And just because it's sometimes nice to let the kids have the final word, I throw out one last question: "Has anyone revised their ideas about the girl?"

"Well, she still may be a troublemaker," Bobby says, "but she hugged the monster, so I think she's also nice."

"And caring," says Monique.

"And helpful," Sylvie says, as everyone nods in agreement.

With that, the students head back to their tables and I gather up their copies of the text. They all will need more opportunities to practice this kind of thinking as they continue to grow as readers and read longer, more complex texts. They'll also need to hear the reading work they've done named for them more than just this once. But if experience is the best teacher, as the old proverb claims, they'll retain what they did here far more than they would if they'd just watched me model—and that, in turn, will increase their ability to transfer the work to other texts.

CORE PRACTICE: **Considering Scaffolds: To Model or Not**

Many of the scaffolding practices commonly used in classrooms—from preteaching vocabulary and background knowledge to modeling a strategy or skill—are specifically designed to simplify, if not avoid, the full complexity of reading. A problem-based approach, however, deliberately wants students to feel the confusion and discomfort a text can spark so they can also feel the sense of accomplishment and pleasure that comes from working their way out of it. So with a problem-based approach you'll want to think twice before automatically offering scaffolds, including modeling.

As you saw in Chapter 4, modeling has been associated with best-practice teaching for years, and it's one of the key tenets of the release of responsibility model, which is sometimes called either to-with-by or I-we-you. In that model, *I*, the teacher, demonstrate *to* you, the student, a reading strategy or behavior I want you to learn. Then I try it out *with* you, as *we* practice together, until I believe *you* are ready to do it *by* yourself, at which point I release responsibility to you.

The problem with this model is that when you practice it before seeing if the students truly need it, you risk creating a culture of dependency or simply having students zone out. And as we noted in *What Readers Really Do* (Barnhouse and Vinton 2012), think-aloud demonstrations (where you model your own thought process) come with another risk: While they're intended to show students *how* readers think, what students often take away is *what* to think (91).

CORE PRACTICE: **Considering Scaffolds: To Model or Not** (Continued)

To address these risks, a problem-based approach reverses the I-we-you model to what my math colleague Lucy West calls a you-we-I model. This reversal invites students to think individually first (you), then share their thinking with the class, a group, or a partner (we), as the teacher (I) notices and names what students have done in a more generalized way so the teaching can be transferred and applied to other texts. And because they've not only experienced it themselves but have felt the satisfaction that comes from figuring something out, students are more likely to retain what they've learned.

There will be times, however, when you will want to offer a brief model. Rather than being planned, however, try to make those decisions in the moment, as a direct response to students either looking at you blankly or having nothing to say. Quite often those blank looks and tied tongues have more to do with students being unaccustomed to sharing thinking in progress than with an inability to think. A quick model, in which you acknowledge that texts are confusing and written in a way that invites questions, can help students open up. So here's my rule of thumb: You can always jump in and offer more support if you see your students really flailing, but you can't retract support once you've given it. So think about how much modeling you'll offer as you plan, rather than just providing it as a matter of course, knowing you can't always see what students can do if you don't give them enough space to show you.

CORE PRACTICE: **Making Student Thinking Visible: Noticing and Naming**

A problem-based approach is all about designing opportunities for students to think. But that doesn't mean there's no teaching involved. In fact, teaching occurs across a session, not just at the start, as the teacher notices and names what students are doing as readers in a way that can apply to other texts— for example, *Oh, so you figured out the narrator's name by spotting it in a line of dialogue spoken by another character.*

Noticing and naming is, thus, a form of feedback—and a powerful one, at that. It helps builds students' sense of agency and identity as readers, makes the invisible work of reading more visible, and by employing generalized language, turns one student's thinking into a strategy that both he and others

CORE PRACTICE: **Making Student Thinking Visible:**
Noticing and Naming (Continued)

can use in other texts. But here's the hitch: In a problem-based approach, you aren't explicitly teaching *how* students should solve problems, so you won't know in advance what the students will do. You will, though, want to notice and name when they're doing the work of the initial teaching point. And by being aware of the problems a text poses and the thinking that might be needed to solve those, you'll have an idea of what to expect and listen for.

As with teaching points, building up a repertoire of things to notice and name develops over time, but a few basic noticings can take you far—and your students will benefit by hearing them repeated. To get you going, here are some things you can notice and name:

- how students navigate or figure out any of the problems the text poses
- how students connect details across a text to develop an idea (even if you know it won't hold up as the text unfolds)
- how and why students revise their thinking
- how and why students use an aspect of critical and/or creative thinking, such as generating possibilities or testing out their ideas
- how and why students use an aspect of complex thinking, such as considering how parts might be connected or noticing patterns of interaction
- the different ideas students have offered

Finally, if you're unsure how to articulate what you heard or saw your students do, follow this advice from Alfie Kohn's *Schooling Beyond Measure*: "When we aren't sure how to solve a problem related to curriculum, pedagogy or classroom conflict, the best response is often to ask the kids" (2015, 64). Ask your students to name what they think they learned about reading or themselves as readers. As you saw with the fifth graders reading "Louisa's Liberation" in Chapter 4, their answers can be wonderful.

UNDERSTANDING A PROBLEM-BASED APPROACH: The Role of Questions

As you read the session transcript, you probably noticed me making several teaching moves, one of which you'll see in every session: Once I set students up to problem solve by articulating an initial teaching point, I shifted into the role of facilitator. You may also have noticed that, as a facilitator, I used a combination of open-ended and text-dependent questions to elicit the students' thinking, and I regularly paused to notice and name both *what* and *how* they were thinking and making meaning.

Noticing and naming is a core practice in a problem-based approach, see page 75. But here we'll explore the key role of questioning to support students' problem solving and make their thinking visible by looking at three kinds of questions you'll want to have up your sleeve:

1. questions that shift students' focus from answers to thinking

2. questions that probe student thinking

3. questions that help students stay in the text

These kinds of questions will serve you and your students well, regardless of the problems your students are wrestling with or the instructional setting (whole class, small group, or a one-to-one conference). And in addition to exploring the purpose and benefits of these questions, we'll take a look at when *not* to raise questions and let the thinking take its course and what to do if students get stuck on an idea or seem at an impasse.

Shifting the Focus from Answers to Thinking

After the students read the first page, the very first words out of my mouth were "What do you think?" This is, perhaps, the most powerful question you can ask in a problem-based session, as it immediately puts the spotlight on thinking. And as the students continued to read and share out their ideas, I continued to keep the focus on thinking by asking

- what they thought of each other's ideas,

- whether anyone else had a different idea, and

- how their thinking might have changed as they encountered new information.

When you ask open-ended questions like these you help students stay open and receptive, and you foster the habits of mind and dispositions associated with creative and critical thinking. You also ensure that students' thinking is self-directed—or as Daniel Willingham says, "the thinker [is] calling the shots" (see "Critical Thinking: What It Is and What It Isn't," on page 31). Of course, calling the shots requires a sense of agency, and these questions help students develop that, too, by sending the implicit yet powerful message that they are people who think. In fact, you could say I was modeling with my question—just not in the usual watch-me-while-I-do-what-I-want-you-to-do way. Instead, through my action and words, I was modeling the value of thinking and my belief in them as thinkers. (See "The Power of Language to Position," on page 52.) And students usually pick up on that quickly. You may have noticed, for instance, that it didn't take long for each child in this session to begin saying, "I think," without being explicitly taught to do so or given sentence stems.

It's worth noting, however, that despite all these benefits, an international study (Alexander 2000) has shown that open-ended questions accounted for only 10 percent of the questions teachers ask. Determining the reasons for that low percentage were beyond the scope of the study, but I have to wonder if it's due to fear: What if students have nothing to say and simply stare at us blankly? What if their ideas don't make any sense, or are far-fetched or silly? And what if, without more direction and guidance, they not only don't meet a lesson's objectives but go off on all sorts of tangents?

Of course, any or all of these can happen. But once again, if we want students to take risks and become flexible thinkers, we must be flexible risk takers, too. And while that can be challenging, what's important to hold onto is that there aren't always right or wrong moves to make, just as there aren't good or bad readers. It's the process of thinking that truly counts, for us as well as our students.

Probing Student Thinking

Asking students what they think about what they're reading accomplishes several things. It helps create a classroom culture of thinking, supports students' identities as thinkers, and makes their thinking more visible. But asking students what they think is only the first step. You'll also want to probe their thinking, as I did in this session in two different ways: I asked them what was behind the "ahs" they all made and regularly followed up a "What are you thinking?" question with "How did you figure that out?"

In the first instance, I probed the students' reaction to the text, knowing that there's often thinking hiding behind an "ah" or a "huh." In fact, you could call these utterances—along with grimaces, smirks, laughter, and nods—authentic reader responses. When you probe them you not only show students that these responses are valuable but also learn a lot about their thinking. And, as happened here when William exclaimed, "They *were* fighting about a pet!" you also create space for students to share and celebrate what they've figured out. So you'll want to pay close attention to the sounds and gestures that indicate thinking and probe those responses right when they happen in order to catch—and celebrate—thinking as it's unfolding.

Whenever students share their thoughts or ideas, you'll also want to ask some variation of "How did you figure that out?" Probing student thinking this way lets you and other students see not just what a student thought but the process of thinking that led there—and once again you can learn a lot. In this session, for instance, probing helped me learn that no one but Sylvie had a solid understanding of how dialogue worked, that Monique might be prone to relying too much on visual clues, which could trip her up as she read more texts with fewer pictures, and that Bobby had a tendency to impose his own experience on a text, which could also interfere with his growth as a reader.

This kind of information rarely shows up in data printouts or analyses from other kinds of assessments, where you might get the names of students, for instance, who haven't met reading standard 1, but not learn how or why. Without that information, you can't always know what instructional steps to take next. But by asking students not only *what* they think but *how* they arrived there, you open the door wide enough for them to show you both what they're able to do and what they still may need to learn. Plus, probing student thinking helps students learn, too. Cognitive scientists have shown that children who can explain their thinking "learn more effectively and generalize more readily to novel situations" (Williams and Lombrozo 2010, 776), or, in this case, to other texts. Thus, the more opportunities students have to talk about their thinking, the more likely they are to transfer that thinking from one text to the next—and isn't that just what we're after?

Helping Students Stay in the Text

If you're new to this kind of teaching, you may be nervous about intervening in students' problem-solving processes lest you tip the balance of voices or interfere with the students' agency. You may have noticed, however, that while I resisted the temptation to jump in and "fix" the students' thinking, I did raise a few questions to encourage more thinking and help students stay in the text.

These particular questions can be open-ended as well as text-dependent, but it's important to note that while text-dependent questions aren't transferrable, the intentions and purposes behind these are. Here, for instance, when I asked the students if they knew why the girl and her mother were fighting, the purpose was not for them to find the answer, but to draw them into the text more by making them realize what the writer hadn't said. And helping students become more aware of what they don't know positions them to read forward more attentively and actively.

Of course, sometimes students answer those questions without really using the text, as Bobby did when he offered an explanation for the fighting that seemed to have as much to do with him as it did with the text. When this happens, you'll want to raise a question like "Has anyone noticed anything *in the text* that might support an idea already on the table or suggest a new one?" The simple qualifier "in the text" redirects students' attention to the page, and in this session, this redirect was incredibly useful, as it led Anya to point out the word *pet*, which then helped her and Sylvie construct a more text-based idea.

You'll note, however, that I didn't use the words *evidence* or *claim* in this session. And this, too, was intentional. A problem-based approach acknowledges that readers need time to think creatively before they critically assert—especially if we want them to see reading as a complex act of understanding, rather than of staking out and defending claims like prospectors during the gold rush (see "Creative Thinking: It's More than Mud in the Tea," on page 32). These students were in the process of developing ideas, not in proving them. At some point, however, after taking the time to consider and test out their own and each other's ideas, they'll be ready to assert claims or draw conclusions, and the details they'll use to develop their ideas can become evidence to support the claims. But until that point, they would be only details, and the students' ideas would not yet be claims, nor should we want them to be. While the ability to academically argue with evidence is certainly an important skill, we might better serve our students as readers if we think of that as a by-product, not the real purpose of reading.

Deciding *Not* to Ask Questions

Sometimes the hardest decision to make in a problem-based approach isn't *what* to say but whether to say anything at all. In fact, if you'd looked into my mind as this session unfolded, you would have seen me wrestling with whether or not to jump in at almost every turn. It's hard, after all, not to respond to student thinking, especially when a student is being insightful, as Sylvie was several times, or when someone goes off in what you know is clearly the wrong direction, as Monique did when she thought Minneapolis

Simpkin might be what the mom was cooking. It's so hard, in fact, that Alfie Kohn also wrote that "terrific teachers often have teeth marks on their tongues" because they "do more listening than talking [while] students do more talking than listening" (2015, 64).

So how do you keep your voice in check—ideally without scarring your tongue? Part of the answer is to always try to hold onto your purpose. The intention of any problem-solving session is not just for the students to get the text, but to give them a chance to build up the muscle to deal with the problems texts like this pose. Jumping in to rescue students or sanction one reader's thinking too early undermines that purpose and risks disenfranchising other students as thinkers. It closes a door, rather than opens one.

Also as students wrestle with problems, try to see their efforts through the lens of creative and critical thinking and focus on their strengths, not their deficits (see "Creative Thinking: It's More than Mud in the Tea" on page 32). In this session, for instance, all of these students were exhibiting a second-grade version of the exact suite of habits and attitudes associated with creative and critical thinking—even Bobby and William. You could see these boys as stubborn or surface thinkers, but when viewed through the lens of creative and critical thinking, you could say they weren't ready to discard a possibility without additional clues. And when more details did appear, they both were able to revise their ideas, which ultimately is more important than getting something "right" right away. Intervening would have disrupted that process and short-changed them both as thinkers and readers, which brings me to the question of trust.

I (mostly) am able to keep my mouth shut because I choose to trust that when we slow the process down, students can put the pieces of a text together in ways that allow them to see connections, relationships, and patterns of interaction (see "Tackling Complexity," on page 4). I also choose to trust the students and myself, believing that even if things don't go as well as they did here, there's always something to learn—if nothing else, what doesn't work. These are the choices I make every day I walk into a classroom, and keeping these choices in the front of my mind helps me hold my tongue.

Managing a Session That Has Gone Off Course

This session shows how students can solve problems with a minimum of scaffolding and support, but not every problem-based session ends on such a high note. Sometimes one or more students get fixed on an idea, such as Bobby almost did here, and refuse to budge. Some will get stuck on a detail that throws them off, while others can't seem to add up the details to their logical conclusion because that conclusion is inconceivable to them—like Minneapolis Simpkin being a name. And sometimes something more basic stands in a student's way, like an inability to navigate pronouns.

When a problem-based session goes off course like this, you may find yourself, as I often do, scrambling for something to say as you debate whether to prompt students more or let the thinking take its course. Usually it's best to choose the latter, but here are some other moves you can make:

- Pose a "What if?" question—such as "What if Minneapolis Simpkin is a name?"—if students get stuck on a detail or are seemingly at an impasse, and let them bat that around.

- Have students read forward until whatever has been indirectly stated appears more explicitly. Then invite them to look back and see if they notice any clues they hadn't spotted before.

- End the session as gracefully as possible and give yourself time to think about how to approach the problem you uncovered, which often involves turning to a less complex text. If everyone had balked at the idea that Minneapolis Simpkin was a name, for instance, I could have brought them together on another day to look at texts where more common names were revealed through dialogue in order to discover how texts work.

- Finally, if you can't hold your tongue and jump in only to regret it, forgive yourself and move forward, remembering how much students can gain when you set them up to solve problems.

 ## WHY THIS WORK MATTERS

Giving students opportunities to wrestle with problems provides them with concrete examples of what monitoring comprehension can look, sound, and feel like, and it lets them experience how thrilling it can be to figure things out on their own, which can help them become lifelong learners. It also allows them to reap what the Roman philosopher Seneca the Younger reputedly said was the true benefit of problem solving: "The important thing about a problem is not its solution, but the strength we gain in finding the solution." And with that in mind, let's imagine these same five children, eight or nine years down the line.

Picture them sitting in a high school English class, just beginning to read Toni Morrison's *Beloved,* a novel whose first page has defeated many a proficient reader because it's so enigmatic and confusing. Let's imagine, too, that the instruction they received as they made their way up the grades continued to build their confidence, resilience, and power as both meaning makers and problem solvers who were capable of figuring things out. What would they do with the first page of *Beloved* (see Figure 5.6)? Throw up their hands and wait for the teacher to tell them what to think? Pretend to read while under their desks they turned on the Spark Notes app on their phones or tweeted about another boring day in English? Or would they welcome this text as a challenge that they were more than ready to meet, knowing that if they paid attention to the details, thought about how they were connected, and then shared those ideas with each other, they'd be able to make some sense of it—and possibly even come to love it?

I know where I'd put my money.

THE FIRST PAGE OF *BELOVED*

124 was spiteful. Full of baby's venom. The women in the house knew it and so did the children. For years each put up with the spite in his own way, but by 1873 Sethe and her daughter Denver were its only victims. The grandmother, Baby Suggs, was dead, and the sons, Howard and Buglar, had run away by the time they were thirteen years old—as soon as merely looking in a mirror shattered it (that was the signal for Buglar); as soon as two tiny hand prints appeared in the cake (that was it for Howard). Neither boy waited to see more; another kettleful of chickpeas smoking in a heap on the floor; soda crackers crumbled and strewn in a line next to the doorsill. Nor did they wait for one of the relief periods: the weeks, months even, when nothing was disturbed. No. Each one fled at once—the moment the house committed what was for him the one insult not to be borne or witnessed a second time. Within two months, in the dead of winter, leaving their grandmother, Baby Suggs; Sethe, their mother; and their little sister, Denver, all by themselves in the gray and white house on Bluestone Road. It didn't have a number then, because Cincinnati didn't stretch that far. In fact, Ohio had been calling itself a state only seventy years when first one brother and then the next stuffed quilt packing into his hat, snatched up his shoes, and crept away from the lively spite the house felt for them.

FIGURE 5.6 *A page from* Beloved

STEERING THE SHIP

TEACHING MOVES TO SUPPORT THINKING AND MEANING MAKING
To shift the focus from answers to thinking, ask students often, "What do you think?"
Ask students what they think of each other's ideas.
Ask if anyone has a different idea.
To help students become aware of what they don't know, ask a "Do we know yet?" question.
Ask students if their thinking has changed as they keep on reading—and if so, have them explain why and how.
Ask students what they're thinking if they respond to the text with gestures, expressions, or exclamations.
Ask students to explain how they figured something out.
To help students stay in the text, ask if anyone's noticed anything in the text that might support an idea on the table or suggest another one.
Ask a "What if?" question if students get stuck on a particular detail.
To help students become more metacognitive, ask them what they think they learned about reading or themselves as readers.

FIGURE 5.7 *Steering the Ship*

Considering Complexity:
More on Figuring Out the Basics

To reach the point where readers are automatically able to make meaning, many children need additional time to deliberately practice connecting textual clues to figure out the who, what, when, where, and why in texts where the writer has conveyed these indirectly. Inviting a small group of students to read a page or two from the beginning of a text whose author employs *in medias res* is a great way to offer that practice.

These texts can be found up and down the level ladder, and to allow students to focus on this critical work without too many other demands, you'll want to offer them a text that's around their reading level. You may also want to give specific students opportunities to practice solving particular kinds of problems, such as figuring out a first-person narrator who hasn't been explicitly named and/or who's saying what to whom in exchanges of dialogue that are untagged or use lots of pronouns. For that, you'd want a text that presented those problems, like the opening of *Leftover Lily*, by Sally Warner (340 Lexile level, Fountas and Pinnell reading level M):

> *"Go away for a second, Lily. There's something I have to ask LaVon," Daisy says.*
>
> *We are playing outside after lunch, the same as usual.*
>
> *My heart goes floop. Up until now, the three of us have shared everything.*
>
> *"Go ahead and ask her—I don't care," I say, shrugging.*
>
> *"No, it's private," Daisy says, and she smiles and shakes her head. Her shiny yellow hair swings back and forth, like in a shampoo commercial. (1)*

Other students may struggle with figuring out where characters are or what's going on, and for those, you'd want to look for a text like Peter Lerangis' *The Sword Thief*, a book in the 39 Clues series (660 Lexile level, Fountas and Pinnell level S):

> *They were toast.*
>
> *Amy Cahill eyed the battered black duffel bag rumbling up the airport conveyor belt. It bulged at the corners. The sign above the belt said THANK YOU FOR VISITING VENICE: RANDOM PIECES OF CHECKED LUGGAGE WILL BE SEARCHED in five languages.*
>
> *"Oh, great," Amy said. "How random is 'random'?"*
>
> *"I told you, a ninja warrior must always keep his swords in his carry-on," whispered her brother, Dan, who had been operating on brain deficit for as long as Amy could remember.*
>
> *"Excuse me, Jackie Chan, but carry-on luggage is always X-rayed," Amy whispered back. "There are extra-special rules about samurai swords in backpacks. Even if they belong to scrawny, delusional eleven-year-olds who think they're ninjas."*
>
> *"What was wrong with 'we need them to slice the veal parmigiana'?" Dan said. "It would have worked fine. The Italians understand food." (1)*

To help you better match students with texts that pose specific problems, the following table lists some other *in medias res* books, along with the specific problems they pose and their reading levels.

TEXT	LEXILE LEVEL	FOUNTAS AND PINNELL LEVEL	PROBLEM POSED
"Worms," from *Hide-and-Seek with Grandpa*, by Rob Lewis	260	I	Invites readers to figure out something before the character does.
The Beast in Ms. Rooney's Room, by Patricia Reilly Giff	290	N	Invites readers to figure out something that happened to a character.
The Name Jar, by Yangsook Choi	290	N	Readers need to figure out an implicit shift in time and place.
"A Bad Road for Cats," from *Every Living Thing*, by Cynthia Rylant	870	R	Readers need to figure out an implicit shift in time and place.
Knights of the Kitchen Table (from the Time Warp Trio series), by Jon Scieszka	630	P	Readers need to figure out who's telling the story, who's saying what to whom, what they're talking about, and what happened.
Just Juice, by Karen Hesse	690	Q	Readers need to figure out who's telling the story, the relationship between characters, what's happening, and why.
"How Th'Irth Wint Rong by Hapless Joey @ Homeskool.guv," by Gregory Maguire, from the YA anthology *After: Nineteen Stories of Apocalypse and Dystopia*	810	Unknown	Readers need to figure everything out—starting with the title.
The Book Thief, by Markus Zusak	730	Z+	Readers need to figure out an unlikely narrator, *Death, The Grim Reaper*.

Creating Opportunities for Readers to Experience Deeper Meaning

Instructions for living a life: Pay attention.
Be astonished. Tell about it.
—Mary Oliver, "Sometimes"

Several months after *What Readers Really Do* was released, I stumbled on a blog post by a literacy coach titled "Confessions of a Plot Junkie." The author bravely and candidly confessed that she didn't think she did what Dorothy and I claimed readers really do—that is, she read for plot, not deeper meaning. She did, though, decide to try to think more deliberately about details and patterns in the next book she read and, as she wrote, what she discovered "was *depth*." She saw and understood more than she had when she had just read for plot—and the thinking she did didn't interfere with her enjoyment of the book. It actually added to it.

I think this coach voiced something many of us may feel. We're not always sure how deeply we read and are often a little uncomfortable when book talks drift to *theme*, which is the academic term we tend to associate with depth. I've felt this myself, especially in high school, when I pictured the act of finding a theme akin to casting a fishing rod into a murky pond and then reeling in what I'd caught. If I was lucky I'd snag a theme, though more often than not I came up empty-handed—or pulled up the equivalent of a rusty tin can, something disposable and worthless. To me, the whole process seemed hit-or-miss and much more reliant on luck than instruction—of which I don't remember any—and it was only years later, when I started writing fiction, that I felt I finally came to understand the term.

These days, of course, we do offer students explicit instruction on identifying themes, though I'm not sure it necessarily leads them to discover the kind of depth the coach wrote about. Consider, for instance, the class of seventh graders I visited who had just finished reading Paula Fox's harrowing historical fiction book *The Slave Dancer*. The book tells the story of Jessie, a thirteen-year-old boy who helps his family make ends meet by playing a flute in New Orleans not far from a slave market. His mother has forbidden him to visit the market, but drawn by his curiosity, Jesse wanders there, only to find himself kidnapped by slave traders who take him to their ship, where he's forced to play his flute while the shackled slaves "dance" to ensure their muscles don't atrophy, which would lessen their value.

Now that the class had finished, their teacher wanted to focus on theme, so I asked the students how they thought readers determined themes, and they said by thinking about what the main character learned. This is a common strategy for finding a theme, but when I then asked what they thought Jessie had learned, the majority said not to disobey his mother. "At what point in the book had he learned that?" I asked, and to answer that, they opened their books and flipped through the pages until they found the moment Jesse had been kidnapped, which happens on page 10.

The problem here is that, in seeking to identify something Jessie learned, the class latched onto a "readily apparent feature" and overlooked the numerous scenes and details that both explicitly and implicitly showed the systematic dehumanization of the slaves and Jessie's desperate attempts to hold onto his humanity, all of which might have led them to a deeper, more penetrating idea. (See "Creative and Critical Thinking in Action," on page 34.) This happens often when students are asked to think about theme at the end of a text, and it also happens when we provide students with lists of abstract words and sayings, such as *courage* and *don't judge a book by its cover*, and then ask them to match one of those to a text (Barnhouse and Vinton 2012). In fact, it's precisely this kind of thinking and teaching around theme that led the writer Flannery O'Connor to say:

> *I prefer to talk about the meaning in a story rather than the theme of a story. People talk about the theme of a story as if the theme were like the string that a sack of chicken feed is tied with. They think that if you can pick out the theme, the way you pick the right thread in the chicken-feed sack, you can rip the story open and feed the chickens. But this is not the way meaning works in fiction.*

> *When you can state the theme of a story, when you can separate it*
> *from the story itself, then you can be sure the story is not a very good*
> *one. The meaning of a story has to be embodied in it, has to be made*
> *concrete in it. . . . When anybody asks what a story is about, the only*
> *proper thing is to tell him to read the story. The meaning of fiction is not*
> *abstract meaning but experienced meaning . . . and the purpose of making*
> *statements about the meaning of a story is only to help you experience that*
> *meaning more fully. (1961, 96)*

Of course, reading the story might not help every reader experience the kind of meaning O'Connor is describing, because like any skill, reading can be done at different levels. We can skim the surface or plumb the depths—but it's only when we dive below the surface that we find deeper meaning. So how do we teach students to do that?

EXPLORING THE PROBLEM:
Experiencing a Text's Deeper Meaning

To answer the question of how to teach students to read for deeper meaning, we need to first understand how writers fashion texts and what the implications of that is on readers. And to do that, it's useful to take a look at the origins of the words *text* and *read*. The word *text* comes from the Latin *texere*, which means to weave and join, which suggests that a writer creates a text by weaving threads of details, images, and words together to convey meaning. *Read*, on the other hand, comes from an Old Teutonic root that means to fit together, consider, or attend to. If we think of reading and writing as reciprocal processes, this suggests that readers need to attend to and fit together the threads and patterns the writer has woven into the story (Barnhouse and Vinton 2012). And they need to start that from the very beginning, which is where many writers introduce the threads that will eventually come together to reveal deeper meaning.

To see what I mean, let's take a look at the prologue from Alison Pollet's chapter book *The Pity Party*. As you read it, try to attend to what details you notice—and if any reoccur to form what you could call a pattern—along with what questions those observations raise. (See Figure 6.1.)

In addition to the multiple book titles, which the author explicitly said was a reading list, you may have noticed the many handwritten notes about orphans. Noticing those, you might have also found yourself wondering if the character who wrote those notes was

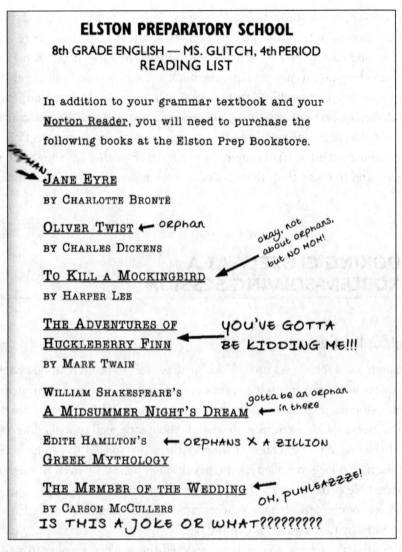

ELSTON PREPARATORY SCHOOL
8th GRADE ENGLISH — MS. GLITCH, 4th PERIOD
READING LIST

In addition to your grammar textbook and your Norton Reader, you will need to purchase the following books at the Elston Prep Bookstore.

orphan

→ JANE EYRE
BY CHARLOTTE BRONTË

OLIVER TWIST ← *orphan*
BY CHARLES DICKENS

okay, not about orphans, but NO MOM!

TO KILL A MOCKINGBIRD
BY HARPER LEE

THE ADVENTURES OF   *YOU'VE GOTTA*
HUCKLEBERRY FINN ←   *BE KIDDING ME!!!*
BY MARK TWAIN

WILLIAM SHAKESPEARE'S   *gotta be an orphan*
A MIDSUMMER NIGHT'S DREAM ← *in there*

EDITH HAMILTON'S ← *ORPHANS X A ZILLION*
GREEK MYTHOLOGY

THE MEMBER OF THE WEDDING ← *OH, PUHLEAZZZE!*
BY CARSON McCULLERS
IS THIS A JOKE OR WHAT?????????

FIGURE 6.1 *Prologue from* The Pity Party

an orphan or if orphans had anything to do with the pity party mentioned in the title. This wouldn't mean you had figured out the theme; for that, you'd need to see *and* experience how what you'd noticed unfolded as you kept on reading and revising your thinking. But noticing all those references to orphans, you'd likely read forward on the lookout for more clues that might explain their significance. And reading that way, with questions in mind, would ultimately help you consider whatever Alison Pollet might be saying about orphans or pity—or any other ideas she might be exploring.

Unfortunately, many students don't pay this kind of attention to details when they read, nor do they raise the kind of questions that might lead them to read forward more actively and closely. In fact, I first came across *The Pity Party* when I conferred with a fifth grader who was just starting the book and had breezed right over this page, without considering its possible significance—just as many students do. But in this chapter's classroom session, you'll see me create an opportunity for students to begin to experience deeper meaning by reading closely, raising questions, and considering possibilities about what the writer might be trying to show them *as* they read, not *after* they've read. And in doing that, they discover some meaningful insights about people and life.

LOOKING CLOSELY AT A PROBLEM-SOLVING SESSION

Planning for the Session

In this chapter, you'll see me set up a class of fifth graders to begin reading closely on the very first page of a new text by noticing, connecting, and questioning details in a way that engages and positions them to consider the text's deeper meaning. The teacher described her students as mostly literal thinkers, some of whom struggled to make inferences and understand the concept of theme. To support them, we looked for a character-driven book that wasn't too long, revealed its themes through patterns woven through the text, and was accessible at the word level. With fewer than two hundred pages, a Lexile level of 520, plus lots of figurative language and themes that seemed perfect for fifth graders, *The Tiger Rising*, by Kate DiCamillo, fit the bill.

I also crafted a teaching point that connected the work of readers to writers, and while I chose the book and how to read it, the students would have plenty of cognitive choices at virtually every step. Additionally I engaged in four more core practices: I made strategic decisions about chunking the text (see page 91); decided to make the students' thinking visible by using a combination of a text-based know/wonder chart (see page 94) and purposeful turn-and-talks (page 97); and crafted a low-stakes writing prompt (see page 101). And with all of these planning decisions in place, I was ready to launch the session.

Implementing and Facilitating the Session

SETTING STUDENTS UP TO BE CURIOUS

I stand between a document camera and an easel equipped with chart paper while the class sits before me on the rug. I explain that we're going to start a new book today called *The Tiger Rising*, and over the next two weeks or so, we're going to be thinking about what the author, Kate DiCamillo, might be trying to show us about people and life through the story. And to start that process, I'm going to ask them to do something readers always do when they begin a new book: keep track of what they're learning or figuring out along

CORE PRACTICE: Chunking the Text

With *No More Monsters for Me!*, I stopped at the end of each page and let the students talk, which works for a short book whose print isn't too dense. But with longer or denser texts, you'll want to make more strategic decisions about where to stop and ask students to talk, especially at the beginning, where writers introduce many of the threads they'll be weaving throughout the text and there's often much to figure out. The beginning is also critical in terms of students' engagement, so you'll want to choose stopping points that will help hook your readers with the book *and* their own thinking. And to do that you'll want to look for places in the text that might help accomplish the goals listed in Figure 6.2.

MAKING PURPOSEFUL CHUNKING DECISIONS AT THE START OF A TEXT

IF MY PURPOSE IS TO . . .	I LOOK FOR THIS IN THE TEXT . . .
Activate students' curiosity and confusion as an intrinsic motivation to read closely	A place early on that raises questions, because something's odd, intriguing, puzzling, or hasn't been explicitly explained
Help students see and experience the process of actively reading for meaning by problem solving	A place that contains answers or clues to one or more of the questions students have
Help me see how students are navigating the problems the text poses	Places where the writer has conveyed information indirectly—e.g., through dialogue, small textual clues, imagery, or figurative language
Help students revise, clarify, or develop ideas they're already circling or maximize the chance of them noticing a particular detail or passage	A place where the writer has provided information or clues that challenge, complicate, or affirm something students have been wondering about

FIGURE 6.2 *Chunking the Text*

with what they're curious or confused about. Readers do this because there's often a lot going on in beginnings, which the writer might not fully explain, and there may be information she introduces that will be important later on. Usually readers do this work in their heads, I tell them, but we'll be doing it out loud together to get a feel for the think-

Understanding a Problem-Based Approach: *"Welcome Curiosity into Your Room," page 105*

ing. Then I make a simple T-chart on the paper with one column labeled "What We KNOW" and the other "What We WONDER," which can include anything they're confused or curious about (see Figure 6.3), page 93 for completed chart.

Then I set the book beneath the document camera and read my first planned chunk out loud:

> That morning, after he discovered the tiger, Rob went and stood under the Kentucky Star Motel sign and waited for the school bus just like it was any other day. The Kentucky Star sign was composed of a yellow neon star that rose and fell over a piece of blue neon in the shape of the state of Kentucky. Rob liked the sign; he harbored a dim but abiding notion that it would bring him good luck. (1)

CORE PRACTICE: **Chunking the Text** (Continued)

Please note that for the last chunking purpose (helping students revise their initial ideas or notice particular details), it's important to remember the old adage "You can lead a horse to water, but you can't make him drink." Here that means that strategically choosing a stopping point doesn't—and shouldn't—ensure that students will notice whatever made you stop there. Readers don't need to catch everything to think deeply about a text, and it's more important to support readers in making something from what *they* notice—be it a question, an inference, or an interpretation—than to help them see whatever you saw.

Also note that when you read a text over several days, you'll want to stop less often since the point is not to dissect the text but to provide students with a meaningful experience. Sometimes that means reading a whole chapter—or more if the chapters are short. The trick is to try to stop often enough for students to engage in meaningful conversation that deepens their understanding without belaboring the text. And while that's an art more than a science, your students can help you with it. Too much groaning means you're stopping too often; too much getting overlooked means you're not stopping enough. Once you're sure, though, that everyone's engaged, you might also let students tell you where they want to stop because they've heard something they think might be important to think and talk about.

I decided to pause here because I thought this paragraph would raise many questions, and when I ask the students to turn and talk about what they think they know or have learned and what they're wondering about, there's a buzz in the room. There's also no shortage of raised hands when I bring them back together, with the choice to share something they either learned or are wondering about, since the order doesn't matter.

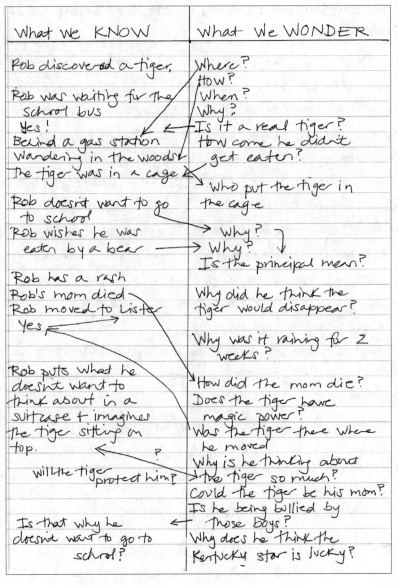

What we KNOW	What We WONDER
Rob discovered a tiger.	Where?
	How?
Rob was waiting for the school bus	When?
Yes!	Why?
Behind a gas station	Is it a real tiger?
Wandering in the woods	How come he didn't get eaten?
The tiger was in a cage	
	Who put the tiger in the cage
Rob doesn't want to go to school	
Rob wishes he was eaten by a bear	Why?
	Why?
	Is the principal mean?
Rob has a rash	
Rob's mom died	Why did he think the tiger would disappear?
Rob moved to Lister	
Yes	
	Why was it raining for 2 weeks?
Rob puts what he doesn't want to think about in a suitcase + imagines the tiger sitting on top.	How did the mom die?
	Does the tiger have magic power?
	Was the tiger there where he moved
	Why is he thinking about the tiger so much?
will the tiger protect him?	Could the tiger be his mom?
	Is he being bullied by those boys?
Is that why he doesn't want to go to school?	Why does he think the Kentucky star is lucky?

FIGURE 6.3 *A Text-Based Know/Wonder Chart for the First Chapter of* The Tiger Rising

I try to capture as much as I can on the chart as students share out, writing down what they've learned—that Rob discovered a tiger and was waiting for the school bus—and what they're wondering, which is a slew of questions about the tiger. This is exactly what I'd hoped for, and with their curiosity now ignited and their thinking recorded, the class quickly settles down to hear more.

CORE PRACTICE: **Making Student Thinking Visible: Text-Based Know/Wonder Charts**

In *Making Thinking Visible*, Ron Ritchhart, Mark Church, and Karin Morrison make a powerful case for "putting thinking at the heart of the educational enterprise" (2011, 23) and making it visible so both we and our students can see what's happening "under the hood" of a student's head. Noticing and naming helps accomplish this, as does orally questioning and probing students' thinking and recapping their ideas. Keeping track of thinking in a longer work, though—and with a lot more students—is harder, and here you'll see me use two indispensable teaching practices, a text-based know/wonder chart, which Dorothy Barnhouse and I shared in *What Readers Really Do* (2012), and the ever useful call to turn and talk.

If you're unfamiliar with text-based know/wonder charts, it's important to first understand how they differ from KWL charts. KWL charts ask students to recall what they know and wonder about a topic *before* they read, and the purposes are to help them access prior knowledge, spark their curiosity, and prepare them to learn from the text they'll be reading, which may or may not address any of the things the students have wondered about or think they know.

On the other hand, a text-based know/wonder chart captures what students are learning or figuring out from the text (what they know) as well as what they're curious or confused about (what they wonder). And its purposes are to

- spark students' curiosity about what the writer hasn't stated explicitly or revealed yet;
- make students become more aware of when they're confused (which is critical for monitoring comprehension);
- position students to read closely and attentively with a minimum of teacher prompting;
- help students hold onto what they're figuring out and learning;

SETTING STUDENTS UP TO DISCOVER ANSWERS THAT RAISE QUESTIONS

I chose my next chunk because here the writer has answered some of the questions the first chunk raised, and I'm hoping students will feel the thrill of finding answers to their questions and begin to experience the recursive way that questions lead to discoveries and new information leads to new questions, which can take them deeper into the text.

> *Finding the tiger had been luck, he knew that. He had been out in the woods behind the Kentucky Star Motel, way out in the woods, not really looking for anything, just wandering, hoping that maybe he would get lost or get eaten by a bear and not have to go to school ever again. That's when he saw the old Beauchamp gas station building, all boarded up and tumbling down; next to it, there was a cage, and inside the cage, unbelievably, there was a tiger—a real-life, very large tiger pacing back and*

CORE PRACTICE: **Making Student Thinking Visible: Text-Based Know/Wonder Charts** (Continued)

- see how meaning and thinking grow and evolve across a text;
- develop a vision of the complex and messy work of reading that's transferrable to other texts; and
- help us see when and how students' comprehension breaks down, as well as any misconceptions they may have about the work of writers or readers.

It's also important to note that the chart can outgrow its usefulness (see Chapter 7), and that, as a scaffold, it should be used only as a temporary support. Once students have internalized the thinking—and can hold the information and questions in their heads—there's no need to chart anymore, though sometimes you'll want to return to it if you're reading a different genre or a text that puts additional demands on students (Barnhouse and Vinton 2102). Over time, though, you can have students chart their thinking in their own notebooks. In fact, students often decide to do this with their independent reading books because they find it useful. And if you're not sure if they need the chart, you can, once again, give them a choice by asking them what they think—and then let them reflect on their decision after they've tried it out.

forth. He was orange and gold and so bright, it was like staring at the sun itself, angry and trapped in a cage.

It was early morning and it looked like it might rain; it had been raining every day for almost two weeks. The sky was gray and the air was thick and still. Fog was hugging the ground. To Rob, it seemed as if the tiger was some magic trick, rising out of the mist. He was so astounded at his discovery, so amazed, that he stood and stared. But only for a minute; he was afraid to look at the tiger for too long, afraid that the tiger would disappear. He stared and then he turned and ran back into the woods, toward the Kentucky Star. And the whole way home, while his brain doubted what he had seen, his heart beat out the truth to him. Ti-ger. Ti-ger.

With the word *tiger* still echoing in the air, I ask the students to turn and talk, this time about three questions:

1. Were any of their wonderings answered?

2. Did they learn anything else?

3. Is there anything new they're wondering about?

Once again the room erupts in talk, with much excitement around the fact that they've discovered some answers to their questions. They now know that Rob found a real tiger in the woods behind a gas station, and he didn't get eaten because the tiger was in a cage, which answered that question while raising another: Who put the tiger there?

I record what they've learned and are wondering about, drawing arrows between what they know and wonder to make the recursive process of questioning–discovering–questioning more visible. I also record two more things they learned—that Rob doesn't want to go to school and wishes he were eaten by a bear—along with the "Why?" questions these details raise. And that prompts a student to wildly wave his hand. He's sure that Rob doesn't want to go to school because the principal is mean. I'm aware there's no evidence for that, but instead of challenging him to provide some, which might shut his thinking down, I recast what, in fact, is a prediction as a wondering, which honors his contribution to the class while reinforcing the idea that what we know must somehow come from the text.

Understanding a Problem-Based Approach: *"Respond Without Judgment,"* page 104

With that settled, students pose two final questions: Why did Rob think the tiger would disappear? and Why was it raining for two weeks? I seize the opportunity this last question offers to notice and name for the class that it's actually the author who has made it rain for two weeks, not, say, a low-pressure front or El Niño. But wondering why she chose to have it rain is a wonderful question we might want to come back to.

SETTING STUDENTS UP TO FIGURE OUT IMPLICITLY CONVEYED INFORMATION

With no further wonderings, I return to the book and read the next chunk out loud.

> *That was what Rob thought about as he stood beneath the Kentucky*
> *Star sign and waited for the bus. The tiger. He did not think about*
> *the rash on his legs, the itchy red blisters that snaked their way into his*
> *shoes. His father said that it would be less likely to itch if he didn't*
> *think about it.*

CORE PRACTICE: Making Student Thinking Visible: Turn-and-Talks

In addition to charting students' thinking, you'll also want to use turn-and-talks whenever you're working with more than a handful of students to ensure that everyone is thinking, not just those who raise their hands. Some of these turn-and-talk stops will be planned and some will be made in the moment, as you sense a possible learning opportunity or recognize students need more time to process. Either way, you'll want to make the turn-and-talks purposeful by asking students to think about something that's text-based, open-ended, and not as specific as "Why was the monster crying in *No More Monsters for Me*?" or as broad as "Turn and talk about what you're thinking."

The planned turn-and-talk stops should coincide with your chunking decisions (that is, you'll want to ask students to turn and talk after each predetermined chunk). As for who should talk to whom, you can be flexible. If students have reading buddies or partners, let them work together. If not, just ask students to turn and talk to one or two people next to them. And in terms of what to talk about, ask students to discuss something that's connected to one of more of the following:

- your initial teaching point
- the work readers do at the point in the reading process they're in (the beginning, middle, or end)

> *And he did not think about his mother. He hadn't thought about her since the morning of the funeral, the morning he couldn't stop crying the great heaving sobs that made his chest and stomach hurt. His father, watching him, standing beside him, had started to cry, too.*
>
> *They were both dressed up in suits that day; his father's suit was too small. And when he slapped Rob to make him stop crying, he ripped a hole underneath the arm of his jacket.*
>
> *"There ain't no point in crying," his father had said afterward. "Crying ain't going to bring her back."*
>
> *It had been six months since that day, six months since he and his father had moved from Jacksonville to Lister, and Rob had not cried since, not once. (2–3)*

I decided to pause here because this passage provides lots of new information and poses some problems that require inferring. The writer indirectly conveys two shifts in time and place here—from the present moment when Rob waits for the school bus to the day of the funeral and then back to the bus stop—along with an important piece of information: Rob's mother has died.

Understanding a Problem-Based Approach: *"Let Students Be the Teacher,"* page 105

Aware of this, I listen carefully to several pairs of students as I once again ask them to turn and talk about our last three questions. Most of them have figured out that Rob's

CORE PRACTICE: **Making Student Thinking Visible** (Continued)

- the purpose behind your chunking decisions (for planned turn-and-talks)

- whatever made you think in the moment that students needed more time to talk (as often revealed by utterances and expressions)

Finally, asking students to turn and talk gives you an opportunity to see not only what students are thinking but how, and to hunker down and listen to students who don't always participate in class. If any of those students have said something intriguing, do share that with the whole class, as that can help quiet or reluctant students build more solid identities and agency as readers. More than anything, though, purposeful turn-and-talks generate thinking, which is critical if, as Bertrand Russell said in Chapter 2's epigraph, we really want children to think. And the turn-and-talk questions are frequently transferrable to other texts, as they support a process of thinking rather than serve as a comprehension check.

mother died, but I overhear one boy confidently say it's "obviously his grandmother's funeral," which his partner seems to accept. So when I bring the class back together to share and someone says we learned Rob's mom is dead, I ask if it actually says, "Rob's mother died," in the book. Everyone's eyes swing back to the screen, and after scanning the text, they shake their heads no, at which point I ask if someone could explain how he or she figured that out.

As one of the students walks the class through her thinking, I grab a new sheet of paper to capture how she added up multiple details to figure out what the writer hadn't said directly, which I write as an equation:

> *Rob doesn't think about his mother + a funeral + Rob and his dad cried +*
> *Rob's dad said, "Crying ain't going to bring her back" = Rob's mother died*

As a standard move, I ask if anyone has other ideas or figured this out differently. Several students also noticed that only Rob and his Dad moved to Lister, which helped them reach the same conclusion, while the boy who was sure Rob's grandmother died is quiet—hopefully because hearing his classmate helped him revise his thinking.

Similarly, when another student says she's confused about where the tiger is, I acknowledge how confusing all the time shifts are and ask if someone can share how he or she figured out the time line and where the tiger was. And as a volunteer explains, I make a mental note of which students may need additional small-group practice in making just these kinds of basic inferences.

SETTING STUDENTS UP TO RAISE DEEPER QUESTIONS

We're ready now to read the final chunk, which will take us to the end of the chapter.

> *The final thing he did not think about that morning was getting onto*
> *the bus. He specifically did not think about Norton and Billy Threemonger*
> *waiting for him like chained and starved guard dogs, eager to attack.*
> *Rob had a way of not-thinking about things. He imagined himself as*
> *a suitcase that was too full, like the one that he had packed when they left*
> *Jacksonville after the funeral. He made all his feelings go inside the suitcase;*
> *he stuffed them in tight and then sat on the suitcase and locked it shut. That*
> *was the way he not-thought about things. Sometimes it was hard to keep the*
> *suitcase shut. But now he had something to put on top of it. The tiger.*
> *So as he waited for the bus under the Kentucky Star sign, and as the*
> *first drops of rain fell from the sullen sky, Rob imagined the tiger on top of*
> *his suitcase, blinking his golden eyes, sitting proud and strong, unaffected*
> *by all the not-thoughts inside straining to come out.* (3–4)

By this point, the students know what to do. The minute I finish, they turn to a classmate and excitedly start talking, and as I listen in to a few conversations, two lines of thinking emerge. Some students gravitate to the figurative language around the Threemonger brothers, which they think might mean they're bullies, and they wonder if that's why Rob doesn't want to go to school. Others focus more on the tiger, wondering why Rob thinks about it so much and speculating on possible answers.

I capture their ideas as questions on the chart when we come back together, writing, "Does the tiger have magic powers?" "Will it protect him?" and "Could it be Rob's mother?" Then I notice and name what the students have done. In the beginning they had lots of questions about the whereabouts of the tiger and how Rob found it, but once they answered many of those, they started asking more "Why?" questions, which is just what readers do because "Why?" questions can help us dig deeper into characters' motivations and feelings—and in the case of the questions about the rain, into the author's deeper purpose. Additionally, with the new tiger questions, they considered possible answers by wondering if Rob's fascination with the tiger is connected to something else in the story, like his mother. "This is also something readers do," I say. "They consider how one part or detail might connect to another, or more generally how *this* could be related to *that*."

When it comes to the Threemonger brothers, however, it's clear that some students have no idea how to navigate that figurative language. So I ask one of the students who thought the boys were bullies to explain what made him think that, and that elicits a chorus of "ahs" as other students entertain a possibility they hadn't seen before. A handful, though, still look puzzled, so I ask the class if they think we should put this idea of Rob being bullied on the "Know" or the "Wonder" side of the chart. A majority, including some who thought the simile suggested bullying, think we should keep it on the "Wonder" side until we get more evidence. I notice and name that as something else readers do: They try to keep their minds open to possibilities until they find more than one clue. I also make a note of those puzzled students, knowing that they'll likely need some small-group sessions on thinking about figurative language (see "Considering Complexity: The Problem of Figurative Language," on page 109).

SETTING STUDENTS UP TO SHARE OPINIONS AND SURPRISES

With the chapter now finished, I end the session by asking the students to take out their reader's notebooks and jot down their thoughts about the low-stakes prompt I crafted:

- Do you think Rob's life is hard and, if so, why?
- How do you think he's dealing with his life?
- Do you think that's a good way to deal with life or not?

In effect, this prompt asks students to share their first impression of Rob and how he's dealing with the situation the writer has put him in, along with their opinion about that, which is work readers do at the beginning. And as they write, I move around the room to see the range of responses and pick a few to share out.

I start the share with a student who wrote that Rob's method of picturing all his bad feelings stuffed into a suitcase was "a good way to lock his feelings inside so they won't get out and he would maybe forget about them." I follow that up with a student who feels

CORE PRACTICE: Making Thinking Visible: Low-Stakes Writing Prompts for Fiction

I believe students need lots of time to talk about their reading, not to present ideas as claims as much as to collaboratively generate and grow them. But writing can help students grow ideas, too, if done in a generative and exploratory spirit. Unfortunately, though, while students are doing more formal, high-stakes writing about texts than ever before—in essays, arguments, and short constructed responses— they're not always invited to use writing as a tool to ponder, deepen, and question their own thinking.

Low-stakes writing can open the door for students to take risks and discover new insights without having to worry about rubrics or grades. So while writing shouldn't replace talk, it's important to give students opportunities to use it as a thinking tool, too. Much of that writing can—and should be—on topics of the students' own choosing. But there are times when it's worthwhile to have students consider a central question at the end of a small-group or read-aloud session, which can

- give you and the class a glimpse of the diverse thinking in the room;
- let you see what's going on in the minds of those who don't participate much;
- let students see how thinking evolves and develops over the course of a text; and
- give students practice in writing to prompts (which, for better or worse, is needed).

The key to crafting effective low-stakes writing prompts is to consider two criteria. First, think about where students are in the text. The work of the reader is different at the beginning, the middle, and the end of a text, and whatever prompt you craft should acknowledge those differences (see "Beyond Before, During, and After: Reenvisioning the Reading Process," on page 39). Beginnings, for instance, are where

CORE PRACTICE: **Making Thinking Visible: Low-Stakes Writing Prompts for Fiction** (Continued)

characters and situations are introduced, so it makes sense to ask readers to consider their first impression of the characters and how they're dealing with whatever situation the writer has put them in. Middles have all sorts of twists and turns that complicate what was introduced in the beginning. So here you could ask students to think about what's changing, plus how and why. Finally, endings resolve many of those complications in ways that give readers a unique window on a writer's messages, so a prompt at the end might ask students to consider the implications of the ending on the entire text.

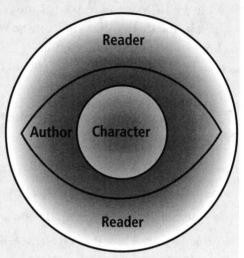

FIGURE 6.3 *Seeing the Text Through the Perspective of the Characters, the Author, and the Reader.*

Second, think about what perspective students should consider (see Figure 6.3). The most natural way to view a work of fiction is through the perspective of a character—which is why we often ask readers to try to walk in a character's shoes. But it's important to remember that it's not just the characters who are developing across the text, it's the reader and the writer as well. So you might also ask students what they think the *writer* thinks about the characters, which can engage them in considering what the writer might be trying to show readers about people or life. You can also ask readers what *they* think about what the writer is showing them, which invites them to talk back to the writer (which readers are entitled to do!) and reflect on how the text has affected them personally or fits into their understanding of the world.

Finally, if students are unaccustomed to low-stakes writing, you'll want to assure them you're not looking for a formal essay, just their thoughts at this point in the text. And as with turn-and-talks, you'll want to walk around the room as students are writing to get a feel for the range of thinking. This can help you choose a few pieces to share out to demonstrate and celebrate the diversity of thinking, versus the quality of the writing, and let you see who defaults to retelling rather than thinking. If any students do retell, pull them together in a small group, where they can have more practice in expressing their thinking versus retelling both orally and then in writing.

the opposite because, as she wrote, "it would be sad if he forgot his mother." After that, we hear from a student who raised a big question: "I don't think skipping school and wanting to die is a good idea because if you skip school you won't get a good education and if you want to die, what's the whole point of living?" And finally we end with a student who actually surprised himself as he wrote, which is just what writing-to-think can do. He shares that as he started writing about Rob's problems, he suddenly thought he understood something he hadn't before: why Rob might be afraid of the tiger disappearing. "Maybe," he wrote, "he thinks the tiger could die just like his mother did."

This powerful insight prompts another round of "ahs" as the class considers another possible connection between the tiger and Rob's mom. It also sparks a wave of new thinking, as other students start to make connections between the tiger and the loss Rob might have felt when he left his friends and old school behind to move. And this contagion of thinking, where you can almost see synapses firing in students' brains, is precisely what can happen when you give students the time and space to think without evaluation, through collaborative talk and low-stakes writing.

UNDERSTANDING A PROBLEM-BASED APPROACH: The Role of Response

The *What* of Response

In the last chapter, we focused on the critical role questions play in a problem-based approach, and here we'll explore the equally important role of response, beginning with looking at *what* to respond to. Here, for instance, you may have noticed that I responded to students by noticing and naming what they were doing as readers, which included how they

- moved from initial *who*, *what*, *when*, and *where* questions to deeper, more probing *why* ones;
- connected and added up details within the text to figure out what the writer hadn't said explicitly;
- pondered possible answers to their questions by considering how one part might be connected to another;
- considered the possible meaning of a simile; and
- decided to stay open to possibilities until they saw more than one clue.

BRINGING IN THE AUTHOR

Additionally, I noticed and named how writers and texts work, which is another powerful way of responding. Specifically, I reminded the class that it was actually the author who made it rain for two weeks, just as she made Rob discover a tiger and have a rash on his legs—and she did all that to show us something about the human condition that she wants us, as readers, to consider.

You could call this response a bring-in-the-author move, and it's incredibly important. Making students more aware there's a writer behind the scenes calling all the shots—and that their job, as readers, is to consider why she made the choices she did—helps students understand and internalize the concept that writers choose details purposefully to convey whatever aspect of people and life they're exploring through the story. So you'll want to try to bring the author in to both your planned teaching points and in-the-moment responses.

The *How* of Response

When it comes to responding to students, it's not just *what* you say, but *how* you say it that counts, as how you respond can make a real difference in whether students feel empowered or not—especially when you're in front of a whole class. In particular, you'll want to respond in ways that help create a safe thinking community whose members are willing to take risks with their thinking and share provisional ideas. To do that, be mindful of how you can inadvertently shut down thinking as well as how you can support it by keeping the following in mind.

RESPOND WITHOUT JUDGMENT

When students share their thinking with you, a small group, or a whole class, it's important to respond in a way that doesn't communicate judgment. That means trying to avoid saying things like, "You got it!" or "You're close," and being aware of your nonverbal signals—you know, those quizzical looks, raised eyebrows, and nods that let students know who's on target or not. Students pick up on judgment very quickly—in fact, I think they read us like hawks—and judging students' thinking directly or indirectly is a surefire way of shutting it down.

You'll also want to avoid assuming the role of cross-examiner or inviting your students to challenge each other at this point in the process, as that can shut thinking down precisely when you want them to stay in that creative thinking mode, receptive to multiple possibilities. This doesn't mean, however, that you need to accept everything students share exactly as they've said it. Here, for instance, I recast a prediction—"The principal is mean"—into a wondering, and I would have done the same with the students' ideas about why Rob seem obsessed with the tiger had they not already picked up and adopted the language "I'm wondering if . . .". Such recastings preserve the student's sense of agency and save you from evaluating thinking that's not ready to be evaluated yet. You will, though, have to trust the process to eventually weed out unsupportable ideas—and trust the community of thinkers in your room (Barnhouse and Vinton 2012).

LET STUDENTS BE THE TEACHER

In the last chapter you saw me use questions to probe student thinking in order to better see what was going on inside individual students' heads. Here, too, I asked students to share their thought processes, but this time to deepen their own learning and help others learn.

Along with research that has shown students retain more learning when they have opportunities to explain their thinking, studies have found they retain even more when they get to teach others, which is exactly what students are doing when they share how they figured something out. Letting students assume the role of teacher also helps create what Peter Johnston calls "a more symmetrical power arrangement" (2012, 56) in classrooms, where the teacher isn't the only expert and both students and teachers are learners. Plus, little can do more to build a student's identity as a thinker and reader than having a chance to teach his classmates.

But the benefits extend to those who listen as well. When students hear a classmate walk them through her thinking, they learn more, too, because I believe that, at the end of the day, they learn more from each other than they do from us. It's important, though, to ask if anyone figured something out in a different way or came to a different conclusion, as you saw me do here, both because you're not fishing for answers, but thinking, and because you want to create a culture of thinking where multiple ideas can exist side by side, without needing to find consensus.

WELCOME CURIOSITY INTO YOUR ROOM

Albert Einstein supposedly attributed his accomplishments not to any "special talent" but to being "passionately curious." And while this might be Einstein being modest, cognitive neuroscience has recently discovered a powerful connection between curiosity, learning, and memory. According to Dr. Matthias Gruber, "curiosity may put the brain in a state that allows it to learn and retain any kind of information, like a vortex that sucks in what you are motivated to learn, and also everything around it" (quoted in Barclay 2014).

Einstein also said, however, "It is a miracle that curiosity survives a formal education," and unfortunately research bears this out, as well. In his book *A More Beautiful*

Question, Warren Berger shares studies that show that while the typical four-year-old asks an average of over three hundred questions a day, a large number of them curiosity-fueled "Why?" ones, the number of questions children ask once they're in school "falls off a cliff" (2014, 44). And that steady decline in student questions is matched with a drop in their engagement and their ability to think creatively as they move through the grades.

This all seems connected to an educational system that values answers over questions. Plus, if we're expected to help students develop skills and acquire great swaths of content knowledge, bringing curiosity into a classroom can seem like opening up Pandora's box. It can lead to distractions or a lack of focus on whatever we're supposed to cover. And even if we're willing to risk that, curiosity, like critical and creative thinking, isn't so easy to teach.

We can, of course, teach questioning skills, such as how to craft open versus closed questions or use sentence stems that correspond to higher-order thinking. But that's different than teaching students to be curious—which seems about as impossible to me as teaching a cat to fetch. That's because curiosity needs to come from inside, which is why it's seen as an *intrinsic* motivator, unlike grades, fancy stickers, or a threat to call parents, all of which come from us. But through your responses and the environment you create in your rooms, you can nurture the very conditions curiosity needs to thrive.

 ## WHY THIS WORK MATTERS

Along with following Mary Oliver's epigraph's advice to pay attention, be astonished, and tell each other about it, these students were engaged in many of the dispositions of creative and critical thinkers. They were also thinking complexly as they began to synthesize parts of the text to see those possible big-picture connections, relationships, and patterns of interaction. And in doing all this, they were absorbed in a grade-appropriate version of the first step in Harvard's close-reading process: They attended to what surprised them, raised questions in their minds, or seemed potentially significant (see "Close Reading as an Outcome, Not a Procedure," on page 37).

But were they meeting the Common Core State Standards (or individual states' rebranding of them)? That's the question on many teachers' and administrators' minds. If you set aside, however, whatever notions you may have about what standards-based instruction should look like and focus instead on what the students were doing, you'll see they were engaged in the work of the CCSS anchor standards for reading, as they did the following:

- "read closely to determine what the text [said] explicitly and to make logical inferences from it" (CCRA.R.1)
- circled ideas that would eventually help them "determine central . . . themes of a text," as they considered the effects of loss and Rob's way of not-thinking about things (CCRA.R.2)
- considered "how and why . . . events . . . develop[ed] and interact[ed] over the course of a text," as they thought about how Rob's mom's death might be connected to his fixation on the tiger (CCRA.R.3)
- "interpret[ed] words and phrases as they [were] used in a text," as they discussed the meaning of those "chained and starved guard dogs" (CCRA.R.4)
- "analyze[d] the structure of texts," as they deconstructed paragraphs to better understand the sequence of events (CCRA.R.5)
- began to "assess how point of view or purpose shape[d] the content," as they wondered about the author's decision to make it constantly rain (CCRA.R.6)

This doesn't mean that every student fully met each of these standards. Many would need more deliberate practice before all of the thinking sank in, and some would need specific practice on dealing with specific problems, such as navigating shifts in time and interpreting figurative language. But when you set students up to authentically read a rich, well-crafted text for meaning, you automatically position them to engage in the work of the first six standards without needing to read the whole text three times. And the minute someone mentions another text or work of art, they'll be engaged in CCRA.R.7 and CCRA.R.8.

This complex thinking across standards is exactly what Timothy Shanahan says expert readers do. The problem, as he sees it, though, is how "to get immature readers to pay attention to the craft and structure while they [are] first making sense of the plot" (2013). Given what these students were able to do, I have to wonder if the problem isn't just in the assumption that students are "immature" but that the techniques and practices we use to "get" them to pay attention, including setting narrow purposes and tasks, don't help them develop the habits of mind complex thinkers and expert readers bring to texts. And that seems like yet another reason to embrace this more dynamic way of teaching: so that students can experience what it means to read closely in more authentic and meaningful ways, using the exact same thinking processes they'll need for college, careers, *and* citizenship.

STEERING THE SHIP

TEACHING MOVES TO SUPPORT STUDENT THINKING AND MEANING MAKING
Notice and name confusion as something every reader experiences—and uses to read closely.
Chart students' thinking without judgment.
Draw arrows to help students see how meaning and thinking evolve as you read.
Ask students to explain their thinking so others can see their thought process.
Notice and name how readers connect details to figure out what the writer hasn't stated explicitly (detail + detail + detail = inference).
Recast students' predictions, speculations, or theories as wondering questions.
Use students' comments to bring in the author, which helps students become more aware of the author's role and choices.
Notice and name when students ask more penetrating "Why?" questions.
Notice and name when students are engaged in thinking about how *this* might be connected to *that* (even if the thinking will later need to be revised).
Notice and name when students are engaged in any of the aspects or dispositions of creative or critical thinking.
Celebrate the diversity of thinking in both talk and writing.

FIGURE 6.5 *Steering the Ship*

Considering Complexity:
The Problem of Figurative Language

Writers often use figurative language to convey information, and this poses problems for many readers. Here, for example, is the beginning of a chapter titled "American Names," from Tony Johnston's *Any Small Kindness* (Lexile level 600, Guided Reading level X, interest level grades 5–7), where the author uses images, similes, and metaphors to convey a range of information.

> My name's Arturo, "Turo" for short. For my father, and my grandfather, and his father, back and back. Arturos—like stacks of strong adobe bricks, forever, my grandmother says.
>
> Really, my name was Arturo. Here's why: Three years ago our family came up from Mexico to L.A. From stories they'd heard, my parents were worried for our safety in Los Angeles. But Papi needed better work. . . . [So] like some random, windblown weeds, we landed in L.A. . . .
>
> In school, I get Miss Pringle. Miss Pringle's okay, I guess, but if scientists studied her brain, I bet they'd find it to be a large percentage of air. She's always kind of floating where she goes. . . .
>
> ANYWAY, first day of school, Miss Pringle, all chipper and bearing a rubbery-dolphin smile, says, "Class, this is Arthur Rodriguez." Probably to make things easier to herself. Without asking. Ya estuvo. Like a used-up word on the chalkboard, Arturo's erased.

> Who cares? Not me. With such a name as Arthur, I'll fit in at this school real
> well. Like a pair of chewed-up Nikes. Not stiff and stumbling new. American
> names are cool. They sound sharp as nails shot from guns.
>
> I'm not the only one who's been gringo-ized. There's Jaime and Alicia and
> Raúl. Presto change-o! With one breath of teacher-magic, there's James and
> Alice and Ralph. . . .
>
> When we're together, we joke about our new names.
>
> "So, 'mano," Raúl says . . . , "how's it feel to be Arthur, like a Round Table guy?"
>
> "Muy cool." I slip into full pocho, an English-Spanish mix. "Hey, Alice," I say.
>
> "Yeah?"
>
> "Seen Alicia?"
>
> She scans the hall. Digs in her backpack. "No, man. She's gone."
>
> We all laugh. But I notice Alicia's eyes, like two dark and hurting bruises. I
> fluff it off, easy as dandruff flakes in a TV ad. (7–10)

Johnston uses figurative language to indirectly convey characters' feelings, traits, and
motivations, as well as possible themes. And to figure out what this language might mean,
a reader would need to do a couple of things:

- Consider what the figurative language might figure by brainstorming
  attributes and associations connected to the language and then consider
  what that suggests about characters and/or themes. Alicia's eyes, for
  instance, are described as being like "two dark and hurting bruises," which
  is an image associated with black eyes and punches. Thus, the figurative
  language suggests that Alicia has been injured or figuratively punched by
  someone. At the same time, the images Johnston uses to describe Miss
  Pringle are all associated with things that are fake or thoughtless.

- Notice patterns and juxtapositions in the figurative language that could
  suggest possible themes. For example, the images Johnston uses to convey
  Alicia's and Arturo's quite different reactions to having their names changed
  suggests that the writer might be exploring how we form our identities and
  the value they do or don't hold for us.

For students who may need practice with considering the meaning of figurative language, here are a few other texts whose authors use imagery, simile, metaphors, and symbols to indirectly convey information and themes.

TEXT	LEXILE LEVEL	FOUNTAS AND PINNELL LEVEL	INTEREST LEVEL
Migrant, a picture book by Maxine Trottier	800	Unknown	PK–2
The Heart and the Bottle, a picture book by Oliver Jeffers	Unknown	Unknown	PK–3
Zero Is the Leaves on the Tree, a picture book by Betsy Franco	700	J	K–3
"Shells," a short story from *Every Living Thing*, by Cynthia Rylant	870	R	4–6
"What Do Fish Have to Do with Anything?," a short story by Avi from the collection of the same name	500	W	5–8
Home of the Brave, a novel written through poems by Katherine Applegate	Unknown	W	6–9
"Ode to Stone," "Black Box," "Inside," and "Self-Portrait: A Poem for My Father," poems from the novel *Bronx Masquerade*, by Nikki Grimes	670	Z	7–10

Creating Opportunities for Readers to Interpret

*We search for patterns, you see, only to find
where the patterns break. And it's there, in that
fissure, that we pitch our tents and wait.*

—Nicole Krauss, *Great House*

One of my fondest memories from grade school is of my fourth-grade teacher, Mrs. Porridge, reading *Mary Poppins* out loud to the class. Previously she'd read *Homer Price* and *Ginger Pie*, both of which I'd enjoyed, but *Mary Poppins* was something else. It was magical, mysterious—and a little frightening, as Mary Poppins could be stern. And the book confirmed something I already suspected but hadn't quite put into words: that growing up is a process of loss, which I poignantly sensed as I read about how, in *Mary Poppins*, children lost their born ability to talk to birds once they got their first teeth.

I loved the book dearly, so much so that when Mrs. Porridge finished it, I made my mother take me to the library, where I promptly checked out and devoured all the other Mary Poppins books. I also saw the Disney movie the very day it came out, and I vividly remember sitting in the theater, barely able to contain my excitement as the lights started to darken. But almost immediately I knew something was wrong. There was Cherry-Tree Lane, just as I'd imagined, and the Banks' house. But the person who entered that house was not my Mary Poppins. Yes, she had the requisite carpetbag and floppy hat with flowers, but my Mary Poppins was plain and strict, not pretty, plucky, and kind. My Mary Poppins would never add sugar to sweeten anything up, nor would she cavort with tap-dancing penguins or romp across rooftops with chimney sweeps. In fact, my Mary Poppins wouldn't even wink, let alone flirt and wear lipstick. But this Mary Poppins did all of that, and as the movie came to an end, I felt not only disappointed, but profoundly betrayed.

I share this because in this chapter we'll explore what it means to interpret, which is what Walt Disney and I had both done with *Mary Poppins*. We'd each read the words on the page through what the authors of *Grand Conversations* describe as "the light of [our] lived or imaginary life, culture, background, hopes, fears, and, at times, guilt" (Peterson and Eeds 2007, 13), and that had led us to different interpretations, not just of what the character looked like but also of the meaning of the book. For Disney, that seemed to be the cheery message that a spoonful of sugar helps the medicine go down, while for me it was more bittersweet: some budding sense that life was full of magic and loss, with the magic helping to make up for the loss, without ever fully erasing it.

Of course, I think my interpretation was better than Disney's because it hewed more to the book. Disney, on the other hand, took too many liberties, which Louise Rosenblatt, who first wrote about reading as a transaction between the reader and the text, cautioned against. Rosenblatt saw meaning making as "'an active, self-ordering and self-correcting process' characterized by subtle adjustments and refinements of meaning in an effort to achieve a coherent interpretation," which she described as one that attempts to take into account all of a text, not just selected parts (McGinley and Tierney 1988, 3). And in my humble opinion, Walt Disney didn't do this. He selected only details that supported his own view of life as one big amusement park. As teachers, however, our goal should be to help students to develop coherent interpretations that are personally meaningful *and* supported by the text. And to do that, we need a more complex understanding of how writers convey meaning indirectly through patterns that change and break.

 ## EXPLORING THE PROBLEM: Developing Penetrating and Supportable Interpretations

In the last chapter you saw a group of students begin to engage in a process of reading that could help them experience and develop interpretations of a text's deeper meaning. That process was connected to a vision of how fiction writers and texts work, with writers weaving threads of details through texts that eventually create patterns. Once those patterns are in place, however, writers play around with them, developing, changing, and breaking them in ways that indirectly convey a deeper meaning (Barnhouse and Vinton 2012). And that begins to happen in books written for even very young readers.

To see what I mean, let's look at Kevin Henkes, who uses patterns to reveal something about human nature in every book he writes. In *Julius, the Baby of the World*, for instance, the main character, Lily, is *always* being sent to the uncooperative chair (a pattern) because she's *always* being mean to her new baby brother, Julius (a pattern), while her parents *always* kiss, admire, and stroke Julius' fur before crooning that "Julius is the baby of the world" (another pattern)—to which Lily *always* says, "Disgusting!" (yet another one).

Something changes, however, when Lily's parents throw a party to celebrate Julius' birth. After watching all the relatives admire Julius, Lily's cousin Garland echoes her sentiments and declares Julius disgusting. But rather than seeing Cousin Garland as a comrade in arms, the pattern breaks as Lily becomes indignant and forces Garland to kiss, admire, and stroke Julius' fur while repeating loudly after her that "Julius is the baby of the world."

This is the fissure novelist Nicole Krauss writes about in the epigraph where we, as readers, should pitch our tents and wait, knowing it's precisely at this moment that we can see whatever an author might be trying to show us. Here, Henkes is showing us that it's one thing to gripe and complain about a family member, but something quite different when someone else does. In fact, hearing others complain about a relative can spark a sense of loyalty and protection we didn't know we possessed—all of which isn't fully captured by the saying "Blood is thicker than water."

Recognizing Patterns in a More Subtle Text

We can see how patterns operate easily in *Julius, the Baby of the World*, because the book is relatively simple and the patterns are all about the characters' thoughts, actions, feelings, and words. Many authors, though, weave subtler patterns involving structure, images, objects, and, as *The Tiger Rising* readers noticed, the weather. And to develop an awareness for those subtler patterns, let's look at writer Eve Bunting's picture book *One Green Apple*, the story of Farah, a young Muslim girl whose family has recently immigrated to the United States. Here's an excerpt from the opening, which I invite you to read while looking for patterns.

> *This is my second day in the new school in the new country.*
>
> *There are to be no lessons today because we are going somewhere. Other days will not be like this one. Tomorrow I will go again to the class where I will learn to speak English.*
>
> *Mothers drive us to the start of an orchard where a hay wagon is waiting. We climb on and lean against the bundles of hay. I think it odd to have boys and girls sit together. It was not like this in my village. . . .*

*I am different, too, in other ways. My jeans and T-shirt look like
theirs, but my dupatta covers my head and shoulders. I have not seen
anyone else wearing a dupatta, though all the girls and women in my
home country do. (5–7)*

On the lookout for patterns, you may have noticed that Farah remarks several times
about differences. The day is different than other days, the way boys and girls sit together
is different, and she, herself, is different, because she wears a headscarf and doesn't
speak English.

The pattern continues when she gets to the orchard and gravitates to a tree that's different: It bears green apples, not red ones. And when her teacher tells her she can pick an
apple, she chooses a green one—or more accurately, Eve Bunting makes her choose the
green apple, just as she made Farah note the differences in the previous passage, because
she may be trying to show us something about what it means to be different.

But then, just as in *Julius, the Baby of the World*, the patterns in *One Green Apple*
start to change and break—though it's subtler than in Henkes' book. If you continued
reading, still looking for patterns, the chances are good you'd begin to notice that instead
of focusing on differences, Farah starts noticing similarities. The dogs in the orchard, for
instance, are similar to the dog she had at home, and the one green apple she chooses is
"small and alone," just as she is. Additionally, as the story winds down, Farah notes that
"laughs sound the same as at home. . . . So do sneezes and belches and lots of things"
(28). And if we remember that it's the author who, like a master puppeteer, is making
Farah think this, it's our job as readers to figure out why. What might Bunting be trying
to show us through these patterns of similarities and differences? Perhaps that our similarities can outweigh our differences, or that we can be different but still belong because
we share so much that's similar.

Readers rarely build such penetrating interpretations from what's most obvious in a
text. (See "Creative Thinking: It's More than Mud in the Tea," on page 32.) For that they
need to notice and question patterns, then keep reading with those questions in mind,
using them, in effect, as lines of inquiry that lead to the deeper layers of a text. And that's
exactly what you'll see me do in this session: help students construct these deeper, more
penetrating interpretations by setting them up to notice patterns, ask questions about
them, and read forward, revising, adjusting, and refining their ideas as they move through
the text (see Figure 7.1).

HOW READERS DEVELOP COHERENT INTERPRETATIONS

WHAT WRITERS CONVEY INDIRECTLY	WHAT READERS, THEREFORE, NEED TO DO
Themes, central ideas, or deeper meanings	Look for patterns and raise pattern-based "Why?" questions
	Use a pattern-based question as a line of inquiry and read forward, looking for clues about possible explanations
	Revise their ideas as they notice new clues, changes, or breaks in the patterns
	Consider the implications of the ending and think, "What might the writer be showing me by ending the story this way?"
	Let go of ideas that don't play out at the end
	Revise their ideas once again to take in the implications of the ending
	Consider how other details fit in with their idea and adjust and revise if needed (discarding ideas that can't accommodate other details)

FIGURE 7.1 *How Readers Develop Coherent Interpretations*

LOOKING CLOSELY AT A PROBLEM-SOLVING SESSION

Planning for the Session

In this session I am working with a class of third graders who have already read the beginning of Cynthia Rylant's picture book *The Old Woman Who Named Things*, using a text-based know/wonder chart to support their thinking. The book tells the story of an old woman who has outlived all of her friends and is so afraid of outliving others that she shies away from forming attachments. Instead, she names inanimate objects that she thinks will outlive her, like her house and her car. At first, this arrangement seems to be working, but things get complicated in the middle when a puppy keeps appearing at the old woman's gate, and these complications only get worse when the puppy doesn't appear one day. This forces the old woman to rethink the decisions she has made in her life—and all of this is conveyed through patterns, which, once established, change and break.

To begin planning, I first assess the students' work to determine next steps, using the Core Practice guidelines below. Then I use my awareness of where the patterns break and change to decide where to chunk the text and have students turn and talk. Additionally, I employ two more Core Practices: I decide how to make students' thinking visible with charts that deepen and extend thinking (page 121) and how much responsibility to give students (page 124).

CORE PRACTICE: Assessing Student Work to Determine Next Steps

Until now you've seen students at the start of the reading process as they grappled with the beginning of a text (see "The Reading Process for Narratives," on page 40). These students, however, are entering the middle, where readers need to pay attention to how writers complicate, develop, and ultimately resolve what they've introduced in the beginning. And because the thinking here is different, you'll want to reframe what you're asking students to do. Deciding how to do that will depend on the thinking your students have already done, and to assess that, look at the thinking captured on your know/wonder chart to see if the chart has accomplished what it was intended for.

- Has it helped students develop a first-draft understanding of the characters and the problems they face?

- Does it contain one or more probing questions (often beginning with *why*) or indicate an awareness of patterns?

The first question is critical because it's hard, if not impossible, to embark on the work of interpretation if the basics aren't in place. Think back, for example, to the second graders reading *No More Monsters for Me!* How far would they get, in terms of deeper meaning, if they thought Minneapolis Simpkin was what was simmering on the stove? On the other hand, the second question helps you segue from the beginning- to the middle-of-the-book work, which is the next step in the process.

To practice assessing student work this way, take a look at the third graders' know/wonder chart, in Figure 7.2. They seem to have a basic understanding of the main character and her problem, and they've also raised a handful of questions, including several beginning with *why*. Additionally, some of what's in the "What We Know" column reflects an awareness of patterns, as indicated by the words *never* and

CORE PRACTICE: **Assessing Student Work** (Continued)

What We KNOW	What We WONDER
The old woman names everything Her chair → Fred Her car → Betsy Her bed → Roxanne Her house → Franklin	Why does she name things? What's her name? Did she give her things the names of her friends?
She never gets any letters, only bill She's outlived her friends She doesn't want to be a lonely old woman There's a picture of her w/ a dog on the cover	Is she pretending the things are her friends because she doesn't have any? Why doesn't she make friends? What does outlive mean? — that her friends have died? — that she lives in the country where no one else does (she lives out)? Were all her friends old too?
A puppy shows up at her gate (!) She feeds the puppy then tells it to go away?	How does she make a living? Will she find a dog to be a friend? Is the puppy a stray? Does it have an owner? Why doesn't she see that the puppy could be her friend?

FIGURE 7.2 *Third-Grade Know/Wonder Chart for* The Old Woman Who Named Things

always (and one implicit *always* in "The old woman names everything").

This indicates the chart has served its purpose and the students are ready to move on. But since classrooms and teaching are complex, you won't always see evidence of a basic understanding, probing questions, and/or an awareness of patterns in every chart. So Figure 7.3 explains how to handle other common scenarios. Regardless of which path your students need, though, you'll ultimately want to take one last look at the know/wonder chart and choose a probing question or pattern to launch the next part of the process. This could be a question that holds the potential to lead students to the heart of a text, like the one I use in this session: "Why doesn't the old woman see that the puppy could be a friend?" Or you could choose a pattern and preface it with the words *Why is* or *How come*.

Using students' own thinking to move the process forward is important for several reasons. It promotes engagement, a sense of agency, and ownership—which all increase the likelihood of students applying and transferring the thinking to other texts. It also gives you a great opportunity to show students what else they can make with what they've noticed, which is the essence of virtually all thinking. At the beginning of a text, for instance, students use what they notice to raise questions and make basic inferences. But as they move forward, you'll want them to experience how they can extend and deepen their thinking by using what they've noticed to develop interpretations.

DETERMINING NEXT STEPS BY ASSESSING STUDENTS' KNOW/WONDER CHART

IF YOU SEE THIS . . .	THEN DO THIS . . .
Students have missed something basic or have focused on only one part of the text	Reframe their thinking around what they missed before moving on to middle-of-the-book work
Students have a basic first-draft understanding but their questions are all about what or when something might happen or are aimed at things beyond the text	Make them aware of what the writer hasn't explicitly stated by asking if they know why a character is doing, saying, or thinking something that appears in the "Know" column. Then invite them to wonder *why* about other things they know
Students still don't have any probing questions or haven't noticed any patterns	Explicitly ask students if they've noticed any patterns—modeling briefly, if needed—then let them turn and talk and record their thinking
Students have a basic first-draft understanding but haven't noticed more than one or two patterns	Use the step above to flush out patterns

FIGURE 7.3 *Determining Next Steps by Assessing Student Work*

Implementing and Facilitating the Session

SETTING STUDENTS UP TO CONSIDER PATTERNS AND BIG QUESTIONS

The third graders have read up to the part where the puppy keeps returning to the old woman's gate and she keeps shooing him away. Now, as the students settle on the rug, I clip the new chart I've made on an easel and introduce it and our next steps this way:

"Yesterday we did some amazing thinking about *The Old Woman Who Named Things*. We figured out lots of things and also had lots of questions, just like readers do when they begin a book. But one of those questions really puzzled us: 'Why doesn't the old woman see that the puppy could be a friend?' Wondering about why a character is or isn't doing something is actually what writers want their readers to do. So today, we're going to keep reading forward to see if we can figure out why the old woman doesn't see that.

> **Understanding a Problem-Based Approach:** *"The Task Is Expansive Rather Than Targeted," page 128*

"Before we start, though, I want to ask if anyone's noticed any patterns—that is, things that keep happening or are repeated. I ask because writers use patterns to show us something about people or life that they want us to think about. And I think this question came up because we'd noticed the old woman was always hoping she'd get letters from friends, which made us wonder why she didn't see that the puppy could be her friend. We didn't call it a pattern before, but that's exactly what I mean by a pattern—something that repeats or keeps happening. So could everyone turn and talk for a moment about what patterns you may have noticed?"

There's a hum in the room as students turn and talk, and when I bring them back together to share out, I add the many patterns they've noticed to the chart (see Figure 7.5).

SETTING STUDENTS UP TO CONSIDER POSSIBILITIES

Next I invite the students to consider our big inquiry question with these patterns in mind: "Wow, you noticed lots of patterns! I think these are really going to help us think about our question, because the answer is probably connected to some of these patterns in some way. In fact, before we start reading again, let's take a moment to turn and talk about why the old woman might not see that the puppy could be her friend. And let's see if any of these patterns can give us some ideas."

The students talk for a few minutes, and when we come back together to share out, I record the students' thinking, prefacing their ideas by the word *maybe* to reinforce that these are provisional, work-in-progress ideas. I also ask each student who shares out how he or she got the idea and capture that thinking in parentheses (see Figure 7.4).

Understanding a Problem-Based Approach: *"Readers Must Be Tentative Before They Are Certain," page 129*

Understanding a Problem-Based Approach: *"Thinking Diverges Before It Coalesces," page 129*

Some students are intrigued by their classmates' ideas, and some question other students' thinking. One student, for instance, thinks that Fred, Betsy, Franklin, and Roxanne are "fake friends," not real ones, that the old woman is using as an excuse. This is clearly insightful thinking, but the majority of students take the old woman at her word. So I notice and name what the students have done: When readers are entering the middle of a book, they may have lots of different ideas about what's going on, and they don't all have to agree. Instead they try to keep their minds open to multiple ideas, because at this point almost anything could happen. And to help the students hold onto this idea, I add it to the chart as a wondering in the first column.

WHAT WE WONDER (OUR BIG QUESTION)	PATTERNS WE'VE NOTICED	WHAT WE THINK (OUR MAYBE STATEMENTS)
Why doesn't the old woman see that the puppy could be a friend? Are Franklin, Betsy, Fred, and Roxanne real friends or fake friends?	She always hopes for letters, but all she gets are bills. She always names things, but she doesn't name the puppy. She's always talking to her car, house, bed, and chair like they're people. She always drives to the post office. She's always alone. She always thinks about outliving. The puppy always comes to her gate. The old woman always feeds it and then tells it to go away. The old woman feels sad.	MAYBE she's afraid the dog will die because it's a living thing. (She only names things that aren't alive.) MAYBE she tells the dog to go away because she doesn't have enough room. (She tells the puppy that Roxanne wasn't big enough for both her and a puppy.) MAYBE she doesn't want to be friends with the puppy because the puppy might not last. (Like she didn't name the gate with the rusted hinges because she thought it "wasn't long for this world.") MAYBE she's afraid it's owned by someone else who will come after it, and she doesn't want to make a friend she'll lose. (Like she lost her old friends.) MAYBE it's because Franklin, Betsy, Fred, and Roxanne don't like dogs. (She tells the puppy that Fred and Franklin don't let puppies sit on them.) MAYBE the dog really is hers and she just doesn't remember. (She's old and talks to her furniture and car.)

FIGURE 7.4 *Third-Grade Chart to Extend and Deepen Thinking*

CORE PRACTICE: **Making Student Thinking Visible: Charts That Extend and Deepen Student Thinking**

Once you've assessed students' know/wonder chart and have chosen a question or pattern to follow as a line of inquiry, you'll need to make a new chart. Depending on your students, the kind of text they're reading, and what you've seen in their know/wonder chart, these charts can take different forms, but they share the same intention: They invite students to focus their attention on details and clues that can help them consider an inquiry question, rather than anything they might notice in the text. This reframing positions students to go deeper, rather than wider, into the text, which is just where you want them to go. In addition to sharing a purpose, these charts also

- capture some of the important thinking students have already done;
- note specific questions, patterns, or details from the text;
- set students up to consider possibilities and develop and/or revise ideas as they move deeper into a text; and
- help students see how thinking evolves across a text.

CORE PRACTICE: **Making Student Thinking Visible: Charts That Extend and Deepen Student Thinking** (Continued)

For picture books that aren't terribly dense, I recommend the kind of chart I used with the third graders, which has three columns instead of two. The first column records a line of inquiry (or in kid-friendly language, a "big question") (see p. 123) taken from the students' know/wonder chart. The second reframes what students know as patterns, and the third is devoted to what students think the answer to their question might be, with those ideas framed as "maybe statements," not theories, to acknowledge they're still works-in-progress (Barnhouse and Vinton 2012).

Chapter books, however, require readers to hold onto more information over many more pages, and the patterns writers weave across those pages are developed in more complex and nuanced ways. So while you'll still want to start with an inquiry question, you'll want to record specific lines in the text that address the pattern, knowing that in longer works, any pattern will eventually lead to deeper layers of the text.

For an example of this kind of chart, let's go back to *The Tiger Rising.* Many of the details Kate DiCamillo wove into the first chapter eventually form patterns. The Kentucky Star, the suitcase, and Rob's rash keep appearing, as do the overcast skies, and in Figure 7.5, you'll find a chart that has turned the pattern about the rash into the inquiry question "Why does Rob *never* want to think about his rash?" In the second column you'll note lines from the text where the pattern appears, and if you read these lines sequentially, you can actually see how writers develop patterns to convey meaning across a text. The first line introduces the rash, while the second suggests it's not a simple skin condition but is somehow connected to Rob's mother and the thoughts he's trying to suppress. The third suggests it's not just thoughts but feelings that Rob is trying to ignore. And by the fourth, readers who are reading closely and thinking about the significance of the pattern learn that the rash flares up whenever he feels something deeply, even if it's good. This could lead readers to consider the possibility that Kate DiCamillo might be trying to show them that ignoring your feelings can leave you unable to feel much of anything at all.

Finally, it's important to remember that readers don't read to fill out charts—or worksheets or graphic organizers. They read to think deeply about what the writer might be trying to show them, and the chart helps them hold onto and revise their thinking as they continue to read. So make sure your charts are serving that purpose and don't become ends unto themselves. And one surefire way to do this is to ask your students if they find them useful and give them a chance to reflect on why and how.

WHAT WE WONDER (OUR INQUIRY QUESTION)	WHAT WE KNOW (PATTERN LINES)	WHAT WE THINK THE WRITER MIGHT BE SHOWING US
Why does Rob *never* want to think about his rash though it *always* bothers him?	"He did not think about the rash on his legs, the itchy red blisters that snaked their way into his shoes." p. 2	
	"He thought about the tiger. And he thought about Sistine. He did not think about his rash. He did not think about his mother." p. 10	
	"'Sadness,' said Willie May, closing her eyes and nodding her head. 'You keeping all that sadness down low in your legs. You not letting it get up to your heart where it belongs.'" p. 37	
	"'You're an artist,' she said. 'Naw,' said Rob. He felt a hot wave of embarrassment and joy roll over him. It lit his rash on fire." p. 43	

FIGURE 7.5 *Chart That Reframes the Task Around a Single Pattern-Based Question in a Chapter Book* (The Tiger Rising)

SETTING STUDENTS UP TO NOTICE PATTERNS BREAKING

Now that students have begun the work of interpretation and are eager to return to the text, I set them up to look for places where they think a pattern might be changing or breaking. I point out that they spotted a change already when they noticed the old woman didn't name the puppy, even though she always names things. Then I ask the students to stop me as I'm reading by giving me a thumbs-up if they think they've noticed a pattern change or break. And a few pages later, thumbs sprout up as I read:

> Then one day that shy brown dog did not come to the old woman's house. She sat in Fred and watched the gate all day long, but the dog never came. The old woman felt sad.
>
> The next day again the dog did not come. The old woman drove Betsy around town looking for the dog, but she did not find it. The old woman felt even sadder.

The class is excited to turn and talk about this new development, but before they do, I notice and name what our author has done and what they, as readers, need to ponder: "So a big pattern broke here and I bet many of you are wondering why the dog stopped coming.

We might find that out as we keep reading, but there's another important question readers need to consider: *Why* did the author do that? Why did Cynthia Rylant make the dog stop coming? She's the one, after all, who created a character who always names things and thinks about outliving her friends. She's the one who made the dog keep coming to the gate and the old woman keep sending him away. And now she has made the puppy not come back. So why do you think she might have done that? What might she want us—or the old woman—to see? And does that help our thinking about our big question?"

CORE PRACTICE: **Deciding How Much Responsibility to Give Students**

If this is your class' first outing at following a line of inquiry to develop interpretations, you'll probably want to choose which student-raised question the class should follow, and you'll also want to be the one who charts the students' thinking. But here are several more ways you can, over time, move beyond the I-choose-and-chart-while-you-think-and-talk structure, each of which progressively gives students more responsibility:

- Let the class decide which pattern and/or line of inquiry to follow.

- Form small groups of students to discuss the whole-class line of inquiry, with the students taking turns charting each other's thoughts or collaboratively creating their own small-group chart.

- Assign different lines of inquiry to different groups of students, with the students taking turns recording the groups' ideas or collaboratively creating a chart.

- Let students choose which line of inquiry they want to follow and have them form groups with like-minded others, choosing how they'll capture their thinking as well.

- Let students talk and then write a notebook entry about how and why their thinking has changed after a whole-class or small-group discussion.

- Let students write or chart in their notebooks instead of turning and talking before they share with either the whole class or a small group.

- Give students copies to annotate by marking details that affirm, extend, or challenge their thinking and then talk or write about how their thinking has changed.

As I listen to the students talk and share out, I hear a range of ideas. Some think Rylant might have done this to jog the old woman's memory so she'll remember the dog is really hers. Some think this is a significant clue that the dog might be owned by someone else, and another builds on that idea by connecting it to a pattern: "Maybe the author did that so the old woman and the dog's owner can be friends." Many more, however, think Rylant wants the old woman to be sad and miss the puppy so she'll realize a living thing is a better friend than a chair or a car. And several students let out another "ooh" as they take in that possibility. So I name for them what they've just done.

"Though people have come up with different ideas, all of them seem connected to at least one pattern we've noticed, which is really important, since Cynthia Rylant probably put those patterns there for a reason. And I'm wondering if some of you said 'ooh' because the idea that she made the dog go away so the old woman would be sad connects to lots of patterns."

"Yeah, and maybe being sad is a pattern, too," says one of the students. "See, it has already come up twice—and the second time she's even sadder," which sets off another round of "oohs."

I agree that this seems possible since we're still in the middle of the book and new patterns may still emerge. Then I explain that we need to hold all these ideas in our heads as we continue reading and see how they might change and grow, and I capture these new possibilities as wonderings and add the new pattern around sadness to the chart.

SETTING STUDENTS UP TO CONSIDER THE ENDING

As we turn back to the book, I remind students to be on the lookout for any signs of patterns breaking; then I start reading again. We learn that after calling the dogcatcher—and hanging up when he asks if the dog has a name—the old woman makes a decision: She drives Betsy to the dogcatcher's and says that she has come to find her dog. And this time, when he asks for the dog's name, she thinks of "all the old, dear friends with names whom she had outlived," and how lucky she'd been to know them—and then tells the dogcatcher that her dog's name is Lucky. And at this point, every thumb in the room pops up.

Everyone realizes this moment is significant, but it also can be interpreted differently. Most of the students, for instance, think this indicates that the old woman realizes she does want the dog as a friend and has overcome her fear of outliving others. But a handful stick to their original thinking—including two

Understanding a Problem-Based Approach: *"Interpretation Precedes Analysis," page 130*

boys who are sure this is the moment when the old woman's memory has kicked in. There is, however, the ending to reckon with, which I now set them up to consider.

"Have you noticed that each time we see a pattern break, we revise or add on to our thinking? That's exactly what readers do! But now we're almost at the end, and while it's possible we'll still see patterns breaking, we'll also get a final chance to revise our thinking when we see how the story turns out. That's because the end of the story can help us see what the writer might be trying to show us. And that might be different depending on the ending.

"Let's say, for instance, that at the end, the old woman finds the dog and starts remembering all sorts of things she'd forgotten. That could mean the author's trying to show us that we might need to almost lose something important in order to get something else back. But if she doesn't find the dog but winds up helping the dogcatcher take care of all the dogs, we'd have a very different idea about what she was trying to show us—maybe something about not always getting what you wished for, but still getting what you need. So let's read to the end now and see what does or doesn't happen and how that might change our thinking."

As we continue, we learn that the dog is, indeed, at the dogcatcher's, that he runs right up to the old woman as soon as he hears her voice, and that "from that day on, Lucky lived with the old woman." No owner returns, no memories resurface—and Fred, Betsy, Roxanne, and Franklin apparently don't mind having a dog around. And after seeing the final illustration of the old woman petting the dog on the bed, the students turn and talk.

Those who had held out for a different ending have to revise their thinking again, which, given how satisfying the ending is, isn't so hard for them to do. But as the students consider what Cynthia Rylant might be showing them about people, they express their ideas in different ways. One student says she thinks Rylant's trying to tell us to remember how lucky we are to have had friends, even if they're not around anymore. Another thinks she may be saying, "Don't be so afraid of losing friends that you're afraid to make new ones." And one of the boys who'd early on thought Betsy, Fred, Roxanne, and Franklin were fake friends thinks she's trying to tell us not to trick ourselves into thinking we're happy if we're alone, because everyone needs a friend. And as everyone puts their own unique spin on their interpretations, the book seems to grow richer and fuller.

UNDERSTANDING A PROBLEM-BASED APPROACH: The Nature of the Task

In many ways this session was very focused in its intentions. I wanted the students to experience how noticing patterns in a text could lead them to deeper thinking through a process of reading in which they were developing and revising ideas *as*, not *after*, they read. But while the session was focused, the thinking the students did was divergent, complex, and rich—and you may be wondering exactly how that happened.

The secret is in the nature of the task itself. It's what, in mathematics, is called a "rich task," one that presents students with an open-ended problem (such as figuring out what an author might be showing) and is accessible to a wide range of students because it provides multiple points of entry and ways of solving—that is, it comes with built-in differentiation. Additionally, according to Jennifer Piggott of the Millennium Mathematics Project at the University of Cambridge (2011), rich tasks do the following—all of which were visible in our third-grade classroom:

- They involve learners in speculating, hypothesis making and testing, proving or explaining, reflecting, and interpreting.

- They offer opportunities to identify elegant or efficient solutions (think back to the "oohs").

- They have the potential to reveal underlying principles (such as the intentionality of the author's choices).

- They have the potential to broaden students' skills and/or deepen and broaden knowledge in the discipline (as in understanding how texts operate).

- They encourage collaboration and discussion.

- They are enjoyable and have an element of surprise—that is, they promote the pleasure factor (see "The Importance of Pleasure," on page 47).

By its very nature, a problem-based approach involves rich tasks, but as Piggott also notes, "much of what it takes to make a rich task 'rich' is the environment in which it is presented," which is ultimately created by you. So now we'll look at a handful of things that you can do as a teacher to both better understand and implement rich reading tasks.

The Task Is Expansive Rather than Targeted

When the lesson began you may have been struck by how much I packed into the intro-duction. In fact, if you look back, you'll see that I

- recapped the work the students had done and situated it within the process of reading (i.e., as something readers do when they start a book);

- introduced the inquiry question and named it as an important kind of ques-tion for readers to ask;

- introduced the concept of patterns and how writers use them; and

- noticed and named an implicit pattern hidden in the inquiry question as an example of a pattern.

I began, as many reading workshop minilessons do, by connecting this day's work to what the students had previously done. After that, however, I departed from the famil-iar structure of a minilesson in several significant ways. I used the students' thinking as a model, not my own, and I took time to situate the work within a larger transferra-ble process when I explained why and how writers use patterns. This could be viewed as an unnecessary detour that might distract the students from the task at hand, but it's important for students to understand *why* the work you're asking them to do matters and develop a more complex understanding of how texts work. And looking at the intro-duction as a whole, it's clear I've broken one of the cardinal minilesson rules: Teach one thing at a time.

Teaching one thing at a time has been recommended as a way of not overwhelm-ing students with too much instruction at once. But this reasoning doesn't work in a problem-solving approach. First, the "one thing" part of the rule usually refers to a strat-egy or skill, but here I'm teaching a process that involves any number of strategies and skills that naturally arise as the students problem solve. This means I teach into what students are doing, not teach them what to do—and given the complexity of reading for meaning, that rarely involves just one thing.

Second, this process involves quite complex thinking, and learning that process requires not only lots of time to deliberately practice but also repeated exposure to the ideas and concepts behind it. If students don't fully understand all of the instructions the first time they hear it, don't worry. They eventually will as they revisit the concepts and experience the thinking again over time.

Thinking Diverges Before It Coalesces

By their very nature, rich tasks presume there are different paths to similar outcomes (and sometimes similar paths to different outcomes). This means that in any problem-solving session, you have to manage students who may be traveling down different paths and trust that they'll all find their way, which can feel disorienting at first if you're more accustomed to everyone practicing the same kind of thinking at the same time.

The chart from this session, for example, displays a range of thinking in the final column (see Figure 7.4). If we generalize and categorize the thinking captured here, we see the students developing ideas that are

- built from one or more patterns (e.g., Maybe she doesn't want to be friends with the puppy because the puppy might not last);
- based on their background knowledge and supported with some textual evidence (e.g., Maybe the dog's really hers, but she doesn't remember because she's old and talks to furniture); and
- based on one detail in the text (e.g., Maybe it's because Franklin, Betsy, Fred, and Roxanne don't like dogs).

Over time, through experience and practice, students will learn to develop ideas that grow out of multiple patterns—versus a handful of details—and that the text will answer most, if not all, of the questions it raises if they're paying attention and reading closely. But it's likely you'll see a spectrum of thinking as students begin this work, especially if you have a diverse group of students. Remember, though, not to sanction one student's interpretation over another's. Instead, try to appreciate all these ideas as approximations of the thinking you want everyone to eventually do—and remember that in almost any text there will be lots of opportunities for students to revise their ideas, including on the last page.

Readers Must Be Tentative Before They Are Certain

Thomas Jefferson once wrote, "The moment a person forms a theory, his imagination sees, in every object, only the traits which favor that theory." More than two hundred years later, we've given this tendency a name, *confirmation bias*, and you're likely to see just this sort of tunnel vision in your classroom. You saw it here, as students ignored details or tried to fit them into theories like square pegs into round holes. There are, however, several moves you can make to help students avoid the trap that comes with forming theories.

In addition to deliberately using the word *maybe* to help students stay in that "Yes and . . ." creative-thinking mode, try to also use words like *could* and *might* when talking about students' ideas. Peter Johnston calls words like these "tentativeness markers," which help children "understand that knowledge is constructed, that it is influenced by one's perspective and by different contexts, and that we should expect and value different perspectives because they help us to expand our understanding" (2012, 59). And just as happened here, if you use them often, your students will pick up on using these words, without needing sentence starters or stems.

You can also help your students become comfortable with the tentative nature of problem solving by commenting often on how their thinking is changing and growing—that is, by focusing on the process, not the product. Additionally, once you've finished a text, consider revisiting your early charts with your students to see more clearly how thinking changes and how they understand things now that they simply could not have understood earlier. Often this is an eye-opener for students who may think they're simply not "good" readers because they didn't get everything right away.

Finally, bring the author in again, by reminding students that she's the mastermind behind what they're reading. While students by third grade can identify the author of a text, and many can name story elements, they—as well as students in higher grades—aren't always aware of how authors purposefully choreograph these elements and weave patterns into texts to convey deeper meaning. Many, for instance, think the author is just recording something that may have happened or making something up to entertain her readers, which I fear is a rather simplistic way of thinking about author's purpose. Instead, over time, we want students to understand that writers are trying to show us something and our job is to consider what that could be by reading closely and thinking deeply.

Interpretation Precedes Analysis

The problem-solving process these third graders engaged in is exactly what Harvard's Patricia Kain has described as the one "that is central . . . to the whole academic enterprise" (1998). See "Close Reading as an Outcome, Not a Procedure," p. 37) They reasoned their way to their own ideas by noticing patterns, asking questions about them, and formulating hypotheses that they then tested out until they had coherent interpretations. In this way, they were also deeply engaged in part of the work of the Common Core's second anchor standard for reading, which asks students to determine central ideas or themes of texts and analyze their development. But did they analyze how the themes they'd determined developed across the text?

The answer is they hadn't yet but were fully equipped to do so now, because once students have interpreted a text this way, by putting pieces together to see the big picture, they can explain how the parts contribute to the whole—that is, they can analyze. In fact, I'd say that asking students to analyze *before* they've interpreted a text is like putting the cart before the horse. Consider, for a moment, the old Indian tale of the blind men and the elephant, where each man tried to understand an elephant by focusing on a separate part. One man touched the trunk and thought an elephant was a snake; another felt the tail and concluded it was a rope; a third stroked the ear and thought it must be a fan. Not one was able to make sense of the whole by analyzing a part.

Analyzing, however, is an easy step to make once you've interpreted the whole. Once a reader has developed a coherent interpretation that takes into account all of a text, not just selected parts, he can turn that into a thesis or claim and repurpose the very same details he used to build his interpretations as evidence to support his claim. And if you felt inclined, you could also ask students to consider how other details they might not have noticed originally fit into the whole. Take this line from *The Old Woman Who Named Things*, for instance: "The old woman was sitting in Fred reading a book on everlasting flowers when she saw the puppy through her window."

When they read this the first time, the students noticed that the puppy had come back, but nobody paid any attention to the book the old woman was reading. After constructing deep interpretations of the story, however, rather than just gotten the gist, they'd probably have a lot to say about why Cynthia Rylant decided to have the old woman read a book about everlasting flowers. And in doing so, they'd also meet the fifth CCSS anchor standard for reading, which asks students to analyze "how specific sentences, paragraphs, and larger portions of the text . . . relate to each other and the whole."

 ## WHY THIS WORK MATTERS

Here you saw what students can do when we set them up to interpret by following pattern-based lines of inquiry. Of course, the question they followed, "Why doesn't the old woman see the puppy could be her friend?" is one that we, as proficient readers with some acquaintance with loss, don't have to stretch ourselves far to answer. But the idea that someone might protect herself from loss by refusing to form attachments is a reach for many third graders—and, as such, is a wonderful example of how texts can deepen and expand our understanding of the human condition, not just echo a known universal truth.

The interpretations they developed are also great examples of what Flannery O'Connor said was the true purpose of making statements about a story: They "help you experience that meaning more fully" (1961, 96), not write a thesis paper (though they can easily be repurposed for that). Unfortunately, though, I don't hear a lot of talk about interpretation in classrooms these days, and I think that's yet another effect of the CCSS.

If you study the Common Core reading standards, for instance, you'll find that the words *interpret* and *interpretation* appear only fifteen times, while the words *analyze* and *analysis* show up over 150 times. Additionally, if you closely read the specific standards that mention interpreting, you'll see that while students are asked to interpret words, phrases, figurative language, figures of speech, and visual information (such as charts, graphs, and diagrams), they're not asked to interpret whole texts.

Students are, however, expected to analyze other writers', artists', and filmmakers' interpretations of texts and real-life events, which means the standards' authors recognize that readers can interpret more than words and phrases. And in real life, versus the classroom, all sorts of people interpret all sorts of things. Doctors interpret their patients' symptoms. Scientists interpret data. Historians interpret the causes of conflicts. Judges interpret the law. In fact, the German philosopher Nietzsche believed that "all things are subject to interpretation. Whichever interpretation prevails at a given time is a function of power and not truth" (1996, 145). And applying this idea to the Common Core standards, the lack of emphasis on interpreting may be far more a reflection of the authors' interpretation of what it means for readers to be college and career ready than of any absolute truth.

In fact, many writers want their readers to interpret and say so explicitly. Take Lois Lowry, for instance, who, when asked why she gave *The Giver* such an ambiguous ending, said:

> *Many kids want a more specific ending to* The Giver. *Some write, or ask me when they see me, to spell it out exactly. And I don't do that. And the reason is because* The Giver *is many things to many different people. People bring to it their own complicated sense of beliefs and hopes and dreams and fears and all of that. So I don't want to put my own feelings into it, my own beliefs, and ruin that for people who create their own endings in their minds. (n.d.)*

And here's another writer who values a reader's right to interpret, Newbery Honor Book awardee Shannon Hale, the author of the Princess Academy books: "I want my stories to ask questions, not force answers. . . . If a person gets insight from a book, it's so much more powerful if that person gleans their own message from the story" (2008).

So if we believe, as these authors do, that reading is a transactional act, with a text's words only coming to life as they interact with a reader's mind and heart, *and* that the students who leave our schools will need to know how to interpret many things, not just analyze them, we need to bring interpretation—and feelings—back into our classrooms.

STEERING THE SHIP

TEACHING MOVES TO SUPPORT STUDENT THINKING AND MEANING MAKING

Relaunch the learning by building on what students have already been thinking (as captured in their know/wonder chart).

Create a new chart as a starting place for deeper thinking.

Choose (or ask the class to choose) one of their "Why?" questions as a line of inquiry.

If students don't have a penetrating "Why?" question, notice and name any implicit patterns on their know/wonder chart (often conveyed through *always* or *never*).

Ask students if they've noticed any patterns.

Show students how any pattern can become a line of inquiry by prefacing it with *why*, and then choose one to track.

Notice and name how readers can begin to see what a writer might be showing them by paying attention to when patterns change and break.

Invite students to pay attention to when patterns change and break.

Frame students' ideas as *maybe* statements to keep their minds open and flexible.

Release more responsibility to students by asking them to let you know when they think patterns are changing and breaking.

Remind students that the writer is the one calling the shots for a purpose, and their job is to consider what that purpose might be.

Notice and name when students' ideas are incorporating one or more patterns.

Notice and name how readers must revise, and sometimes let go of, ideas when they learn how the story ends.

Explain how an ending can reveal what the writer wants us to see.

Invite students to express their final ideas and celebrate both the diversity of thinking and how that's expressed.

FIGURE 7.6 *Steering the Ship*

Considering Complexity:
The Significance of Details

Teacher and fellow blogger Steve Peterson once posed a question about two of his third graders who were partner reading the early chapter book *The Blue Ghost*, by Marion Dane Bauer. The book tells the story of a girl named Liz who, while staying at her grandmother's log cabin deep in the Minnesota woods, keeps being woken in the middle of the night by a blue ghost whispering, "Elizabeth." Both of the students were sure the ghost was Liz's mother, despite any number of clues that suggested otherwise. Eventually the ghost's identity was revealed, and the students revised their thinking, but Steve wondered how to help students not only pay more attention to details but also understand that the writer has intentionally placed them there for the reader to notice and question.

Return to the Beginning to Spot Overlooked Clues

For students who seem to brush over details, get stuck on ideas that don't have much evidence, and/or don't seem terribly curious, invite them to reread the beginning of a book they've finished to become more aware of how writers plant clues they hadn't noticed before. Steve's two students, for instance, noticed all sorts of details they'd ignored before—such as the ghost's "long old-fashioned dress"—which, on rereading, they recognized was a clue that the ghost was someone from the past, not Liz's mom. They also noticed other details that played an important role later in the story, such as the large wooden trunk the ghost hovers over, which contains an object that's critical to the plot. Seeing how much they'd missed the first time made them realize how much more there was to notice and wonder about as readers.

Read Prologues That Invite "Why?" Questions

Ultimately we want students to read with the question, "Why is the writer telling me this?" in their heads. You can help students practice this habit of mind by reading prologues (or chapters that act like prologues) in small groups in order to raise questions and ponder possibilities and then read forward to a passage that answers some of those questions. For example, you could ask students to look at the prologue to Alison Pollet's *Pity Party* and then read this excerpt from the book:

> *Cass was used to people feeling sorry for her, of course. Her parents had died in a car accident when she was eight years old. "A tragic car accident," it was usually called. That was shorthand for "it wasn't just a fender bender—people were hurt, and not just moderately but tragically."*
>
> *Tell people your parents are dead, and it's always the same. After the "I'm sorry's" and the "How horrible's," they run out of things to say. That's how the looks start. They gaze at you with woeful eyes, frowning to show you how sorry they feel, then scrounge for something to nervously fiddle with. . . . Cass hated people feeling sorry for her, and she hated the looks. (7)*

If the passage confirms students' thinking from the prologue, it validates them as thinkers—and if not, they can return to the prologue to look for the clues the author planted. The following table includes other texts that offer beginnings, excerpts, or prologues that almost beg students to ask "Why?" questions and bat around ideas.

use facts to persuade or inspire their audience, often by using rhetorical devices. Feature articles, on the other hand, and many kinds of essays use facts to explore a topic or issue the writer may have an opinion about, through a mix of narrative and expository prose. Textbooks and what are often called all-about books, such as those by Gail Gibbons and Seymour Simon, use facts to purportedly give readers undisputed and unbiased information primarily through exposition. And narrative nonfiction—which includes biographies, memoirs, and books like Steve Sheinkin's *Bomb*, which tells the story of the race to build the atomic bomb—uses many of the techniques of fiction.

Each of these subgenres comes with its own particular set of problems, which affects what and how you set students up to problem solve. The good news is that many of the problem-solving approaches we've explored with fiction can be used with narrative nonfiction as well. But expository nonfiction operates differently, and in this chapter we'll look at the specific problems these texts pose for readers who want to really understand, not just know some facts, along with what they need to do to navigate those problems.

EXPLORING THE PROBLEM:
Considering the Implications of Facts

While some of the problems nonfiction texts pose are the same as fiction (like pronouns, which can trip readers up in nonfiction just as in fiction), the differences outweigh the similarities. Much of what a reader has to figure out in fiction is connected to the characters—from where they are to how they're related to why they're doing what they're doing—while in expository nonfiction, readers need to figure out things about the facts, such as

- how they are related (through cause and effect, parts to whole, idea and example, etc.);
- what they might imply (e.g., any conclusions or generalizations readers might draw from the facts); and
- how a phenomenon, process, or event works or happens.

Figuring out any of these usually requires some logical reasoning, which is challenging for many children, but what makes expository nonfiction even harder is that it's often a challenge simply to recognize that there might be something to figure out. In fact, unless they're reading closely and actively, readers often read right through facts, unaware they don't fully understand them.

To see what I mean, let's look at an excerpt from *Starfish*, by Edith Thacher Hurd, a picture book that appears in the Common Core's list of exemplar nonfiction texts for kindergarten and first grade and comes with a Lexile level of 170. On the surface, it seems like a simple book, with lots of short, declarative sentences that directly convey information. But there's an implicit conclusion or two to draw from these explicit facts, and I invite you to read it, paying attention to what the facts seem to imply that the writer hasn't said directly.

> *Starfish live in the sea.*
>
> *Starfish live deep down in the sea. . . .*
>
> *Starfish have many arms.*
>
> *The arms are called rays.*
>
> *Starfish have arms, but no legs.*
>
> *Starfish have feet, but no toes.*
>
> *They glide and slide on tiny tube feet.*
>
> *They move as slowly as a snail.*
>
> *The basket star looks like a starfish, but it is a little different.*
>
> *It doesn't have tube feet.*
>
> *It moves with its rays.*
>
> *It has rays that go up and rays that go down.*
>
> *Tiny brittle stars are like the basket star.*
>
> *They hide under rocks in pools by the sea.*
>
> *The mud star hides in the mud.*
>
> *It is a starfish.*
>
> *It has tiny tube feet.* (5, 9–15)

As a proficient reader who was asked to consider the implications of these facts, you may have drawn two conclusions that weren't explicitly stated: that a starfish's feet are on its arms and that starfish are starfish because they have tube feet, versus other kinds of ocean stars that don't. Both are examples of a particular type of inference expository nonfiction readers often need to make—what we can call an "If *this* and *this*, then *that*" conclusion. That is, *if* starfish have arms, but no legs and *if* they have feet, but no toes, *then* their feet must be on their arms. If, however, I hadn't asked you to look for places where the writer left something unstated, you might have just registered those facts without thinking more about them, which is quite easy to do. In fact, I'd say it comes with the territory of reading this kind of nonfiction.

You see, unlike fiction, expository nonfiction writers frequently give readers only one chance to catch something that has been stated indirectly. That's because fiction *unfolds*, with whatever the writer might be showing her readers becoming more apparent as you keep reading (Barnhouse and Vinton 2012). Expository fiction, on the other hand, often compartmentalizes information into subcategories or sections so readers have only one opportunity to figure out something that has been stated indirectly. The passage here from *Starfish*, for instance, is the only place that mentions other stars. After this, the text turns to other matters, like what starfish eat and how they reproduce, without ever returning to what makes a starfish a starfish.

Additionally, expository nonfiction doesn't always tap into our curiosity the way fiction does. Fiction writers deliberately write in a way designed to make us curious, choosing details purposefully and withholding information to create tension or suspense so that we'll keep turning the pages to find out what happens. But while expository nonfiction writers may invite us to marvel at the information they present, their authoritative, often nothing-but-the-facts tone can actually discourage questions. Instead, they seem to want us to take the facts at face value, precisely because they're facts, without necessarily questioning their veracity or our own understanding of them.

Shifting from Knowing to Understanding

If you're wondering if first graders really need to figure out the difference between starfish and other kinds of stars—and if so, if they might learn that better by visiting an aquarium, not reading a book—you're not alone. But we do need to make sure we're not spreading what author David Perkins calls "aboutitis," the endless learning *about* something without necessarily developing "an empowering and enlightening body of understanding" (2010, 6).

And that's especially when students are engaged in some kind of in-depth study around a topic or issue, whether that's in language arts, social studies, or science.

Like elementitis, a term he also coined (see "A Focus on Pieces," on page 5), aboutitis is a condition he frequently sees in schools, and to explore the distinction he's making here, let's take a look at a more complex text, "What Big Brains You Have," an excerpt from Jody Morgan's *Elephant Rescue: Changing the Future for Endangered Wildlife*, which is aimed at students in grades 4 through 8. As you read it, try to consider not just what you're learning about elephants, but what these facts help you understand about these animals' intelligence, along with what you have to do, as a reader, to understand that.

> It's not just the elephant's size that inspires awe and wonder. Its intelligence and personality, its elaborate social life, the way it cares for its young and grieves for its dead, its sophisticated communication—all of these qualities set elephants apart from other animals.
>
> An animal's intelligence is related to brain size, and at between 9 and 13 pounds, an elephant's brain is the biggest among land animals. Like those of humans, apes and dolphins, elephant brains are also extremely complex—this, too, is a measure of its intelligence. . . .
>
> In Asia, young working elephants learned to stuff the wooden bells around their necks with mud to stop them from ringing. They could then steal silently into farmers' fields at night to take bananas. Elephants have been known to hold tree branches in their trunks in order to scratch hard-to-reach spots or remove parasites. Matriarchs, the lead females in the social groups, can remember and guide their families to prime feeding areas and watering holes—even if years have passed since their last visit.
>
> Like humans, elephants care for one another. The matriarch, in particular, will put herself at risk, facing down poachers while the rest of her family escapes. Elephants may gather around a wounded comrade to offer support. After a death, surviving members often stand by for days in a clear display of grief. Likewise, they will cover their dead with branches, leaves and grass, as if burying them. When they come across elephant bones, they sniff and stroke them with their trunks, and may even pull out the tusks to shatter them against a tree or rock. (8)

HOW EXPOSITORY NONFICTION READERS FIGURE OUT
THE IMPLICATIONS OF FACTS

WHAT WRITERS MAY CONVEY INDIRECTLY	WHAT A READER THEREFORE HAS TO DO
The meaning of individual words	Look for context clues throughout the text.
How facts could be connected or related (e.g., through cause and effect, idea and example, parts to whole)	Think: How might *this* be connected to or related to *that*? Could there be a missing *because* or *for example*?
What the facts might imply (e.g., conclusions or generalizations that can be drawn)	Think: If *this* is a fact and *this* is a fact, could *this* be a fact, too? or Does this mean something even bigger about the topic?
How and/or why a phenomenon, process, or event works	Think: How and/or why does this actually happen or work?
For all of the above	Be aware of when you're confused or suspect the writer has left something unsaid.

FIGURE 8.1 *How Expository Nonfiction Readers Figure Out the Implications of Facts*

If you're like me, you came away from this piece with an increased sense of wonder and awe about these remarkable creatures. But to deeply understand how intelligent they are, a reader would need to think about at least some of the things the writer conveys implicitly. For instance, while the writer says that both brain size and complexity are measures of intelligence, she doesn't explain what she means by complex brains, but rather leaves that to readers to figure out through the examples she offers. She also doesn't really explain how the various facts in paragraph 3 demonstrate intelligence and complex brains—and if you hadn't considered that before, just think about what those young elephants had to figure out about people's behavior and acoustics in order to get those bananas. She also doesn't make explicit how the final paragraph is connected to intelligence. In fact, she begins with a sentence that might lead readers to think that she has left intelligence behind and moved on to social behaviors. Yet these facts all have implications for elephants' brains and intelligence, which a reader would want to ponder to truly build that "empowering and enlightening body of understanding," not just learn some facts about elephants, like the weight of their brains.

LOOKING CLOSELY AT A PROBLEM-SOLVING SESSION

Planning for the Session

The fourth graders I work with in this session have been studying frogs and the impact humans have on them as part of a nonfiction reading-and-writing unit that will culminate in students researching other animals and writing persuasive pieces about them. My goal is to help them become more aware of the thinking needed to truly understand facts, not just collect them, and to do that I've selected an article from *National Geographic Kids* called "Lungless Frog," about a rare kind of frog that breathes through its skin.

By using the text "Core Practice: Assessing the Problems of a Text," I've become aware of specific places where the writer has conveyed something in-directly or simply not connected all the dots, and I use that awareness to decide how to chunk the text and frame the turn-and-talks. Additionally, I make three other planning decisions that you can learn more about in this chapter:

- considering whether or not to preteach vocabulary (see page 146)
- considering how to activate background knowledge (see page 150)
- making thinking visible through a confused/understand chart (see page 152)

CORE PRACTICE: **Assessing the Problems of a Text**

With both *Starfish* and "What Big Brains You Have," you saw how easy it can be for readers to simply read facts without thinking about them more deeply because nonfiction doesn't unfold like fiction and often adopts an authoritative tone. So if you want to help students understand, not just know, the facts they read, you'll need to be aware of where there's more to consider in the texts you're planning to use. This means reading the text to identify the particular places where a reader might

- need to figure out how one or more facts relate to others;
- draw a conclusion or generalization from the facts;
- or consider how and/or why something actually works or happens.

CORE PRACTICE: **Assessing the Problems of a Text** (Continued)

Academically speaking, this involves knowing where a reader must infer to truly understand the facts. But given that inferences come in many shapes and sizes—from the meaning of a pronoun to a whole text's themes—it's useful to use these specific descriptors, which can give both you and your students something more precise to look for. Then once you've assessed a text this way, you can use what you learned about the problems it poses to make strategic decisions about how to chunk it and what to ask students to turn and talk about—that is, to have a plan.

Figure 8.2 can give you a sense of what a plan might look like for "What Big Brains You Have." In terms of chunking, you'll see that I decided to stop at the three places where I'd noticed the writer had conveyed something implicitly or simply left something unsaid, and at each of those stopping points, I planned an initial, open-ended question as well as a second, more text-specific one to use as a follow-up, if needed. Each is an example of the more generalized questions found in Figure 8.1, and you'll see me use both kinds of questions in the classroom example.

"WHAT BIG BRAINS YOU HAVE" FROM *ELEPHANT RESCUE*, BY JODY MORGAN

TURN-AND-TALK STOPPING POINTS	INITIAL QUESTION	FOLLOW-UP QUESTION (IF NEEDED)
End of paragraph 2 (Writer hasn't explained or defined what makes a brain complex.)	Is there anything we're confused about or don't think we really understand? ("Be aware of when you're confused.")	The author has come right out and told us that elephants' brains are complex, but do we really understand what that means? ("Be aware of what hasn't been said.")
End of paragraph 3 (Writer hasn't explicitly stated how the facts demonstrate complex brains and intelligence.)	Does any of this information help us better understand why and how elephants are intelligent and what makes a brain complex? ("How does *this* connect to *that*?")	We know that elephants have learned how to steal bananas, but can we turn and talk about all the things they had to figure out to do that to better understand how intelligent and complex their brains are? ("How does this phenomenon or process work?")
The end of the piece (Writer hasn't explicitly explained what these facts reveal about complex brains and intelligence.)	Do we think this paragraph has anything to add to our ideas about elephants' intelligence and brains? ("How does *this* connect to *that*?")	Can you and your partner choose one of these facts and think about what elephants might have to understand in their brains to care for each other the way they do? ("What might be the implications of these facts?")

FIGURE 8.2 *Planning Sheet for "What Big Brains You Have"*

Implementing and Facilitating the Session

SETTING STUDENTS UP TO BE AWARE OF THEIR CONFUSION

To begin the session, I share with the students that I know they've been studying frogs, and that today we'll be reading an article about another kind of frog. Before we start reading, though, I address the two preteaching decisions I made. First, I see if anyone knows the words *dissection* and *adaptation*, and then I ask them to recall what they know about breathing.

Most students know the two words already, and those who don't are brought up to speed by their classmates. They also know a lot about breathing: That it's vital for life because all animals need oxygen to survive, that we get that needed oxygen from the air we breathe, and that the air enters our bodies through our noses and then travels to our lungs through tubes. Once that has been established, I pass out copies of the text to the students and project it on a screen. Then I offer the following teaching point.

CORE PRACTICE: **Considering Scaffolds: Preteaching Vocabulary (or Not)**

Like considering whether to model or not, you'll want to make deliberate case-by-case decisions about preteaching vocabulary rather than just doing so as a matter of course. First read the text and note the words students might not know. Then for each word, consider two guiding questions:

1. Is it absolutely critical for thinking about the deeper meaning of the text (e.g., the author's purpose, message, meaning, or themes)?

2. If so, could a reader figure the word out through context clues across the text or could it be assigned a placeholder?

With "Lungless Frog," I noted the words *lunglessness, dissection, colleague, deemed, specimen, sacrifice, adaptation, dissolved, metabolic, biology, doubtless, rational, hampered, rarity*, and a handful of proper nouns that refer to names of people or places. Then I used the strategies from "Considering Complexity: The Problem of Vocabulary" (see page X) to see how many words students might be able to read around and still get the gist, which allowed me to scratch these words off the list: *specimen, colleague, deemed, sacrifice, dissolved, metabolic, biology, doubtless, rational, hampered,* and *rarity*.

"We know nonfiction writers want to inform their readers about the topic they're writing about by giving us lots of facts and information, but they don't always explain those facts in a really clear, understandable way. That means that, as readers, we could know those facts well enough to answer a question or use them in our writing, but not fully understand them. So today I'm going to ask us to do something that readers of non-fiction do all the time in their heads: They ask themselves the question, 'Do I really get this or am I confused?' And they ask this because they know that paying attention to when they're confused will help them figure out things and understand more."

Then I create a confused/understand T-chart (see Figure 8.3) and explain that we'll use this to keep track of our thinking. And with this in place, I read my first planned chunk, stopping at the end of the paragraph in which the word *lunglessness* appears.

> *An animal that can breathe through its skin and not through its lungs might sound a little alien-like, but strangely enough, this animal lives on Earth and is known as* Barbourula kalimantanensis, *the frog without lungs.*
>
> *The first recorded species of frog that breathes without lungs was found in a clear, cold-water stream on the island of Borneo in Indonesia. It gets all of its oxygen through its skin.*

CORE PRACTICE: **Core Practice**: **Considering Scaffolds: Preteaching Vocabulary (or Not)** (Continued)

What you're left with are usually words that are critical for understanding the facts, and with this text I still had *lunglessness*, *dissection*, and *adaptation*. *Lunglessness*, however, came with context clues, which means I could let students have a go at it rather than teaching it in advance. But *dissection* and *adaptation* both seemed important, and for words like these, see if anyone knows the word and can explain it to those who don't, and if that fails, preteach whatever words are left.

Remember, though, that if a word you've decided not to preteach becomes a real stumbling block, you can always jump in after the students have had a chance to wrestle with it—and research has shown that students are more likely to remember something you've taught them if they've had a chance to grapple with it first, even if they haven't figured it out (Paul 2012). Additionally, after they've read the text, return to some of the Tiers 2 and 3 words you scratched off your list (such as *rational* and *biology*), as you do want to build students' vocabulary along with their ability to navigate unknown words.

"Nobody knew about the lunglessness before we accidently discovered it doing routine dissections," study lead author David Bickford, a biologist at the National University of Singapore, said in an email.

Lunglessness is a word that meets my vocabulary criteria: It is critical for true understanding but can be figured out from context clues. My hope is that someone will find the word confusing, which could spur some problem solving, but when I ask the students to turn and talk about what may be confusing them, all of the groups I listen to are focused on why the author said the frog might seem "a little alien-like"—and none refer to what the author said explicitly, that the frog was "an animal that can breathe through its skin and not through its lungs." Instead they are focusing on the photograph of the frog at the top of the article, which shows a creature whose huge wide-set eyes and nostrils-only flat nose make many students think of E.T., which I note as a question on our chart.

SETTING STUDENTS UP TO CLARIFY THEIR CONFUSION

Once the students finish analyzing the picture, I ask if anything else confused them, and several point to the word *lunglessness*. So I seize this opportunity to offer a second teaching point.

"I think we're confused because this is one of those places where the writer hasn't come out and directly told us something. Instead he expects us to figure it out, and nonfiction readers often do that by thinking about how a word or fact connects to other parts of the text. So with a partner, can we take a look at what we've read so far and see if we can connect this to anything else that could help us figure out that strange word?"

Motivated by their confusion, the students go back and partially solve the problem—that is, they figure out that the word refers to the frog not having lungs. But knowing a word doesn't necessarily mean they understand how lunglessness works, so I ask: "Do we think we all really understand how this frog breathes now?"

Most of the students nod their heads yes and many volunteer to explain, but when I call on one boy, this is what he reveals: "Oxygen from the air and water comes in through the frog's skin and then it goes to the —." He stops himself, the word *lungs* in his throat. "No, wait," he says, "it goes in through the skin—and then I'm not really sure." With no other hands in the air at that point, I ask everyone to turn and talk at their tables, and after a few moments of much back-and-forth, I bring them together and ask for another volunteer. The student says, "It's like its skin is both its nose and lungs. It actually breathes through its skin because it doesn't have lungs."

WHAT WE'RE CONFUSED ABOUT	WHAT WE UNDERSTAND
Why does the writer say the frog seems alien-like?	Did he think it looked like E.T.?
What does "lunglessness" mean?	Lungless = no lungs Lunglessness = having no lungs! The frog has no lungs! It gets oxygen through its skin and turns it into CO_2 there, too! Maybe that's why the writer said it was like an alien!
Why did the scientists partially dissect the frog when they were so valuable?	Maybe a frog could live if it was only partially dissected. Maybe the scientist wanted to see the lunglessness for himself, even if he killed it.
What does being flat have to do with being lungless?	A flat frog has more skin that is in contact with the water than a "blobby" frog does. That means there's more skin for the oxygen to come through.

FIGURE 8.3 *Confused/Understand Chart*

An "ah" of understanding ripples across the room, and I notice and name what the students have done. They've moved from just knowing some facts to really understanding them, and that took a lot of work to figure out because the whole concept of breathing through skin is really strange. This new understanding leads one girl to wonder if this is why people thought the frog was like an alien, which others now think is quite possible.

Understanding a Problem-Based Approach: *"Understand the Text and the Context,"* page 155

RESPONDING TO STUDENTS' NEEDS WITH A FOLLOW-UP QUESTION

With this misunderstanding cleared up, I read my next planned chunk, stopping at a place where I'm aware the author has left it up to his readers to draw some possible "If *this* and *this*, then *that*" conclusions.

> His colleague Djoko Iskandar at the Bandung Institute of Technology in Indonesia first described the frog in 1978 from one specimen. About 15 years later, fishermen found another individual.
>
> "Each specimen was deemed so valuable that scientists did not want to sacrifice the animals for dissections," Bickford said.

> But the biologist immediately partly dissected several frogs when he
> found the species on a recent expedition to Borneo.

Again I invite students to turn and talk about what seems confusing that we might need to figure out. Here I'm hoping that at least one student might question why the scientist dissected a frog, knowing how valuable it was, but no one raises a hand. So I ask a follow-up text-specific question.

"I think I see another one of those places where the writer hasn't come out and directly told us something but expects us to figure it out again. Do you see this fact, here, about each frog being so valuable that scientists didn't want to dissect them, and then right after that, this fact about the scientist partially dissecting a bunch of them? Do we think there's something the writer hasn't explained that we may need to figure out?"

This is all the students need to realize they, too, are confused, and once again they consider possibilities. "Maybe you could do a partial dissection without killing the frogs," some think; others suggest, "Maybe the scientist was too excited about finding the frogs that he did it anyway, because he wanted to see the lungless-ness for himself." I hadn't considered this second idea when I had first read the piece, and I share that with the class before adding it to our chart, which helps students see me as a fellow learner, not the keeper of answers.

Understanding a Problem-Based Approach: *"Create an Environment That Promotes Thinking and Independence,"* page 157

CORE PRACTICE: **Considering Scaffolds: Activating Background Knowledge**

With fiction, I rarely ask students to access their background knowledge before they read, because fiction operates as a kind of self-contained world, where writers provide readers with enough details to figure out what's going on within the world of the book (Barnhouse and Vinton 2012, 92). Many nonfiction writers, however, don't; they assume readers have some background knowledge, which many do not. So with nonfiction it is sometimes useful to ask students what they might know about a topic to create a context for what they'll be reading.

You will, however, want to think about what schema you'd like students to access before they start reading, and my rule of thumb is to make that decision based on what you think will be the most

SETTING STUDENTS UP TO DO MORE OF THE WORK

Given how challenging this text is, the students have been doing great work, and so for the next chunk, I decide to make a critical move. Instead of asking them to consider what the writer hasn't said about a problem I noticed, I invite the students to see if they notice any places where we might need to figure something out that the writer hasn't fully explained. And to guide our thinking, I suggest we ask ourselves three questions:

1. Do we really get this or are we confused?

2. Why might the writer be telling us this?

3. How might this part connect to what we've figured out so far?

CORE PRACTICE: **Considering Scaffolds: Activating Background Knowledge** (Continued)

challenging aspect of the text for students to understand, even if it's not the central topic. For example, if you were planning to read an article from *Ranger Rick* about black-footed ferrets, it might seem logical to ask students what they know about ferrets. It would, however, be more helpful to ask them what they know about prairies because the article describes how the loss of prairie lands to development led to the loss of prairie dogs, which are the ferrets' main source of food. Thus, understanding the environment is key to understanding why the ferrets are in danger. And in this session you'll see me ask students to recall not what they know about frogs, but what they know about breathing, which is where the challenge to understanding really lies.

Of course, there's no guarantee that asking students to activate their prior knowledge will help them understand a text more. The fact is, like confirmation bias, it's often hard for both children and adults to move beyond what they think they already know, unless they're reading actively and closely. And sometimes students have little to say because the request to activate prior knowledge before reading simply isn't engaging enough for them to dig into their memory banks. More often than not, though, you'll find students automatically drawing on their background knowledge in order to solve problems if they're genuinely curious or confused—that is, they'll use the strategy strategically when and if a situation calls for it.

I write these questions on the whiteboard so students can hold onto them, and then I read my next planned chunk of text, where again the writer doesn't fully connect the dots of facts to draw conclusions as explicitly as he might:

> The researchers suggest lunglessness in B. kalimantanensis *may be an adaptation to the higher oxygen content in fast-flowing, cold water.*
>
> *"Cold water can hold more dissolved oxygen than warm water,"* Bickford explained.
>
> *The frog also has a low metabolic rate, which means it needs less oxygen.*

CORE PRACTICE: **Making Student Thinking Visible: Confused/Understand Charts**

Know/wonder charts help students read fiction more actively and closely by tapping into their curiosity at the beginning of a text, and they can work equally well with narrative nonfiction, which uses many of the same techniques to engage readers. Expository nonfiction, however, may pique students' curiosity, but because it doesn't unfold as a narrative, much of what they're curious about will remain unanswered. Students reading *Starfish*, for instance, might be curious about many things—why the animals' arms are called rays, why their toes are called tube feet, and why brittle stars hide under rocks—but the text will answer none of these. So rather than asking students what they wonder at the beginning of an expository nonfiction text, I ask them what they're confused about and use another simple T-chart, with the first column titled "What We're Confused About" and the second, "What We Understand."

Like other charts you've seen, this one supports multiple goals by helping students

- hold onto their thinking,
- see the benefits of recognizing confusion,
- become more aware of when a writer has left something unsaid, and
- better see and understand the process of meaning making.

Additionally, the chart is another example of how to use your understanding of how different kinds of texts work to make informed teaching decisions. And when you bring that understanding to your planning and instruction, you display, in the words of teacher-effectiveness writer Charlotte Danielson, "solid knowledge of the important concepts in the discipline and how these relate to one another" (2011, 5).

> *What's more, the species is severely flat compared to other frogs, which increases the surface area of the skin.*
>
> *Thus loss of lungs as an adaptation to the cold, fast-flowing water "seems like a rational hypothesis to me," he said.*

As students turn and talk about the three questions, I hear lots of thinking and questions. Some students, for instance, are flummoxed by the sentence "The researchers suggest lunglessness in *B. kalimantanensis* may be an adaptation to the high oxygen content in fast-flowing, cold water," but others think they get it. When asked to share, one of those students explains that *B. kalimantanensis* is the name of the frog without lungs, and that scientists think it learned to breathe without lungs *because* it lives in a stream where there's lots of oxygen for its skin to take in—and with that implicit *because* now made visible, many children say "ah."

I notice and name what that student has done: He's recognized that all of these facts are related through cause and effect, even though the writer didn't make that clear by using the word *because*. But there's something else the students are confused about. They think the writer hasn't made clear what the frog being flat has to do with anything—or as one boy puts it, "Yeah, why's the writer telling us that?"

At this point, the students don't need to be invited by me to turn and talk; they naturally do so now. This allows some students to think that somehow the frog's flatness is connected to its lunglessness—though they don't fully understand how. So at this point, I step in again to notice and name what they've done and set them up for one last round of problem solving.

"By asking, 'Why is the writer telling us this?' and paying attention to when we're confused, we've found another place where the writer hasn't explained something. We think the flatness is connected to the frog not having lungs because that's what the writer's talking about here. But we don't really understand how. And that's another one of the things writers often leave it up to us to figure out: How does this actually work? How might being flat help the frog breathe through its skin?"

As I walk around the room while the students talk, it's clear the problem really puzzles them. And that means I have to go into problem-solving mode myself and figure out how to help them wrestle with the concept of surface area without giving the whole thing away.

> **Understanding a Problem-Based Approach:** *"Be Present in the Thick of the Thinking,"* page 156

Knowing that manipulatives and visuals can be useful, I give each group two pieces of paper and ask them to lay one flat on the table and crumple the other one up in a ball, then imagine the flat piece is our lungless frog and the crumpled one is like most other frogs. This helps a few groups come to the conclusion that there's more exposed paper on the flat piece than the crumpled up one, which means there's more skin for oxygen to enter a flat frog than a more rounded one, which helps it breathe without lungs.

With that problem solved, I read the article's last sentence: "Further studies of the frog to test the hypothesis, however, may be hampered by the species' rarity and endangered habitat, according to Bickford and colleagues." Then I ask the students a final question, which invites them to consider their own opinions about the facts the writer presented: "What do you think is more important: learning more about how the frog evolved without lungs, which requires at least partial dissections, or protecting the species from extinction—and why?" And they jump into that discussion with the vigor that only engaged, invested readers who truly understand can.

UNDERSTANDING A PROBLEM-BASED APPROACH: The Role of Preparation

Once again, you see students engaged in complex thinking and problem solving as they consider relationships and patterns of interaction between facts to figure out what the writer hasn't said in order to understand. That thinking also engaged students in the work of multiple reading standards—and it engaged me in some problem solving as well, as I had to think on my feet several times to solve problems posed by *teaching*, not the text. Having a plan helped with that, but in addition to planning, I also was prepared, which is actually different. According to change leader Tim Merry, for instance, there are inherent dangers in relying just on planning: "We can get so involved in making plans for where we should go and how we're going to respond and what we're going to do . . . that when we actually go out and start delivering it, [our plans] can undermine our ability to address the reality as it arises" (2015). On the other hand, he says, "preparation is a full analysis and understanding of the context . . . that allows us to be adaptive and responsive as situations arise. . . . [It's] the platform on which a flexible adaptive approach is built." So to better understand a problem-based approach, which by its very nature is flexible and adaptive, let's take a look at several things you can do to not just plan, but prepare.

Understand the Text and the Context

Assessing texts for the problems they pose is a core practice of a problem-based approach that actually serves two functions: it helps you plan *and* be prepared. In this session, for instance, I'd planned to stop at the end of the paragraph where the word *lungless-ness* appeared because I knew it hadn't been explicitly defined, despite being critical to understanding the article. I hadn't, however, anticipated the reality that arose when the students became fixated on the detail about the frog seeming alien-like—but I was prepared. Having initially asked if anything confused them, I asked if anything besides that detail did, which surfaced the word *lunglessness*. I was prepared, though, to go even further and ask a more text-specific follow-up, "Do we know what this strange word *lunglessness* means?" and then have the students turn and talk. Similarly, I followed up my open-ended question about confusion with a text-specific one when students weren't aware of the gap in the facts around the partial dissections.

Truly understanding the content of the text and the problems it poses for readers prepares you to raise questions such as these, whether you write them down on a planning sheet or hold them in your head. You also, though, want to remember the context: your ultimate goal is to help students become inquiring, inquisitive, and independent readers who seek to understand through their own agency—and recognize there's more to understanding than simply knowing facts. This means that unlike Common Core–style text-dependent questions, these serve a different purpose and context. The Common Core-style questions are intended to

- help students get whatever you or the packaged curriculum have determined they need to get;
- provide practice in backing up claims with evidence;
- prepare them to complete a performance-based writing task; and
- meet individual standards.

In contrast, the text-specific questions I'm recommending here help students become more aware of

- how expository nonfiction texts operate, with writers often leaving gaps between facts;
- what they don't understand or are confused about;

- how to use that confusion to fuel a process that leads to deeper understanding; and
- how it feels as a reader to really understand versus just know the facts.

These text-specific questions are more oriented toward process than products—that is, they're not intended as comprehension checks as much as gauges of understanding—and the answers they invite are often *not* found in the text, which is why I call them text-specific versus text-dependent. They're not aimed at having students embark on answer-getting missions; instead they offer students a chance to think about, explain, and question what they're getting in their own words, which requires a deeper level of understanding and gives you a better picture of what's going on in their heads. And in this way, your preparation is preparing students to read other texts with more depth and independence.

Be Present in the Thick of the Thinking

Inevitably there are limits to the support you can offer students from the front of the class. So you'll want to walk around the room and listen to students' conversations as they wrestle with the text. You'll hear all kinds of interesting thinking you might miss if you listened only when students shared with the whole class. But if you're committed to being responsive, rather than sticking to your plans regardless of what happens, you'll inevitably find a moment, as I did here, when you have to think on your feet. In this case, I recognized that every student was struggling to understand how this frog's flatness was connected to its lunglessness—and fortunately I was able, in the moment, to offer a manipulative that helped them out.

You could say I was lucky (which, in fact, was how I felt), but if luck is what happens when preparation meets opportunity, as many people, from the Roman philosopher Seneca to Oprah Winfrey, have supposedly said, preparation played a role here, too. I could never have made the move I did had I not paused at that fact myself as I first read the text and realized the writer hadn't explained the connection between flatness and surface area, which would pose a problem for readers who didn't understand or even know about the concept of surface area. He also didn't explicitly explain how having more skin surface area helped the frog to evolve without lungs, which meant readers would have to reason their way toward yet another conclusion. And all that preparation helped me respond in the moment.

Of course, when you're moving around the room, fully present in the thick of the thinking, you may not always be able to come up with something to support students' problem solving. Being prepared will increase your chances, but if nothing comes to mind in the moment, remember that students gain much—and retain more—when they grapple with a problem, even if they can't quite solve it. And you can always table the problem for the moment and return to it once you've had more time to think about how to address it.

You'll want to do this too if, as you listen, you hear students who aren't getting the hang of the thinking. The entire class, for instance, missed that the writer had explicitly connected the frog seeming alien with its lunglessness in the first sentence. I was also aware that some students were better able than others to reason their way to possible implications, recognize that the writer had left something unsaid, and/or explain their thinking. If you recognize that a whole class could benefit from some additional instruction on a particular problem (such as navigating syntactically complex sentences, which may be why the class went off on its E.T. tangent), return to what the students struggled with and address it through a whole-class minilesson. And if you realize some students are following along more than thinking on their own, give them time to practice thinking in small groups, where they can't just observe. For the students in this class, for instance, the teacher and I considered forming needs-based groups for students to practice one or more of the following:

- becoming more aware of what a writer has left unsaid in a less complex text (such as *Starfish*)
- trying to figure out what the presented facts might imply by reasoning (again in a less complex text)
- explaining what they think they've figured out and how, using either the whole-class text or another less complex one
- reading around unknown words, assigning placeholders when needed
- navigating syntactically complex sentences

Create an Environment That Promotes Thinking and Independence

Like many teachers, you probably spend time thinking about your classroom—how to arrange the students' seating, what to put on the walls, and so on. That's because you know that classroom environment directly affects students' thinking and learning. It sets the tone and establishes the culture, all of which is another way of preparing: You create the conditions for thinking and learning to flourish.

In earlier chapters, you saw different ways to create these conditions, from using charts that honor student thinking and make the path to meaning making visible to responding to students without judgment. And to that list, you can add the following:

- Use the words *we* and *us* instead of *you*—as in, "Are any of us confused here?"—as a way of creating an environment in which everyone is a thinker and a learner.

- Acknowledge students' confusion as a natural reaction to nonfiction texts because nonfiction writers don't always fully explain their facts.

- Explain the connection between confusion and learning (which I often do by sharing this quote from Tom Peters: "If you're not confused, you're not paying attention.").

- Acknowledge when the real world seems stranger than fiction.

- Ask students in a genuinely curious way whether they're confused about something you anticipated they might be.

- Admit when you're confused and when a student has an idea you hadn't considered before.

After sessions such as these, you'll also want to create the kind of anchor charts found in *What Readers Really Do* (Barnhouse and Vinton 2012), which not only capture what students did as readers in student-friendly language but also provide specific examples of the thinking they did (see Figure 8.4). Using the students' own thinking as a model supports the thinking and learning environment and provides students with an experiential reference point, which can remind them of what they did—and prepare them to do it again.

WHAT WE DID AS READERS TO UNDERSTAND, NOT JUST KNOW, THE FACTS IN EXPOSITORY NONFICTION
Pay attention to when you are confused because the writer hasn't explained something directly, and ask: "How might *this* connect to *that*?" Example from "Lungless Frogs": The frog had no lungs = the frog was lungless = it had the trait of lunglessness
Look for places where the writer gives you facts but leaves it up to you to figure out the implication of those facts and ask: "If *this* and *this*, then what?" Example from "Lungless Frogs": Lungless frogs were too valuable to be dissected + scientist partially dissected them = the frogs might live through a partial dissection, or the scientist didn't care
Look for places where the writer hasn't explained why or how something happened and ask: "Why and how did this happen?" Example from "Lungless Frogs": Being flat helped the frog live without lungs because it had more exposed skin to breathe through and get oxygen

FIGURE 8.4 *"What We Did to Understand Expository Nonfiction" Chart*

Finally, if we're serious about helping students become independent readers who seek to understand through their own agency, we have to be willing to release responsibility to them before we're absolutely sure they can do it on their own. With this class, for instance, I gave the students more responsibility two-thirds of the way through the session by asking them to see if they spotted something the writer hadn't fully explained, despite some uncertainty about how that might go. The worst that would happen, though, is that I'd step in, which I was prepared to do—and you can do, too, at any point in a problem-solving session. So try to take a "nothing ventured, nothing gained" approach when it comes to giving students more responsibility for thinking. And who knows? They may do more than you think they will because you've created an environment that values learning, risk taking, and complex thinking.

WHY THIS WORK MATTERS

Like curiosity, confusion can play a powerful but underappreciated role in learning. According to a recent study, for instance, "Confusion is likely to promote learning at deeper levels of comprehension," especially when it comes to "complex learning tasks [that] require learners to generate inferences, answer causal questions, diagnose and solve problems [and] generate coherent explanations" (D'Mello et al. 2014, 154), which understanding this text clearly did. Researcher Derek Muller (quoted in Kolowich 2014) has also found that five problematic things tend to happen when confusion is absent or unacknowledged:

> *One, students think they know it. Two, they don't pay their utmost attention.*
> *Three, they don't recognize that what was presented differs from what they*
> *were already thinking. Four, they don't learn a thing. And five, perhaps most*
> *troublingly, they get more confident in the ideas they were thinking before.*

Both the benefits of confusion and the problems that can occur when it's not present can be seen in this session. Students needed to be aware of their confusion in order to recognize that what was presented differed from what they already knew, and their confusion helped them pay more attention to the text in front of them. Additionally, confusion allowed them to generate inferences and explanations, answer causal questions, and not only solve problems, but diagnose them as well—all of which led to deeper understanding.

Despite all these benefits, however, we don't always invite confusion into our rooms, because it comes with problems for both us and students. Students, for instance, can experience confusion quite differently than curiosity. Curiosity frequently feels like an itch that's begging to be scratched; it's energizing and can motivate students to read more actively and closely. Confusion, on the other hand, can stir up discomfort, frustration, and even feelings of failure. Students don't want to scratch it as much as resolve or avoid it altogether. And confusion can be risky for us as well.

Like inviting curiosity, opening the door to confusion can wreak havoc with our pacing guides. Also, if we believe the skill of citing evidence to support a claim is more important than understanding the facts in the first place, confusion can feel like a waste of time. Imagine, however, these fourth graders being asked, "Why did scientists think the frog's lunglessness might be an adaptation to its habitat?" Some could probably answer that question by pulling evidence from the text, but without going through the process of thinking that was fueled by their confusion, they might answer the question "correctly" but still think the frog had lungs. And how would that serve them as thinkers and learners?

I think we risk something even more profound when we turn a blind eye to students' confusion as long as they're able to cite evidence from a text: We encourage students to think school is a place where things don't always make sense. We also risk giving them a warped vision of what it means to succeed, especially in college, where they'll be expected to do their own thinking and use their own words to explain things.

So instead, I believe we need to open the door to confusion as wide as we possibly can so that we and our students can see how a mind works as it strives to understand. And we'd also do well to encourage our students to follow these words from the writer George Saunders—and to follow them ourselves—"Don't be afraid to be confused. Try to remain permanently confused. Anything is possible. Stay open, forever, so open it hurts, and then open up some more" (2005).

STEERING THE SHIP

TEACHING MOVES TO SUPPORT STUDENT THINKING AND MEANING MAKING
Explain (or invite students to consider) the difference between knowing and understanding.
Explain how confusion can support understanding by helping readers pay more attention.
Open with an open-ended question (such as, "Is there anything we're confused about?").
Be prepared to offer a more text-specific follow-up question, if needed.
Notice places where the writer hasn't explicitly explained something and name them as examples of specific kinds of problems expository nonfiction readers face.
Notice and name how students figured out what the writer hasn't stated (e.g., "If *this* if a fact and *this* is a fact, then *that* might be a fact, too.").
Move from asking students to talk about their confusion to asking them where they think the writer has left gaps in the facts.
Give students lots of opportunities to explain their thinking to others.
Try to support problem solving in the moment (possibly by using manipulatives or other resources such as maps, diagrams, graphs, and other visuals).
Give students a chance to share their own opinions about what they've come to understand.
Use student thinking as examples on charts that generalize the kind of thinking nonfiction readers need to engage in.

FIGURE 8.5 *Steering the Ship*

Considering Complexity:
More Expository Nonfiction Problems

Much of the expository nonfiction students read is connected to a unit of study or a content area topic. So rather than offering a list of texts or strategies, this interlude explores a few additional problems that nonfiction poses across the disciplines and grades.

Figuring Out Figurative Language

To make expository nonfiction more lively and engaging, many writers use figurative language, idioms, and puns to make facts seem less dry. And while this might make a text more fun to read, it doesn't always make it easier to understand. Here, for example, is an excerpt about lungs from one of the popular Basher Science books, *Biology: Life as We Know It.*

> We are a set of beautiful twins that give your body a good airing. Life's a gas for us—we take oxygen from the air and pass it to Red Blood Cell. At the same time, we get rid of suffocating carbon-dioxide waste. . . . We're made of pink foamy flesh, but if you smoke, you'll make us a sooty mess, turning a softly purring machine into wheezing windbags. (64)

When students encounter this kind of language, they'll need to slow down, acknowledge confusion, and first try to sort out what's literal from what's figurative ("carbon-dioxide waste" versus "give your body a good airing"). Then invite them to use the strategies from "The Problem of Figurative Language" (see page 109) and explain in their own words what they think the writer is trying to convey.

Overlooking Key Small Words

Between gaps in facts and figurative language, there are lots of opportunities for readers to misunderstand expository nonfiction. But sometimes students don't understand, not because a writer has left something out or used confusing language, but because they've glossed over prepositions that establish how facts are related. Here, for instance, is an excerpt about minerals from a New York City fourth-grade science textbook:

> Do you remember the last time you picked up a pebble? Maybe it had sparkling specks or wavy lines. Maybe it was as clear as glass. Minerals formed the colors and patterns in the pebble. A **mineral** is a sold, nonliving substance that occurs naturally in rocks or in the ground. Every mineral has unique properties. Earth's surface is **rock**, a solid substance made of minerals. Rock can be made of many minerals or of one mineral with different-sized grains. Look at the granite. Each of its colors is a different mineral. (194)

The authors have highlighted the key vocabulary (shown here in bold), as well as provided lots of pictures of minerals. If asked what a mineral is, however, many students will look at the key words and pictures and say that a mineral is a rock or a kind of rock, missing the small but important word *in*. This is surprisingly common, so you'll need to be aware of when a relationship between words and facts is directly conveyed through prepositions and be prepared to ask a question, like "Do we understand how minerals are related to rocks?"

Understanding Concepts

Understanding facts isn't always easy, but expository nonfiction also deals in concepts—such as surface area and adaptation in "Lungless Frog"—that writers also don't always explain. Here, for instance, is a seemingly straightforward introduction to Mesopotamia from *Ancient Mesopotamia*, by Allison Lassieur, that contains two big social studies concept terms that aren't defined but could be grappled with—if you help students become aware of them.

> *Ancient Mesopotamia was one of the world's first great civilizations. Its people were responsible for early innovations in writing, **agriculture**, city building, and the recording of history. Tens of thousands of people lived in its enormous, beautiful cities.*
>
> *Throughout Mesopotamian history, politics changed and many different rulers rose to power and eventually fell. Cultures grew, became powerful, and were overthrown by stronger cultures that moved in to take their places. . . . A long line of kings and cultures attacked and overtook the city of Babylon, only for each culture to be overthrown by a later rival. Despite the various origins of these people, however, they all considered themselves to be Mesopotamian. (12–13)*

The word *agriculture* is defined in the margin, but *civilization* and *culture* aren't, despite the fact that understanding the difference and connection between the two is conceptually important in social studies. There are, however, context clues that could help students wrestle with this. And while it's possible some students will say they're confused about the difference between those terms, you'll want to be prepared to ask a question for conceptual words like these that students may "know" but don't fully understand.

Creating Opportunities for Readers to Consider Ideas and Opinions in Nonfiction

If you're purely after facts, please buy yourself the phone directory of Manhattan. It has four million times correct facts. But it doesn't illuminate.

—Werner Herzog

If you watch TV, you may recall a GE commercial that begins with two worried nurses standing beside a hospital bassinet in which a strange, white, feathered and furry creature opens up its newborn eyes. The creature, it turns out, is an idea, and as an oboe starts to play a sad dirge, a voiceover tells us, "Ideas are scary. They come into this world ugly and messy [and] are frightening because they threaten what's known." The music continues as the poor idea goes out into the world, where it finds itself shunned, rejected, and feared—until, that is, it finds a home at GE, where people understand that "under proper care [ideas can] become something beautiful."

Ideas take center stage in this chapter, which will look at the problems posed by non-fiction writers whose purpose is not just to inform or report on a topic or event, but also to explore topics or issues they may have their own ideas and opinions about. To dive into that, though, we need to consider what we mean by an idea. According to *Random House's Unabridged Dictionary*, the word *idea* means a thought, conception, or notion, or an opinion, view, or belief, which, to add Herzog's idea from the epigraph, should illuminate. If you ask students, however, what a main idea is, they'll often say it's what a text or a paragraph is "mostly about," which is frequently how we teach it. That teaching would likely lead readers of "What Big Brains You Have" to think that the main idea of the last paragraph is how elephants take care of each other—and in thinking that, they'd have missed how those facts also illuminate the intelligence of elephants in a way that could actually change how we think about those remarkable creatures.

Like teaching students to think of themes as sayings or one-word abstractions, we tend to offer shortcuts for the complex, messy work of engaging with an author's ideas, and then we ask students to practice the shortcut as a skill. Such a skill might be useful when studying content and answering test questions, but it doesn't help readers who are reading to expand their understanding of the world. And perhaps that's why students have trouble with it: Identifying main ideas as a skill just doesn't seem terribly meaningful. It might offer the satisfaction of completing a task, but it doesn't provide the aha feeling that accompanies illumination. For that, we need a more complex understanding not only of what ideas are but of how readers can engage with them based on how writers convey them.

EXPLORING THE PROBLEM: Considering an Author's Ideas and Opinions

In the last chapter, we saw several writers present information about a topic without conveying overarching ideas and opinions beyond "Elephants are really smart." To see how that's different from texts in which a writer implicitly conveys more complex and sometimes slanted ideas, let's take a look at an intriguing short text called "The Price of War" from the anthology *Things Get Hectic: Teens Write About the Violence That Surrounds Them*. The piece presents a series of facts the writers have ordered in a particular way for a particular purpose—and as such, it poses that ultimate problem: What might the writers want us to understand about these facts? Keep that question in mind as you read it now, and try to pay attention to what you do as a reader to arrive at a possible answer.

THE PRICE OF WAR

One Patriot missile fired: $600,000
One year of Board of Ed. Saturday SAT review course: $368,907

One jet: $25,000,000
High school drug abuse program for five years: $27,371,850

Daily fuel bill during air war: $10,000,000
Library books for high schools for five years: $9,857,562

Building one Stealth bomber: $530,000,000
Salaries of all high school academic teachers, 1989–90: $525,814,000

Long-term care and compensation for 6,000 American casualties:
$2,000,000,000
Annual budget for School Food and Nutrition Services: $205,535,422

One ground-to-ground missile fired: $100,000
Salaries for two school librarians, 1989–90: $85,237

> Sources: *Military figures:* New York Newsday *and Council on Economic Priorities.*
> *Board of Education figures:* Budget Estimate for Fiscal Year 1990–1991,
> New York City Board of Education, *Volumes 1 and 2.*

Whether you did this automatically or with some conscious awareness, the first thing you probably noticed was a pattern. The writers shared pairs of spending facts, one for the military and one for education. Looking more closely, you might also have noticed a pattern within that pattern. In each case, there was an incongruity in volume, with many of the military facts about a single thing—one jet, one missile, one day's worth of fuel—while the educational facts were mostly about multiple items or units of time. Clearly the authors are comparing and contrasting what's being spent for what, but to what end? Are they simply informing us of these facts or do they have an opinion about them that they want us to consider?

The choice and juxtaposition of facts suggest an idea and opinion by themselves. But there's another thing we can do as readers to consider an author's opinion: pay careful attention to the writer's choice of words. All of the words in the body of the text have been taken directly from outside sources, but the writers have chosen to title these facts "The Price of War." By this, the writers seem to be conveying that we spend less on education *because* of our military spending, and the wording also suggests the opinion that we do so to the detriment of children and society. Our thinking, however, about the writers' opinion would have been different if they'd chosen a title with more positive connotations, like "Keeping the Peace" or "Making Our Nation Safe." That's because words can convey opinions, which is why they're so important.

Considering Ideas and Opinions in a Longer Text

"The Price of War" is a clear example of how writers use facts to explore an idea they have an opinion about, but it's not your typical nonfiction text. So to see how writers do that in a more developed text—and how shortcuts can often backfire—let's look at an article called "Goat Throwing in Spain," which a small group of seventh graders read. The piece is about a village in Spain that holds an annual festival honoring the village's patron saint, which they kick off with a strange tradition. Every year, teenage boys from the village toss a live goat from the top of a church's bell tower, and the villagers below attempt (and sometimes fail) to catch it with a canvas sheet.

After reading the piece, the students were asked to create a chart that identified the main idea and supporting details. Take a look at the chart (in Figure 9.1) and consider what it seems to reveal about the students' understanding of the text's ideas and of thinking about main ideas in general.

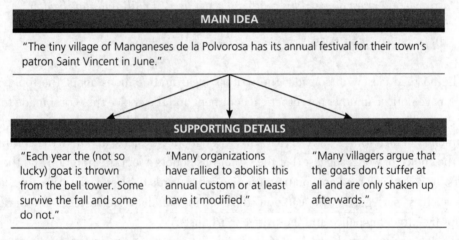

MAIN IDEA

"The tiny village of Manganeses de la Polvorosa has its annual festival for their town's patron Saint Vincent in June."

SUPPORTING DETAILS

"Each year the (not so lucky) goat is thrown from the bell tower. Some survive the fall and some do not."

"Many organizations have rallied to abolish this annual custom or at least have it modified."

"Many villagers argue that the goats don't suffer at all and are only shaken up afterwards."

FIGURE 9.1 *Main Idea Chart*

Even without having read the piece, you may have noticed several things that raised questions. The students, for instance, cited a line from the text as the main idea, which suggests they think main ideas are conveyed directly in single sentences. And the line they picked isn't really an idea; it's a fact that's connected to the general topic, which suggests the students are also fuzzy about the difference between topics, facts, and ideas. Additionally, the lines they cited as supporting details aren't actually connected to what they thought the main idea was. What's interesting, though, is if you look at those three details, you can see that the writer is giving us more than the basic who, what, when, and where facts about the festival. Those details actually suggest an idea: the writer wants us to understand that this village's tradition is quite controversial—and the parenthetical "(not so lucky) goat" remark suggests the writer may have an opinion about that.

If the group had begun with those three details (which seem to have stood out for them), and considered what they were conveying, they would have likely understood at least some of the ideas in the text. That's because readers don't really *find* ideas in texts; they *construct* them from the details they notice. But they also have to take into account other parts of the text, such as the following paragraph, which looks at the history behind the tradition.

> As to when and how this began, no one can actually confirm, though each
> villager is absolutely sure that their rendition of the story behind the tradition
> is true and undisputable. . . . One version claims that this custom began in the
> 18th century (others say hundreds of years ago and others as little as 20 years
> ago) when a priest donated his goats' milk to a needy family and shortly after
> the goat fell from the church bell tower but was miraculously saved by the poor
> villagers who caught the goat.

If you read closely to consider the writer's ideas and opinions about the topic, you might have noticed another parenthetical comment and the choice the writer made to say that each villager was "absolutely" sure of his or her "undisputable" rendition. Parenthetical comments, in fact, form a pattern that runs throughout the piece, and here the comment and the choice of words suggest that the writer has doubts about the tradition and the villagers. In fact, if you read on, you might notice other words he uses to describe the villagers—such as "partygoers" who "catapult" the goat and "retaliate" against the animal rights groups by "attacking police and inquisitive journalists."

These are all examples of loaded language, where the writer has chosen particular words that carry specific connotations. *Catapult*, for instance, is more extreme than *toss* and conjures up images of medieval battles. *Retaliate* is more violent than *respond*, and you wouldn't expect to find *partygoers* at a religious event. Instead the word brings to mind drunken revelers, and as such, it raises additional questions about the tradition and the villagers. And when taken all together, the word choices and the pattern of parenthetical comments might lead you to conclude the writer wants you to understand that the tradition is not only controversial but cruel.

Of course, readers don't have to agree with an author's opinion, but they should always consider it in order to understand the complexity of a topic or issue. And that requires much more thinking than deciding which individual sentence best captures a vague notion of an idea. Readers of this kind of nonfiction (which includes magazine articles, investigative journalism, and many kinds of essays) have to actively draft and revise their thinking as they move through a text, adding on to their ideas as they do— sort of like a snowball that accumulates more substance and weight as it rolls down a hill. These cumulative understandings are, by their very nature, more deep and penetrating—and more nuanced and complex—than those focused on readily apparent features, and it's these understandings I aim for as I work with a class of sixth graders in this chapter's classroom example.

HOW NONFICTION READERS FIGURE OUT THE IDEAS A WRITER MIGHT BE EXPLORING

WHAT WRITERS MAY CONVEY INDIRECTLY	WHAT A READER THEREFORE HAS TO DO
The ideas they're exploring about a topic or issue	Notice how the facts have been structured or arranged.
Their opinions about those ideas	Notice patterns (both between and within the facts).
	Think: What might the writer want me to understand about the facts she shares?
	Add ideas together to arrive at more complex and nuanced understandings.
	Notice the writer's choice of words, especially those that may carry positive or negative connotations.
	Think: Could these words point to an opinion or bias?

FIGURE 9.2 *How Nonfiction Readers Figure Out the Ideas a Writer Might Be Exploring*

LOOKING CLOSELY AT A PROBLEM-SOLVING SESSION

Planning for the Session

The sixth-grade class I work with here is currently reading Linda Sue Park's fact-based novel *A Long Walk to Water,* which tells the story of Salva and Nya, two children who grew up in different decades but were both affected by the conflicts in Sudan. So for this foray into nonfiction, I've chosen a feature article from *Junior Scholastic* by Sean McCollum called "The Lost Boys Look for Home," which should pair well with the book.

The article is divided into four sections with subheadings that capture what each is mainly about, such as "A Terrible Fate" and "Kids on the Run," and these divisions make for natural turn-and-talk stopping points. By assessing the text, though, I'm aware there are a few places where the writer has left it up to his readers to consider the implications of facts, just as the writer of "Lungless Frog" did. At one point, for instance, the author cites a report that says, "The smallest boys are placed closest to the enemy. In war, they are said to be fearless. . . . They are cheaper to keep, as they eat less, and are easier to manipulate. . . . Some are sent into battle high on drugs to give them courage." The author doesn't explicitly say that the boys are being exploited, but a close, attentive reader would want to consider the possibility that the boys aren't actually fearless; rather, they're being drugged and used.

I'm also aware there's another problem that's specific to this kind of text. To figure out where the author might stand on the issue or topic he's writing about, a reader needs to pay attention to who's saying what—the author or any experts or bystanders he quotes—in order to attribute the ideas and opinions to the right person.

I'll bring my awareness of these problems with me when I step into the classroom so I'm prepared for whatever twists and turns the students' meaning making might take. To finalize my planning, however, I engage in two more core planning practices, which you can read about here. First, I decide to make the students' thinking visible by using two different kinds of charts (see page 174), and then I craft a low-stakes writing prompt, following the tips for nonfiction (see page 180).

Implementing and Facilitating the Session

SETTING STUDENTS UP TO CONSIDER IDEAS

With the sixth graders sitting at desks grouped together, I begin the session with a question: "What do you think a main idea is?"

And, unsurprisingly, they repeat what they've been taught: "It's what an article is mostly about."

When I ask, however, how readers find them in texts when the writer doesn't come right out and state them, most of the students seem flummoxed. One suggests looking for key words and then putting them together in a sentence, while another suggests reading between the lines.

When I ask him how readers do that, he says, "You read between the lines by thinking about what might be between them," which even he realizes doesn't explain much. Then, with their current understanding (or lack thereof) of how readers engage with implicitly conveyed ideas now visible, I explain what we're going to do today and why.

Understanding a Problem-Based Approach: *"Frame the Work Around Concepts in Reading,"* page 183

"I asked you those questions because we're going to read an article about the lost boys of Sudan, whom I know you've been reading about in *A Long Walk to Water*. That book is a novel based on a true story, but the article we'll read today is nonfiction, and it's one of those texts where the writer doesn't come right out and say what the main idea is. Instead he offers us a bunch of facts he's deliberately chosen because he wants us to understand something about them. And to figure that out, readers don't really try to find an idea hidden between the lines. Instead, they think about what the writer might want us to understand, paragraph by paragraph or section by section. Then they try to combine and connect those ideas to create one that captures the whole text. And that's what we're going to try to do today, starting with the first section."

Understanding a Problem-Based Approach: *"Frame the Work Around the Writer,"* page 184

I then pass out copies of the text to the class and project the first section on the whiteboard, which includes the following three paragraphs. I ask the students to think about what the writer might want them to understand as I read the section out loud.

> *Children driven from war-torn countries tell fearful tales of life on the run. Now, some of the "Lost Boys" of Sudan are beginning new lives in the U.S.*
>
> *Emmanuel was only 4 years old when his childhood ended. His village, in the African country of Sudan, was attacked by government soldiers. They destroyed his home and scattered his family. During the next two years, he and his sister followed a river of refugees—including 12,000 children, mostly boys. They walked more than 600 miles to find food and safety.*
>
> *"There was no food, no medical help. We were eating green leaves," Emmanuel, now 17, remembers. "Many people died. Some were eaten by wild animals. Many drowned when we tried to cross the rivers." All the while, the refugees were hounded by the government army and its aircraft.*

Once I finish the rest of the section, I ask the students to turn and talk about what the writer might want them to understand and I eavesdrop on a few groups. Then I bring them back together to share out and write down their ideas on chart paper, once again trying to capture as much as I can without cherry-picking or judging, despite the wide range of thinking. Some students, for instance, focus on a single detail, such as "The writer wants us to understand that they had to eat leaves because there was no food," while others offer more encompassing ideas, such as "I think the writer wants us to understand that this was really horrible." Once everyone has had a chance to speak and I've recorded all of their thoughts, I set them up for their next steps.

SETTING STUDENTS UP TO SORT AND GROUP IDEAS

With the chart positioned in front of the room, I frame the next part of the process. "When I asked you to think about what the writer wanted you to understand, it seems like you had many more ideas than you might have had if I'd asked you about the main idea. I think that's because everyone paid attention to details that really stuck out to them, which is great. But now I'm wondering: Do you think these are all separate ideas or could some be connected? Like, could some be examples of others? If so, do you think we could sort and group them into categories, the way you might have done with words or shapes when you were younger? Can we try that by turning and talking?"

CORE PRACTICE: Making Student Thinking Visible: Charts That Help Students Sort and Synthesize

As you've now seen, this kind of nonfiction doesn't unfold as narratives do, and that has implications for your charts. With fiction, for instance, I use two basic kinds of charts: a know/wonder chart that supports the thinking readers need to do at the beginnings of texts, and one that reframes their thinking around an inquiry question or pattern to support the work needed in the middle right up until the end. Here I also use two charts: one that, chunk by chunk, captures what students think the writer might want them to understand and uses arrows to then sort and group those ideas (see Figure 9.4) and another that helps students combine those ideas in order to add layers of nuance and complexity to their thinking (see Figure 9.5).

For the first, I use a piece of chart paper to record whatever the students think the writer wants them to understand, transcribing those thoughts as they share out. Then, once I invite them to sort and group those ideas into categories, I move to a second chart where I've drawn the kind of brackets used to track sports team play-offs—not for the purpose of eliminating ideas, but of adding and combining them, so the end result is a synthesis of ideas, not one idea that trumped all the others. And to segue from one chart to the other, I import the ideas from the first chart to the second, using the students' thinking to continue the process, just as I lifted a question or pattern from the students' know/wonder chart to reframe their work around an inquiry with fiction.

As I move around the room, I hear many students say that lots of the ideas on the chart could be examples of how really horrible life was for the lost boys, and a few others think some are also connected to one of the other ideas on the chart: that the lost boys had to grow up really fast. These two big ideas emerge, as well, when the whole class shares out, and I circle them on the chart with a different-color marker to distinguish them from the others, then I draw arrows to show how all the other ideas they came up with are connected to one or both of these. Then I notice and name what they've just done: They've figured out that the writer wants us to understand these two really big ideas, and all these other details helped us to see them more clearly. (See Figure 9.3.)

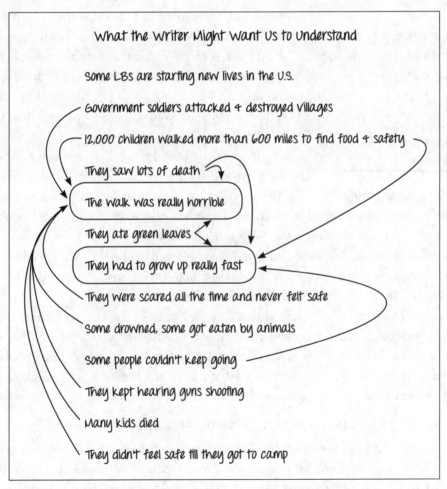

FIGURE 9.3 *"What the Writer Might Want Us to Understand" Chart*

SETTING STUDENTS UP TO COMBINE IDEAS

Now that the students have teased out some big ideas, it's time to explain how readers can synthesize even more by combining the larger, overarching ideas. To demonstrate that process, I take out my second chart, where I've drawn several sets of play-off team brackets, and after asking a sports fan volunteer to explain how brackets work to those not in the know, I offer a teaching point.

"After all that talking and thinking, we think the writer wants us to understand two really big ideas: that what happened to these kids was utterly horrible and they had to grow up really fast. So I'm going to write these first two lines. We're not, though, going to do a play-off here and debate which idea is more important and has a chance to move to the finals. Instead we're going to try to combine these ideas because writers often want us to understand more than one thing, especially when they're writing about something complex that may have multiple perspectives, causes and effects, and problems and solutions. To help us with that, I've put some combining words that might help us put these ideas together: *and, but, because, so, while, when, although, until,* and *since.*

"So take a moment to turn and talk with your group about how you might combine these ideas using one or more of these words and then write down that combined idea."

Understanding a Problem-
Based Approach: *"Framing Versus
Scaffolding,"* page 182

As I circulate through the room, I hear several groups using the most accessible word, *and,* but many also gravitate to *because,* saying things like, "The lost boys had to grow up really fast because of all the terrible things that happened to them on the walk." Additionally, one group combines ideas with *when* as well as *and,* as in "When the lost boys tried to run from the war, they still saw lots of people dying and that made them grow up really fast." Also, in addition to using different combining words and sentence structures, different groups bring in other useful words, like *survival* and *war,* to their statements.

I notice and name these subtle differences for the class; then we try to interactively incorporate some of these variations in the idea I finally write on the chart. This celebrates and honors the diversity of thinking and demonstrates the power of collaboration to develop more complex understandings, which, I explain, is exactly why people say two heads are better than one. (See Figure 9.4.)

SETTING STUDENTS UP TO TRANSFER AND APPLY THE THINKING

With the first section of the article finished, we move to the second part, where I explain that we'll do the same thing we just did. As I read the next part, students should think about what the writer might want them to understand and then share their ideas with

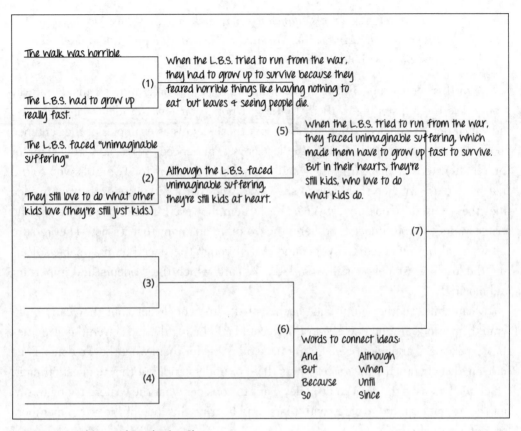

FIGURE 9.4 *Combine and Synthesize Chart*

their groupmates. But this time, I'd like them to try sorting, grouping, and combining their ideas with their group and record their thinking on a sentence strip.

As I read, the class learns that the lost boys were named after the boys in Peter Pan who had lost their parents, and that not only were many of the Sudanese boys orphaned, but some were forced to become soldiers and kill, while others were raped or found life so unbearable they took their own lives. Then the writer says this:

> All of these children face suffering unimaginable to the average American teen.
>
> Even so, says Molly Daggett, a social worker who has helped children in the Kakuma camp, "These children are remarkably resilient (able to recover). They want you to know that they love to sing, dance, and play sports—just like other kids."

> *Emmanuel now has his chance to enjoy such activities. Last month, he and his sister arrived in Seattle, Washington, as part of a program to resettle 3,500 of the Lost Boys in the U.S.*

With this section now finished, the students turn and talk, and as I make my way around the room, listening to their thinking, I notice far fewer students latching onto individual details. They do, though, talk about those details as examples of the sentence about the "unimaginable suffering" the lost boys experienced—especially how some of the children took their own lives, which many have reactions to. Two girls who found that particular sentence striking also share with me that it's like the explicit main idea lines they're used to looking for. When I ask them, however, if that's the only thing the writer wants them to understand here, they're quite adamant that it's not. They're sure the writer also wants them to understand that although they faced unimaginable suffering, the lost boys somehow still were kids at heart, which the students find important and moving.

Meanwhile, another group has reached that same conclusion, but they can't quite wrap their minds around how the lost boys could still be regular kids given the atrocities they experienced and witnessed. So I notice and name for them what they've done: They have an idea about what the writer wants them to understand, but they're questioning it, which readers have the right to do. They want to consider what the writer's trying to say, but they're not required to agree with that—and hearing this, one of the group members lets out a sigh of relief.

SETTING STUDENTS UP TO CONSIDER THE AUTHOR

Without knowing it, these groups have stumbled on one of the problems I was aware of when I assessed the text. If readers don't closely attend to who's saying what, they can misattribute thoughts and ideas to the author. Of course, an author might agree with someone he has quoted. In fact, he might have chosen the quote precisely because it's a point he wants to make, and he knows it will carry more weight if it comes from an expert. But that's not always the case. And being aware of this particular problem, I decide to use this opportunity to distinguish an author's point of view from that of someone he's quoted.

"It sounds like many of us think the writer wants us to understand that, *while* the suffering these children went through is unimaginable, they also just want to be seen as kids. But some think that, with all the lost boys have gone through, that's unimaginable, too. And that's OK. In fact, readers can always have their own opinion about the facts themselves and what the writer wants us to understand. But I want to ask an important question here: Did the writer say they're just like other kids?"

Virtually everyone nods his or her head yes, so I ask them to take another look at the text, at which point they realize those are actually the words of Molly Daggett, the social worker, not the author. So I continue.

"The writer may want us to know that the lost boys think they're just like other kids—and Molly Daggett seems to believe that because she says they're 'remarkably resilient.' But I'm not sure we absolutely know the writer's opinion about all these facts. So before we finish for today, can we take one last look at what we've read so far and see if we spot anything that might be a clue to what the author thinks?"

The room is quiet as the students go back and look at the article more closely, and when I ask them to come back together, I can tell by their faces that many have come up empty-handed. Two students, however, think they've spotted something. One points out a sentence in the first section, where the author has written, "Emmanuel was only 4 years old when his childhood ended." She thinks this could be a clue that the writer doesn't think they're just like other kids because "his childhood ended" are definitely the writer's words. The other student, meanwhile, has noticed that the writer didn't say that here in the United States, Emmanuel was singing, dancing, and playing sports, but that he had a "chance" to do that, which could mean the author's not sure he does. And this time the students' faces tell me they're considering their classmates' ideas, with many students nodding and others murmuring "hmm."

SETTING STUDENTS UP TO REACT TO THE TEXT

With these ideas now out on the table, I decide to wrap up the session halfway through the text and let the students ponder these ideas further in writing through a low-stakes prompt. I ask them, "At this point in the text, what do you think the writer wants us to understand about the lost boys? And what do you think about that—as in, do you agree or disagree with what the writer seems to be saying? And, as always, why?"

This prompt asks students to look at the text through both the author's and their own perspectives, and again I assure them I'm not looking for an essay, just their thoughts, feelings, questions, or opinions.

Understanding a Problem-Based Approach: *"Frame the Work Around the Reader," page 185*

Given how quickly the room grows quiet once they've pulled out their notebooks, the students seem to have much to say, and I once again circulate to get a feel for their thinking. Many attempt to put themselves in the lost boys' shoes, trying to imagine what it must have been like to lose their families, have nothing to eat, and make the decision to end your own life. Some say they're not sure what the author thinks but they want to believe that once they reached the camp, the lost boys could be kids again, as the social worker said. Some, however, think that's not possible, and a few of those students think the writer wants them to understand that in addition to all that the lost boys lost—homes, families, friends—they also lost their childhood. That makes one student reflect back on her life and write, "I'm lucky that I get just to be a kid," and I ask that student if she'd be willing to read what she wrote to start off our share.

CORE PRACTICE: **Making Thinking Visible: Low-Stakes Writing Prompts for Nonfiction**

Just as with fiction, you'll occasionally want to ask students to respond to a low-stakes writing prompt at the end of a nonfiction problem-based session so that both you and your students can better see the range of thinking in the room. And once again, you'll want to craft those prompts in a general, non-text-dependent way, so the thinking you're asking for can be transferred and applied to different texts in the same subgenre. You won't, however, have to consider where students are in the text (i.e., the beginning, middle, or end) as you would in fiction, since these texts aren't structured that way. But you'll still want to consider what perspective(s) you want the students to think about, which can be visualized

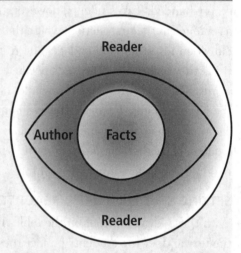

FIGURE 9.5 *Seeing Nonfiction Texts Through Different Perspectives*

in a graphic similar to the one you saw with fiction (see Figure 9.5). This means you could ask students to consider any one of the following:

- What do you think about the facts the author has presented (as in, what's your opinion or reaction to them) and why?

- What do you think the author thinks about the facts and why?

- Do you think the author sees things the same way you and/or the people he has quoted do or not, and why or why not?

CORE PRACTICE: **Making Thinking Visible: Low-Stakes Writing Prompts for Nonfiction** (Continued)

- What do you think about what you think the author seems to think (again, your opinion or reaction) and why?

As you may have noticed, each prompt is progressively more complex, and once students have experienced and engaged with the thinking through both talk and writing, you can also let them choose which one they want to consider, which allows for built-in differentiation. And again, if needed, offer a reminder that you're not looking for a formal essay here, just their thoughts on paper—which also means you won't grade it.

UNDERSTANDING A PROBLEM-BASED APPROACH: The Role of Framing

All of the elements of problem-based teaching that we've explored so far were on full display in this session. My planning helped me be prepared to offer a wide range of questions and responses as students engaged in a rich task that provided multiple points of access and pathways to meaning. And to round out your understanding of this dynamic approach, let's take a look here at the important role of framing.

By framing, I don't mean the positive versus negative ways to frame feedback or responses to student behavior, as Doug Lemov does in *Teach Like a Champion* (2010). Nor am I referring to the kind of lesson framing recommended in books like *The Fundamental Five: The Formula for Quality Instruction* (Cain and Laird 2011), where teachers are advised to frame lessons around a single—and often narrow—learning objective that is then assessed at the end of a lesson. Instead I mean the different ways we can focus students' attention to help them think deeply about what they're reading in specific, genre-related ways that are transferrable to other texts.

Project Zero's David Perkins calls these "thinking frames," which he says are "intended to guide the process of thought, supporting, organizing, and catalyzing that process" (1986, 7). I've used them throughout the sessions in this book as I've set students up to do different kinds of thinking while they've made their way toward deeper meaning by grappling with various problems in their texts. Here we'll explore some key concepts and ways of framing, beginning with digging more into the idea of frames.

Framing Versus Scaffolding

If I were to ask you to name an instructional practice that supports students in taking on deeper thinking, the chances are good that you wouldn't say framing, but you might very well say scaffolding. Both are intended to support students, but I think there's a critical difference. Consider a frame as the specific thinking work of reading you're inviting students to engage in (that is, a frame is the *what*), while a scaffold or a strategy is a tool that can help students do that (it addresses the *how*). This distinction is important because, as Jeremy Greensmith says in *The Teacher You Want to Be: Essays About Children, Learning and Teaching*, "the danger with a lot of what gets done at the moment is that there's so much scaffolding that you end up just teaching the scaffold, and you really don't teach the way of thinking and the way of reading and writing—you just teach [students] to deliver the tool you taught them" (quoted in White 2015, 103).

With this class, for instance, I did offer several scaffolds to support the thinking I was asking the students to do, such as the charts, the list of linking words, and the question about the author's opinion. But I didn't model how to fill out the chart, nor did I offer any sentence stems or templates to show students how to use the words. Those are examples of scaffolds, as well, but they're not really tools for doing the thinking; they're tools for doing the scaffold. And as such, they can limit and constrain thinking, rather than catalyze it, by making the expression of thought mechanical in ways that don't necessarily help students become more flexible, fluent, and diverse thinkers.

Framing, on the other hand, breaks down complex thinking into manageable pieces without ever losing sight of the whole, and it invites students to engage in the actual thinking work that's behind what we often teach as skills. In this session, for instance, you could say that one of the things I taught the class was how to determine importance. But beyond the charts, I didn't offer other scaffolds, such as teaching the strategy of focusing on text features, text structures, or key words, or the skills of scanning and skimming. Instead I framed the work as steps in a process of thought that begins with brainstorming, then sorting and grouping, which is the invisible thinking work involved in determining importance. You and I and some students can do this unconsciously, while others can't, and those thinking frames help guide and support students through that process.

Frame the Work Around Concepts in Reading

Here I kicked off a session with a question that invited students to share what they knew (or thought they knew), about reading itself, not about the topic of the text they'd be reading. I asked them what they thought a main idea was and how readers figure out implicitly conveyed ones. Since I often work with students I don't already know, these questions give me a window into how they conceive of the work of reading, which helps me adapt to where they are. But they're also great formative assessment questions, which I think are underutilized in classrooms, where we tend to assess students' reading solely through their performance. If, however, Einstein is right that "if you can't explain [something] to a six-year-old, you don't understand it yourself," questions that ask students to articulate their understanding about an aspect of reading give both us and students valuable information.

Here, for instance, this question made the students aware they weren't really sure how to figure out implicitly conveyed ideas in nonfiction—and moving from not knowing what you don't know to consciously knowing that is the first step toward mastering anything (see "The Necessity of Time and Repetition," on page 46). Additionally, as we've seen, students retain more when they have opportunities to metacognitively reflect on and explain concepts and their own thinking.

Of course, there are students who can explain the thinking without necessarily being able to do it themselves. But I wonder if we don't ask students questions like this because they can reveal the limits of our teaching—that is, we might face the uncomfortable truth that students didn't learn what we taught. If we're committed, however, to learning and meeting students where they are, not where we think they should be, launching a problem-based session with a question about reading should be in your repertoire. And here are a few others you can use to frame a session around concepts in reading, each of which should be followed by a question that asks students to explain their thinking further, such as "Why?" or "How?"

- Do you think there's a difference between knowing and understanding?
- Do you think the experience of reading fiction is different than that of reading nonfiction?

- Do you think there's a difference between a topic and an idea (or facts and ideas) in nonfiction?

- Do you think authors want to do more than persuade, inform, or entertain their readers? (It's often useful to ask students to think back to a text they've read in common to ground their thinking in something specific.)

- Do you think identifying themes in fiction or ideas in nonfiction helps you as a reader—or in your own life?

Frame the Work Around the Writer

Framing the whole session around the question of what the writer might want you to understand immediately puts the author on the students' radar. But it's often harder to spot writers in nonfiction than in fiction—especially in the kind of nonfiction we're looking at here, where writers use facts to explore topics or issues they may or may not have an opinion about. In fiction, after all, the writer has chosen everything—from who the characters are to the problems they face and how they do or don't solve them, along with a bevy of smaller details (like having an old woman who fears outliving things read a book about everlasting flowers) that support what she's trying to convey. In nonfiction, however, the writer is constrained by the facts and sometimes only peeks out through one or two of the following:

- the arrangement of facts
- parenthetical comments
- word choice
- the selective inclusion or omission of facts or points of view
- the structure of the piece, including how much space is given to different aspects of a topic or issue
- the last note struck by the ending

This makes figuring out where an author might stand on an issue or topic a little like playing Where's Waldo? And this problem is further compounded when readers aren't paying close attention to who's actually saying what, as happened here. In this text, for instance, the writer quotes a variety of people who have different perspectives and viewpoints, including two Sudanese boys who experienced the effects of the conflict firsthand, the social worker in the refugee camp, and an aid worker with the United Nations High Commission for Refugees. The social worker is quoted as saying that the lost boys "are remarkably resilient," while the aid worker thinks something quite different. "Many of these child soldiers," the writer quotes him saying, "learn to handle guns before they learn to handle toys . . . and it's very difficult to rehabilitate these young soldiers after the war is over."

Figuring out where the writer might stand along this spectrum of viewpoints is critical to fully considering what he wants his readers to understand. And while as proficient readers, we're able to distinguish the words of the author from those of people he quotes without much conscious effort, many students don't make these distinctions—or are even aware there are distinctions to make. So you'll want to be aware of who's saying what as you assess the text in order to be prepared to draw students' attention there—which you'll do by framing what you could call a task within the larger task.

Frame the Work Around the Reader

After asking the students to share their understanding of how readers figure out implicitly conveyed ideas, I framed the thinking work around the question "What do you think the writer wants you to understand?," which is quite different than asking students, "What's the main idea?" When you ask students to identify a main idea, for instance, you're asking them to objectively *extract* something from the text, but when you ask what the writer might want them to understand, you're inviting them to *transact* with the text by considering what stood out for them more subjectively as readers. This automatically makes the work more accessible, meaningful, and engaging because it brings the reader into the equation. Additionally, it sets students up to enter the text with a more inquisitive stance, while avoiding the right-or-wrong-answer trap that can shut down the creative thinking needed to generate, speculate, and form hypotheses (see "Creative Thinking: It's More than Mud in the Tea," on page X). It also taps into what I believe is the basic but essential process for all thinking: paying attention to what you notice and then making something of that, be it a question, a reaction, an inference, a hypothesis, or an interpretation—which, in fact, is what readers are making when they consider what a writer might want them to understand.

I also brought the reader in through the way I invited students to determine importance. When we teach this as a skill, we frequently warn students not to get distracted by small details and distinguish between what's really important and what's simply interesting. Here, though, I made no such distinctions because this is problematic advice if we think about reading for meaning, which entails noticing the details a writer has chosen and then considering why he chose them. The details are, in effect, portals to ideas, and readers are more likely to take on this thinking if we invite them to pay attention to what interests or moves them, rather than suggest they ignore or skip over what they find intriguing, mysterious, poignant, or appalling. In fact, according to Annie Murphy Paul in her *Mind/Shift* article "How the Power of Interest Drives Learning" (2013), "interest effectively turbocharges our thinking," and here it gave students access to thinking work that might have eluded or thwarted them before when it was taught as a skill.

Finally, I framed the thinking work around the reader when I opened the door for students to share their opinions about what they just read in writing, which involved yet another slight shift: I asked the students to *react* to the facts, rather than *respond* to them. You could see this as another semantic splitting of hairs, but I think the difference is again important. Reacting invites students to attend to their emotions—that is, what the facts make them feel—while responding is typically grounded in reasoning and logic, not feelings. We do, of course, want students to develop the ability to reason and apply logic to all sorts of situations, problems, and texts. But if we also want them to develop a sense of compassion, empathy, and social justice—plus see reading as personally meaningful—we need to create space for students to feel. In fact, in her essay "What Price Beauty? A Call for Aesthetic Education," Ellin Keene suggests that true engagement requires not only students' intellectual involvement but their emotional involvement as well—and that involvement should lead to a change in students' outlooks or perspectives and/or an aesthetic experience where students perceive something as "deeply meaningful, personal, and beautiful" (2015, 87).

Of course, given the nature of this text, many students perceived what the lost boys had experienced as horrific, not beautiful. But they were deeply moved in a way that changed their perception not only of what humans are capable of—in terms of both survival and cruelty—but also of childhood itself as a special and precious time of life. And it's just this kind of experience that, as Keene writes, has "everything to do with whether we remember and put our ideas out in the world" (92).

 ## WHY THIS WORK MATTERS

The Common Core State Standards place great emphasis on having students analyze and evaluate writers' arguments. In fact, these are seen as two of the most important academic skills needed for college and careers. Analyzing and evaluating are also important life skills, as we live in a world where we're bombarded with information and *mis*information, which manipulates, circumvents, or distorts facts. And to address both the standards' concerns and our seemingly post-fact world, we often teach students to read with a wary and critical stance, ever on the lookout for manipulative language, bias, and dubious claims.

In *Reading Nonfiction: Notice & Note Stances, Signposts, and Strategies*, Kylene Beers and Bob Probst wisely suggest that students need to read nonfiction "with a skeptical eye and an open mind" (2016, 72). But in too many classrooms I see much more emphasis placed on the former than the latter. Students are asked to read texts for the explicit purpose of questioning and judging the author's word choice or to gather evidence for their own arguments or talking points in debates. In fact, much classroom discourse is now framed around debates, with students having lots of opportunities to practice and hone their debating skills over others, like their interpretative skills, that I believe are equally important but too often overlooked and undervalued.

In his thought-provoking essay "Young Minds in Critical Condition," writer and Wesleyan University president Michael S. Roth directly addresses what he, too, sees as an imbalance between critiquing and understanding. He writes, "In overdeveloping the capacity to show how texts, institutions or people fail to accomplish what they set out to do, we may be depriving students of the chance to learn as much as possible from what they study . . . [and] become absorbed in the works in literature, art and science" (2014, SR5).

Put another way, by encouraging students to be what Roth calls "critical unmaskers" and "debunkers," we may be discouraging them from engaging with texts in ways that can both illuminate their understanding of the world and lead to that "education of the heart."

I have to believe that all the book lovers out there don't want that to happen. We want our students to consider the possibilities inherent in the different perspectives and experiences they can encounter in books—and be open enough to be changed and affected by what they read. But we also want them not to be gullible or at risk for being manipulated by some sly, clever wordsmith. So while you help your students become critical readers, be sure you're giving them as many opportunities to develop that open mind as you do that skeptical stance by letting students grapple with the ideas in a text before they start debating and debunking. Help them to see skepticism as the work of a consumer (as in, "let the buyer beware") and take to heart C. S. Lewis' belief that "the true reader reads every work seriously in the sense that he reads it whole-heartedly, making himself as receptive as he can" (1961, 11).

STEERING THE SHIP

TEACHING MOVES TO SUPPORT STUDENT THINKING AND MEANING MAKING
Ask students what they think the writer wants them to understand, not what the main idea is (letting them gravitate to what stands out to them, not what seems important).
Invite students to sort, group, and categorize ideas that seem to have something in common.
Help students see how ideas can be grouped by drawing arrows between ideas that could be examples of or support for larger ones.
Notice and name how writers show us larger ideas through the details they've chosen.
Invite students to combine (i.e., add up) larger ideas together in order to draft more complex and nuanced understandings.
Offer some basic linking words (if needed).
Notice and name not only the diversity of thought but of how that thought is expressed.
Seize opportunities to help students become more aware of the author's presence in a text, including distinguishing the author's words from those of others she cites or quotes.
Release additional responsibility to the students by letting them work in groups or pairs, and then try to make the thinking public.
Ask students to write about a variety of perspectives on the facts an author presents (e.g., their own, the author's, the people the author quotes, and their own take on the author's perspectives).
Let students react versus respond to facts and ideas in writing and in talk (knowing that facts without feelings don't illuminate and ideas can be both beautiful and scary).

FIGURE 9.6 *Steering the Ship*

Considering Complexity:
The Problem of Loaded Language

To help students become complex readers of nonfiction who come to texts with an open mind *and* a discerning, if not skeptical, eye for the language writers use, you'll want to offer them opportunities to practice considering what perspective or bias a writer's choice of words reveals by reading texts or excerpts that do that in small groups.

Advertisements, both in print and on air, can be useful for becoming more aware of loaded language, as can looking at newspaper headlines whose wording conveys different points of view or judgments about the same event. But if you want students to become aware of the kinds of subtle words we saw in the last chapters, you'll want to look at more than headlines and ads. Following is an annotated list of texts that run the gambit from picture books to historical documents and a couple of paired texts, where students can see writers holding and conveying quite different points of view about the same topic.

TEXT	GRADE LEVEL	DESCRIPTION
Dear Mrs. LaRue: Letters from Obedience School, a picture book by Mark Teague	2–4	This book is about a dog named Ike who manipulates language in order to convince his owner to rescue him from obedience school, which Ike describes as a *"prison"* where the "warden *barks orders*" and he's "*forced* to perform the *most meaningless tasks*"—though the illustrations make it look like a country club.
Who Was George Washington Carver? by Jim Gigolotti, and *A Weed Is a Flower*, by Aliki	3–6	These two biographies draw on the same facts but use language and details to create very different views of the inventor who was born a slave. Gigolotti's book, for instance, opens with an anecdote that shows how helpful and handy Carver was as a child—without ever mentioning he'd been a slave—while Aliki's book begins by recounting the obstacles Carver faced. One is a book about a man who "never lost that helpful spirit . . . and used his passion for nature to become one of the most famous, and helping, scientists in the world"; the other is about "a man who devoted his whole life to helping his people and the world around him."
"A New World," by Alice Crowell Hoffman, and "Columbus Day," by Jimmie Durham	4–6	One of these poems is by a turn-of-the-century poet who admiringly writes that "Columbus found a new world/Because he *dared to do/A thing that was unheard of/A thing that was quite new.*" The other is by a member of the Cherokee Nation who sees Columbus, Cortez, and other explorers as *"filthy murderers,"* whose "heroic discoveries/Made by *liars and crooks*" he learned about in school.
"Breakfast on Mars: Why We Should Colonize the Red Planet" and "Robots Only: Why We Shouldn't Colonize Mars," both by Chris Higgins, from the essay anthology *Breakfast on Mars*	5–8	These two essays not only present the pros and cons of colonizing Mars but also use language to convey very different points of view about humans. The pro essay suggests that we humans deserve a *"a stretch of new frontier into which we can explore"* and *"Mars is there for the taking,"* while the con sees us as *"basically big, weighty bags of water,"* who are *"emotionally needy"* and *"overbearing."*
"Sis! Boom! Bah! Humbug!" by Rick Reilly	5–8	This essay describes cheerleading as "about *as safe as porcupine juggling,*" with "*Velcroed-on smiles*" and "*bizarre arm movements stolen from the Navy signalmen's handbook.*"
"More U.S. Children Being Diagnosed with Youthful Tendency Disorder"	7–10	This anonymously written satirical article from *The Onion* suggests play is a psychological disorder characterized by "a variety of senseless, unproductive physical and mental exercises," and a "love/hate relationship with reality."

Creating Opportunities for Readers to Solve Problems in Their Independent Reading Books

The book to read is not the one that thinks for
you, but the one which makes you think.

—Harper Lee

If we believe the ultimate aim of instruction is the transfer of learning, it follows that we must carve out time for students to read independently as we sit down beside them and confer to see if transfer is happening. On the one hand, this seems like a no-brainer, but, of course, it's more complex than that. Time is always an issue in schools and conferring isn't easy, which I learned many years ago when I worked for the Teachers College Reading and Writing Project alongside all-stars like Shelley Harwayne, Georgia Heard, and, of course, Lucy Calkins, who pushed my thinking and challenged me to do more than I ever thought I could.

Lucy said that every conference should change a student's life, which seemed a pretty tall order to me. In fact, to this day, I sometimes bumble through a conference, unsure of what to say until hours later, when the perfect words suddenly dawn on me. Over time, though, I've come to believe that just sitting beside students and listening to what they have to say about themselves as readers and how they're transacting with a text can, indeed, be life-changing. And this is particularly true if we listen, as Stephen Covey, author of *The 7 Habits of Highly Effective People*, says, not with "the intent to reply"—that is, until we hear something to teach—but with "the intent to understand" (1989, 251).

Through a combination of conference examples, some core practices, and a look at the role of research in conferences, this chapter will show you how to apply a problem-based approach to reading conferences focused on meaning. Your aim in these conferences will be to set students up to wrestle with whatever problems might limit or deepen their thinking. And to reach that aim, we'll explore how to listen with the intent to understand how students are navigating the problems their books pose and to elicit that information through research questions throughout the conference. But first, let's look at the central problem meaning-focused conferences pose for us as teachers.

EXPLORING THE PROBLEM: Assessing the Text

So far, we've focused on the problems texts pose for readers, but here we'll explore the central problem independent reading poses for us as teachers: we haven't chosen what students are reading. In whole-class and small-group settings, after all, you're the one who selects the text, and the choice you make is informed by your awareness of the problems it poses. In independent reading, however, students choose their own books, and frequently you'll find yourself conferring with students who are reading something you haven't read or aren't familiar with. This means you won't know beforehand what sorts of problems a student's book contains, nor will you know the spectrum of meaning a reader might make of it. And even if you've read what a student is reading, it's unlikely you'll remember the particular problems you had to solve to make meaning, and that creates several challenges.

Other approaches address these challenges by having teachers set an agenda in advance. A teacher, for instance, might come to a conference having already decided to focus on fluency or see if a student is practicing something that's been an instructional focus or a student's reading goal. In a problem-based approach whose goal is meaning, however, you'll want to hold off on deciding what to teach until you have a sense of how a student is navigating the problems he's encountering and what meaning he's making as he reads. And to do that, you'll need to get a quick feel for the text as well as the reader.

Reading Alongside a Reader to Understand a Text's Problems

Even speed readers can't skim a whole book in the time it takes for a conference, and while a book's flap or cover often offers a summary, that won't tell you what you'd have to figure out as a reader to reach that understanding. If we think, however, that what makes texts complex is the amount of information a writer conveys indirectly, here's a way to assess any text and the meaning a student is making of it. First, ask the student you're conferring with to open his book to wherever he stopped reading (be it on page 5 or page 105) and read forward a few paragraphs to a page, as you read the passage alongside him.

You'll both be reading to consider what it means, with the student thinking about how this part adds on, complicates, or challenges what he has already read, while you develop a first-draft understanding of this particular passage. Then, once you ask the student to stop, use the draft you just created to begin to compare and assess whatever meaning the student has made of it.

Of course, this means jumping into a book on what, to you, is a random page—and that can feel like parachuting into unknown terrain. You've literally landed in the middle of things, with only the words on the page and the cover as a compass. Just remember how much you can figure by piecing details together in the same way you do in the opening of books whose authors used *in medias res*. And while there may be things that puzzle you, you'll undoubtedly get enough to create a first-draft understanding of the passage to see what problems it poses.

To see what I mean, take a look at this passage from the middle of Cynthia Lord's book *Rules*, which I read in a conference alongside a student named Marianna. The book comes with a Lexile level of 780 and a Fountas and Pinnell reading level of R, and the back-cover blurb explains that the main character makes rules for her brother, who she wishes will one day be what she calls "a regular brother." With that in mind, try reading it now to see how much you can figure out about the characters, where they are, and what's going on, and if you notice any patterns that might intimate larger themes.

> *"I have a new neighbor who's my age," I say. "I haven't met her yet, but I'm hoping she's nice."*
>
> *He smiles.* **Catherine. Friend.**
>
> *"I do have friends—my best friend is Melissa—but no one that lives near me. My neighborhood is mostly old people and families with little kids. Well, except the boy who lives on the corner. He's my age but he—"*
> **Stinks a big one!!!**
>
> *I put that card as far from my name as possible. "You'll have to be careful when you use this one. The last time I yelled this, I had to sit in the front seat of the bus."*
> **No. I mean. Catherine. My. Friend.**
>
> *My lips feel dry. I lick them, though Mom always tells me not to. "Sure," I say, even if I think of us more as clinic friends than always friends. Seeing Jason's finger on the word, I wonder why he didn't already have it.*
> *(69–70)*

Having jumped into this page without knowing what came before it, you're probably unsure of some things, but it's likely you figured out at least some of the following, all of which was conveyed indirectly:

- The narrator's name is Catherine.

- Catherine is having a conversation with Jason, who may have a problem speaking.

- The different font and how it's punctuated represent cards that Jason is using for his side of the conversation.

- They may be at some kind of clinic that treats people with disabilities.

- Catherine isn't totally sure how she feels about being Jason's friend.

- The author might be exploring what it means to be a friend, as the word appears in this passage six times.

Being aware of the problems this section holds—and having drafted your own understanding of it—you're now in a position to assess the depth of a student's thinking and the meaning she has made. This doesn't mean your drafts have to match; the student, after all, has read all the pages leading up to the one you've landed on. But as you'll see as you read on, your first draft gives you a basis from which to continue your research and decide what to teach.

 # PLANNING FOR INDIVIDUAL READING CONFERENCES

Because you can never predict exactly how a meaning-based conference will go, you can't plan ahead for the teaching you'll do when you sit down with a student. But there are some practices you can implement to help you focus on problem solving and meaning as you work with readers. Many of these are in-the-moment teaching moves you'll make as you talk with students, but here are three things you can do to set the stage and be prepared for meaning-based conferences:

1. Follow a predictable conference structure that's designed to help you see how students are transacting with the book they're reading.

2. Create an independent reading culture focused on meaning by teaching students a meaning-based way of finding a just-right book.

3. Have a repertoire of predictable research questions to ask for each stage of the conference.

In terms of structure, I recommend a more complex version of the research-compliment-decide-teach structure you may already know. In this version, you stay in research mode throughout the conference, rather than just at the beginning, as you probe students' thinking and listen carefully to understand who they are as readers and how they're thinking about what they're reading, while following these steps:

1. Research the student as a reader.

2. Notice and name (versus compliment) what the student is doing.

3. Read alongside the student.

4. Research the meaning she has made of what she has read.

5. Notice and name what she has done to make this meaning.

6. Use what you've learned to set the student up to problem solve.

7. Research the student's response to your teaching and agree on a plan.

The core practice sections in this chapter have information and tips on teaching students a meaning-based way of choosing a book (page 196), noticing and naming (page 207), reading alongside students (page 199), and setting students up to problem solve (page 201). But here let's take an extended look at the critical role of research.

UNDERSTANDING A PROBLEM-BASED APPROACH: The Role of Research

Whenever you probe a student's thinking in a whole-class or small-group setting, you're engaging in research that helps you learn more about the student. Independent reading conferences, however, offer a unique opportunity to learn about a student's meaning-making process as well as how he perceives the work of reading and himself as a reader. So you'll want to conduct three rounds of research across the conference, each of which has a specific purpose.

Research the Reader, Not the Book

Many reading conferences open with a question about what a student is reading, such as, "So tell me about your book?" On the one hand, this seems like a natural way to begin a reading conference, but on the other, it's a question about the book, not the reader—and it's the reader you need to learn about. Your goal is to understand how deeply or not students are thinking about themselves as readers along with what they're reading. So in this initial round of research, focus on the reader with questions like these:

- Is there something *you're* trying to do or work on as a reader?

- Are *you* wondering about anything?

- What have *you* figured out so far?

- Is there something *you're* hoping *you'll* understand more or figure out as *you* keep reading?

- Have *you* noticed any patterns or things that are repeated?

- Do *you* have any ideas about what the author might be trying to show *you*?

Such open-ended, reader-focused questions can help you gauge how metacognitive students are about themselves as readers, how actively they're reading, and what they have (or haven't) absorbed from whole-class and small-group experiences. Sometimes,

CORE INDEPENDENT READING PRACTICE: Teach Students How to Choose a Book Based on Meaning

Many teachers give students explicit instruction on choosing a just-right book by using the five-finger rule, which asks students to read a page of a book and count the number of unfamiliar words they encounter. Four or five words, and the book is too hard; only one, and the book is too easy. And for books that fall in the sweet spot in between, students are also taught to ask themselves, "Does it make sense?" as a comprehension check.

This is an easy way of helping students pick a book, but as you've seen, easy can come at a price. In this case, the five-finger rule suggests that reading is all about knowing words, rather than thinking about meaning, and it can unnecessarily limit the books students choose. Consider, for instance, the first page of Kate DiCamillo's *The Tiger Rising*. There are conceivably six words readers might not know in the first paragraph alone: *composed, neon, harbored, dim, abiding,* and *notion.* Applying the five-finger rule, those readers might put the book back on the shelf or bin, thereby missing a phenomenal book. If,

CORE INDEPENDENT READING PRACTICE: **Teach Students How to Choose a Book Based on Meaning** (Continued)

however, you want students to think about meaning in addition to words, you could teach the vocabulary strategy I shared and see how much they can figure out from what they do understand. For *The Tiger Rising*, students who didn't know those six words could focus instead on what remains in bold: "**The Kentucky Star sign was** *composed* **of a yellow** *neon* **star in the shape of the state of Kentucky. Rob liked the sign; he** *harbored* a *dim* but *abiding notion* **that it would bring him good luck.**"

By focusing on what they know instead of what they don't, many students can get the gist—and that combined with interest can take them far.

On the other hand, asking, "Does it make sense?" puts the focus on meaning, but as you've seen from the snapshots of students who were lost in just-right books, readers can think their book makes sense without that sense necessarily corresponding to the words on the page. And to shift the expectations around choosing a book from counting words to meaning, you can also ask students to do the following:

- First, have them read the opening page or two to see if they can figure out who the characters are, how they're related, and what seems to be happening to them, when, and where.

- If they're unsure but are intrigued, ask them to read forward to see if they can figure out more, following the reading equivalent of the screenwriter's "seventeen-page rule," which states that by page 17, a screenplay should have established who the main characters are, what sort of problems they face, and why. Then students can decide if the book is just right.

Framing the choice of a book this way makes the vague "Does it make sense?" more concrete, and it sends out the message that reading is more than figuring out words. And since reading a book is like entering a relationship, this approach invites students to go on a first date with a writer before making a serious commitment. (Though, as someone who often abandons books way beyond page 17, I think students have the right to end the relationship if the writer ends up disappointing them.)

This framing also allows you to establish the more general expectation that as students read, they should always have a sense of who's in any given scene, where and when it's taking place, and what's going on—and if not, they should pause and reread to figure out what they missed. This, in effect, gives students a strategy for monitoring their comprehension.

however, students don't say much—and some don't even understand the questions. If that happens, you have a perfect opportunity to make more explicit the mental work of reading and the thinking expectations around independent reading.

These questions also shift the focus of a conference from *what* students are reading to *how* they're making meaning, which sends out the message that the thinking students are doing with the book is as important, if not more so, than the book itself. Asking reader-focused questions also lessens the chance that students will launch into a retelling, which is critical. Conference time is precious, and unless you're quite familiar with a book, there's no way you can assess if a student's retelling is built on solid comprehension or not. And even if you know the book, inviting a retelling won't necessarily give you a window into *how* the student is making meaning, only that he has made it or not.

Research the Meaning the Student Has Made

BEGIN WITH A QUESTION ABOUT THE GIST

After students have read a short section of their book, as you read alongside them, launch your second round of research by asking a general question such as, "Can you tell me what's going on here?" This question invites students to share what they've made of the section, and their response will help you begin to see what they've comprehended and how they've dealt with the problems they encountered. When I asked our *Rules* reader Marianna what was happening in the passage you just read, she said Catherine was at the clinic where her autistic brother goes with a boy named Jason who, as she put it, "isn't autistic; he just can't walk or talk." This corresponded to what I'd pieced together and had gleaned from the book's back cover—and this meant Marianna had figured out several problems, such as the narrator's name. I couldn't, however, yet see how she'd handled some of the other problems I'd noticed. And in cases like this, where a student's answer to your first question seems incomplete or doesn't reveal how she's handling other problems you noticed, ask one or more follow-up questions to get a better picture.

FOLLOW UP WITH MORE TEXT-SPECIFIC QUESTIONS

Often a simple "Can you say more?" suffices. But you may need to ask a more text-specific question about a problem the student didn't address. With Marianna that would mean asking a question about the pronouns, the font, the dialogue, or the characters' feelings—any of which would help you learn more. Try to think, though, about which question might give you the most information and help the student think more deeply.

With Marianna, for instance, I thought a reader might not be able to consider the characters' feelings and the implications of the dialogue if she hadn't comprehended that the words on the cards represented Jason's side of a conversation. Because of that, I decided to follow up my first question with a text-specific one that zoomed directly into that problem: Did she know why some words were printed a different way?

Marianna admitted she didn't know, revealing that her basic comprehension wasn't solid, and you've seen before how difficult it is to engage in deeper thinking without the basics in place. So my research helped me decide to focus my teaching on shoring up her comprehension.

LET THE STUDENT'S RESPONSES DETERMINE YOUR QUESTIONS

If Marianna's response, however, had shown that she knew Catherine and Jason were conversing, I would have gone in a different direction (see Figure 10.1). That's because, if a student's comprehension is in place, you'll want to set her up to think more deeply across the whole text by developing a line of inquiry or becoming more aware of the patterns the author has woven into the text. With *Rules*, for instance, I might ask a reader whose baseline comprehension was intact what she made of the last paragraph, where Catherine licks her lips and reveals she thinks of Jason as a clinic friend, not an always friend. This paragraph hints at some internal conflict, and thinking about characters' conflicts or problems engages readers in those deeper levels, which ultimately is where you want them to go.

CORE INDEPENDENT READING PRACTICE: **Reading Alongside Students**

You've seen how reading a passage alongside students can give you a window into how they're handling the problems that section poses as well as how deeply they're thinking. Here, though, you'll find some answers and tips to three critical questions teachers often ask about this practice.

Why should students read from where they last stopped?

I rarely confer with students on their writing without looking at what they've written because I know there are students who can talk the talk without quite walking the walk, and the same holds true in reading. It's not enough to ask students to tell you what they're thinking or doing, nor to ask them to open their book to a favorite scene they've already processed. We need to look at the drafts of meaning they're making *as* they're reading to better see what's happening in their minds as they encounter and absorb new information, as that's when our feedback is most needed.

Again, your next move would be determined by the student's response. A student might have lots of ideas about why Catherine is licking her lips and making a distinction between clinic and always friends. You might even have someone who has already noticed all the details and patterns around friends and is intrigued by this new development. With those students, you'd simply want them to continue following that line of inquiry more deliberately, by jotting down specific lines in their notebooks, and wondering what

CORE INDEPENDENT READING PRACTICE: **Reading Alongside Students** (Continued)

Should students read the passage out loud?

Given how much choice can affect students' motivation and engagement, I recommend letting students decide how they want to read the text. Do, though, be aware of what comes with each choice. If students choose to read out loud, you'll get a sense of their fluency, which can impact comprehension. Sometimes, though, students comprehend less when they're reading out loud because they focus on reading the words smoothly instead of making meaning of the whole. So if students choose to read out loud but then don't have much to say about the passage, invite them to read it again silently, which could lead to different results.

How do you determine how much they should read?

Your goal is to see how students are navigating problems in order to make meaning, so you'll want them to read long enough to encounter a few places where the writer has conveyed something indirectly. Depending on the text, you might find that in a paragraph or two, though it can take a full page or more. That's because not every text will have as many problems as the page of *Rules* did. You will, though, find that on almost any page of any work of fiction, the writer is conveying something implicitly, which can pose a problem for readers. And at least half the time, you'll also notice clues to some of the larger ideas or themes the writer might be exploring.

You can also use your confusion as a guide. After all, if you, as a proficient reader, are struggling to figure out what's going on and who the characters are, there's a chance a more novice reader is, too. So if that happens, stop and tell your students you're confused. Sharing that helps normalize confusion as something even strong readers feel, and that admission can make your research questions seem less like an interrogation and more like an invitation to bring you up to speed.

the writer was showing them. But if you had students who weren't sure what to make of that paragraph, you could ask another follow-up question, such as one of these:

- Does that part make you wonder anything?
- Does it connect or fit with anything else you've noticed or have thought about?
- Does it add to or change anything you might be thinking?
- Are the characters doing anything similar or different here? If so, how and why?

Finally, whether you're focusing on basic comprehension or deeper interpretive work, keep one more question up your sleeve: "Do you have any ideas about what it could mean?" This question implicitly sends the message that thinking is as important as answers, gives students an opportunity to share thinking in progress, and helps you see how students deal with problems, not just if they've solved them or not.

When I asked Marianna about the font, for example, she said she thought it might be Catherine's thoughts, which she'd seen authors do through italics. But, as when Billy tried substituting "Oh, my gosh" for Minneapolis Simpkin, this didn't make sense when she tried it. She did, though, share that she'd figured out another font representing the rules Catherine writes for her brother, which showed she had some experience in solving problems. This gave me a more complex picture of her as a reader and informed not just what I decided to teach but how to frame it.

CORE INDEPENDENT READING PRACTICE: Set Students Up to Problem Solve

As you looked at the role research plays in a conference, you saw two ways a conference might go. My actual conference with Marianna revealed that her basic comprehension wasn't solid, so I decided to focus my teaching on setting her up to solve the problem of what that strange font meant, knowing that her thinking could only go so far without comprehending that. Had her response, however, demonstrated more solid comprehension, I would have set her up to follow a line of inquiry framed around a question like, "Why does Catherine only think of Jason as a clinic friend?" which would engage her in the deeper problem of what the writer might be trying to show her about friendship and/or disabilities. So your general decision-making rule of thumb should be that if a student's comprehension is in place, go for deeper thinking, as that's where the real payoff is for readers.

CORE INDEPENDENT READING PRACTICE: **Set Students Up to Problem Solve** (Continued)

Once you've decided *what* to teach, think about *how* to teach it. With students like Marianna, who have missed something significant, you could certainly prompt them with questions that could lead them to whatever they have missed. But while prompting might help them get the answer, it wouldn't help them build a sense of agency or identity as strong, resourceful readers—and by directing students to something you'd noticed, you would have done half the work.

You could also give students a quick lesson on the importance of monitoring comprehension, but that would focus on their deficits, not strengths—and figuring out what they'd missed on their own would be a more effective way of bringing home the importance of monitoring. Instead, you might offer something like I did with Marianna:

> "You've recognized that the way these words are written probably means something specific, just like those other words do, which is great. And that question—'What does it mean?' or 'Why did the author do that?'—is always important for readers to consider. So I'm thinking it might be worth your time to try to figure out what words printed this way mean, just as you figured out what the others meant, and that might mean going back and looking for other places where words are printed this way and seeing what you can figure out. But I think it would be a worthwhile thing to do. What do you think about that?"

If we analyze this teaching line by line, you'll see that in the first line I notice and name something specific she has done. The second line explains in a more generalized way how that's connected to the work of reading. The third sets her up to problem solve by asking her to do what she has already done more deliberately. And the last asks her what she thinks of that suggestion, which is important if she is to own the teaching.

Of course, depending on what your students say, you may not always be able to connect the work you're suggesting with something they've done before. Had Marianna, for example, said she had no idea what the font meant, I could have noticed and named for her how important it is for readers to be aware of what they don't know and why, which would have recast something that could have felt like a deficit into a strength, and then continued my teaching.

RESEARCH THE STUDENT'S UNDERSTANDING OF YOUR TEACHING

Deciding what to teach, thus, grows directly out of what you've come to understand by listening carefully to a student's responses to your research questions. But after you've made a teaching decision, you'll want to engage in one more round of research before you close the conference and explicitly ask the student what she thinks of your suggestion. The response to this question can help you determine the level of student buy-in, without which even the best teaching can fail. The good news, though, is that most students are willing to try something that comes from their own thinking, especially with a book they've chosen.

I also recommend asking students to tell you or write down in their notebooks what they're going to do in their own words. This lets you see if they've really understood what you've suggested, and it also helps students hold onto the teaching so that you, in turn, can hold them more accountable for following through. (And for younger students, transcribe what they say in their notebooks so they have a record, as well.)

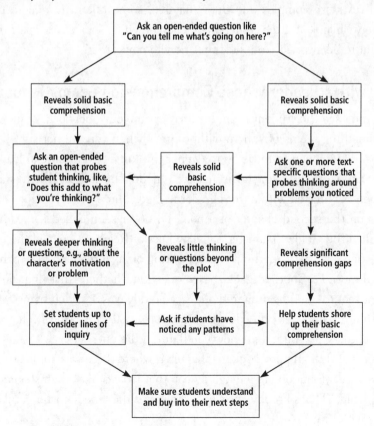

FIGURE 10.1 *Different Paths a Reading Conference Can Take*

If students both like and understand your suggestion, you're both good to go. But if a student hasn't quite understood, you have a chance to clarify instead of waiting a week or two to discover he didn't know what you meant. And if a student understands but doesn't like the suggestion, ask him what he'd like to think about as he moves through the book. It's yet another question that opens the door to thinking—and the answers are often surprising.

LOOKING CLOSELY AT OTHER CONFERENCE SCENARIOS

While this way of conferring may seem complicated, the process of thinking and the moves you make in response to what your research reveals can be generalized (see Figure 10.1). Most conferences will follow these steps, but because the transactions between students and texts are complex and unpredictable, some take a few more twists and turns. So here we'll look at three conferences, each of which showcases a particular problem you'll want to be aware of and illustrates how to navigate it.

Conferring with a Reader Whose Comprehension Seems Tenuous

Whether it's the page the student is on, his answers to your questions, or just a nagging sense that something seems off, there will be times when you are not sure if a student has comprehended enough to move on to deeper thinking—and that can leave you in a quandary. To handle that, try to stay in research mode a bit longer, which is just what I had to do when I conferred with a third grader named Julio.

Julio was on the second chapter of a book I'd never seen called *I, Freddy,* the first in a series called the Golden Hamster Saga, by Dietlof Reiche. I opened the conference with the question, "Is there anything you're working on as a reader?" to which Julio just shrugged. So I moved to another reader-based question, "Is there anything you've figured out so far?" At that, he said he'd figured out that Freddy was a golden hamster who lived in a cage with other hamsters who didn't want to play with him. And I followed that up with the standard, "Can you tell me how you figured that out?"

To answer that, Julio flipped back to Chapter 1, where there was an illustration of ten hamsters in a cage, all but one in a tangled heap that looked like a hamster version of an NFL tackle pileup. "That's Freddy," he said, pointing at the lone hamster, "and the others aren't playing with him."

Whenever a student relies on an illustration to explain his thinking, your comprehension alarm should go off, as this may be a sign of a student overly relying on picture clues. But instead of jumping in to teach right away, stay in research mode and ask, "Is there anything in the words that made you think that, too?" That question refocuses students on the text, and in this case it led Julio to reread a paragraph above the illustration, which I read alongside him:

> *I know: Biology teachers call these scuffles "mock trials of strength," and they're*
> *supposed to be genetically programmed. Maybe, but I found them irritating.*
> *It wasn't that I couldn't hold my own; I simply preferred to think my own*
> *thoughts in peace. (4)*

As you may be thinking, this was not an easy read. In addition to a number of challenging words, there was an idiom ("hold my own") and sophisticated syntax—and between this complexity and my concern about picture clues, I was already thinking that not only might Julio need help with comprehension, but he might also need a different book. But before I could ask him what he thought, he stopped and said, "Oh, wait, Freddy's not playing because he doesn't want to, not because they're not letting him. Now I think he just wants to be left alone and not be with those other crazy hamsters."

This is a classic example of what can be gained by not rushing in to teach the first thing you've noticed—that is, just to listen for a chance to reply. Staying in listening-to-understand mode allowed me to see that Julio could navigate this paragraph, despite its many challenges, and he could revise his thinking when encountering new information, which is huge. And seeing that, I was curious to see what else he could do. So I asked him to go back to where he'd left off and read the next few paragraphs, which I invite you to draft your own understanding of and see if you notice any whiffs of conflicts that might indicate possible themes.

> *Sometime before I was sold, Great-Grandmother went into Eternal*
> *Hibernation. At first I thought she was simply taking an unusually long*
> *time to wake up. The pet shop's fat salesclerk knew at once what was*
> *wrong, however, and before I could utter a squeak Great-Grandmother*
> *had disappeared.*
>
> *I took it hard, unlike the rest of our clan, who barely noticed. Golden*
> *hamsters, as Great-Grandmother had often told me, are loners by nature.*
>
> *I missed Great-Grandmother. With her I'd been able to discuss every*
> *aspect of golden hamsterdom. When I tried to do this with my fellow*

hamsters, my lack of success was spectacular. "Discuss things?" I was told.
"Nah, I just work out. You should try it yourself." (5)

When Julio finished, I asked him what was going on here, and he said that Freddy's great-grandmother had disappeared and he really missed her because she was the only one he could talk to. Julio clearly got the gist of the passage, but you probably inferred something Julio seemed to miss: that Freddy's great-grandmother died.

On the one hand, you could see this as another sign that his comprehension wasn't quite in place—and when you see students who miss an inference like this, you may feel an urge to jump in and teach. But first consider the overall importance of the missed inference and remember you're teaching for meaning, not skills. Marianna's inability to infer the font and realize that Catherine and Jason were conversing directly impacted her ability to consider what the author might be showing her about the meaning of friendship or the challenges of disabilities. Julio, on the other hand, understood the impact of Freddy's great-grandmother's disappearance, and ultimately that seemed more important than knowing exactly how she disappeared. So here's an addendum to that earlier rule: If making a particular inference doesn't impact a student's ability to think more deeply, let the inference go and focus on the bigger, more complex thinking.

To do that, I asked Julio, "How does that connect or fit with what you were thinking before?"

Julio replied, "I know Freddy just wanted to be left alone, but now that his great-grandmother's gone, he has no one to talk to. So now I'm thinking he's going to be lonely and I'm wondering if he'll still want to be left alone or will he want a friend."

Although I'd first questioned his comprehension, Julio had extended his thinking again by recognizing what might be a real problem for Freddy—and by doing so he also wondered something that would make a great line of inquiry: Will Freddy still want to be left alone or will he want a friend? Had I jumped in to teach at the first sign of trouble, I never would have seen that depth. And having now seen it, I took what I'd learned and suggested that Julio try reading forward with that question in mind.

Julio liked that idea, so I set him up to more deliberately track the development of this problem by creating a three-column chart in his notebook. The first column was for recording clues that suggested Freddy still wanted to be left alone, while the second would capture those that suggested he might now want a friend. The last was reserved for Julio's own ideas and questions about what Freddy was doing and why—and, taken as a whole, the chart would help him see how much he could make from what he noticed, which would help him notice even more.

Simple charts like these help students keep track of their specific thinking *and* reinforce a more generalized way of thinking about texts. And while it took a while to get Julio there, he was now where we want all students to be: deeply thinking about a text's meaning.

Conferring with a Disengaged Reader

Chris Lehman, coauthor of *Falling in Love with Close Reading*, has said that "engagement isn't a thing, it's the only thing" (2013). This succinctly captures what many of us feel: that learning doesn't happen if students aren't engaged. Engagement is also connected to motivation, which in turn is affected by choice, and research has shown that engagement and choice—or a lack thereof—are also related to student achievement (Guthrie 2001). Unfortunately, as teachers are required or feel compelled to have students read complex whole-class texts, student choice has eroded, and this has resulted in a drop in motivation and engagement. And because engagement is so critical, if you come across students who seem disengaged, set everything else on the back burner and focus on engagement first.

CORE INDEPENDENT READING PRACTICE: Notice and Name Instead of Compliment

Just as you notice and name what students are doing throughout whole-class and small-group sessions, you'll want to do that throughout a conference, rather than at just one point. This noticing and naming serves a different purpose than a traditional conference's compliment. In a research-compliment-decide-teach conference, the compliment is meant to recognize and reinforce what students are doing or approximating in order to position them to be receptive to whatever instruction is offered. Or as Peter Johnston more bluntly puts it in *Opening Minds*, it's "to bolster the child's self-esteem before presumably bruising it with a critique" (2012, 46). Noticing and naming, on the other hand, serves what Johnston describes as the purpose of positive feedback: "[to] improve conceptual understanding or increase strategic options while developing stamina, resilience, and motivation—expanding the vision of what is possible and how to get there . . . and establishing the foundation on which to build" (48).

Noticing and naming is thus both feedback and what Johnston calls "*feedforward.*" It helps students develop a vision of the whole complex work of reading, understand how that's connected to what they're doing, and consider what else they could do. Of course, what you notice and name will depend on what

This doesn't mean you should try to "hook" readers with provocative questions or anecdotes related to the text. I've certainly done that myself, but I've found that whatever interest or curiosity that stirs up is often short-lived. That's because a student's interest in a topic doesn't guarantee she'll be engaged with a text—especially if we use the definition of engagement that Charlotte Danielson provides in *Enhancing Professional Practice*:

> *Student engagement is not the same as . . . "time on task." . . . Mere activity . . . is inadequate for engagement. Nor is simple participation sufficient. The activity should represent new learning. What is required for student engagement is* intellectual involvement *with the content or active construction of understanding.* (2007, 83)

To build that intellectual involvement, you'll need to help students become engaged with the power of their own thinking, and that means leaning into whatever students think or feel, even if it's negative. Think of it as turning into a skid when your car hits a patch of ice. Ignore the impulse to steer away, and drive directly into the student's reaction. And to better see what that can accomplish, let's look at a conference I had with a seventh grader named Yusef, whose class was reading "The Lottery," Shirley Jackson's short story about a village that, for reasons no one remembers, holds a lottery every year and stones the winner to death.

Like many Common Core texts, "The Lottery" used to be read more in high school than in middle school because of its vocabulary, syntax, and tone. And while some students

CORE INDEPENDENT READING PRACTICE: **Notice and Name Instead of Compliment** (Continued)

a student says or does, but any of the notice-and-name moves you've seen in other chapters can be used in a conference, as well. And here are some that often are useful during your first round of research:

- If a student shares something he's working on, you can notice and name how that's connected to the thinking work of reading, the way writers write, and/or how texts work.

- If a student shares a wondering that is—or could be framed as—a "Why?" question, notice and name that, as well as why that's important.

- If a student expresses confusion, you can notice and name why that's so important for readers to pay attention to.

who make it to the end like it because of its creepiness, getting there is frequently hard—and Yusef was having a hard enough time getting to the third paragraph. When I sat next to him, he pushed the text as far away on his desk as he could, and when I asked if he was wondering anything, he simply said, "This story's too weird."

I followed that up with, "What do you mean, weird?"

He looked at me out of the corner of his eye and said, "You don't know what weird means?"

This clearly was a student who had no interest in what he was reading, possibly because of the challenges it presented. But here's what happened when I leaned in and drove directly into his reaction. I assured him I knew the meaning of weird and then asked if he could give me an example, and with that he pulled the story back and accusingly pointed to the second line of the story's second paragraph.

> *The children assembled first, of course. School was recently over for the*
> *summer, and the feeling of liberty sat uneasily on most of them; they tended*
> *to gather together quietly for a while before they broke into boisterous*
> *play, and their talk was still of the classroom and the teacher, of books and*
> *reprimands. Bobby Martin had already stuffed his pockets full of stones,*
> *and the other boys soon followed his example, selecting the smoothest and*
> *roundest stones; Bobby and Harry Jones and Dickie Delacroix—the villagers*
> *pronounced this name "Dellacroy"—eventually made a great pile of stones*
> *in one corner of the square and guarded it against the raids of the other*
> *boys. (289)*

"Right there," Yusef said. "That's weird. They just got out of school and it's like they don't like it. Man, when I get out of school for the summer, the last thing I want to do is talk about it."

Here again, we see that listening to understand—and probing a student's thinking while reserving judgment—can reveal surprises. I learned that Yusef's disengagement wasn't connected to the challenges the vocabulary and syntax posed. What he didn't know, though, was how to use his response to engage with the text. And for students like Yusef, you'll want not only to probe their thinking but also to validate their response as reasonable. I acknowledged, for instance, that that was pretty weird and then asked him if he'd noticed anything else, to which he answered, "Yeah, what's with the stones?"

You may be thinking here just what I did: that beneath all of that attitude, there was an astute reader who was unaware of that. But noticing and naming could help him begin to see that. So I told Yusef what he'd done: "You've noticed what seems to be a pattern of weirdness, with kids not doing what they usually do, and another pattern around the stones." Then I connected that to the larger work of reading and writing: "Writers often use patterns to try to show us something they don't want to come right out and say, and I think it's possible that the writer actually wants you to pick up all this weirdness and to figure out why she put it there." And I built on what Yusef was already doing to offer a suggestion: "How about you keep on reading, paying attention to whatever seems weird, maybe even making some notes in the margins to both note those places and think about why all the weirdness might be there?" Then I asked him what he thought about that.

Yusef agreed and went back to the text with a pencil in hand and a new sense of purpose and competence. Of course, I didn't know if this conference would carry him to the end of the story because the Yusefs in our classrooms need many opportunities to have their thinking listened to and validated before they begin to consider that they may, in fact, be insightful readers. And until the tide changes and the powers that be acknowledge what's lost when we systematically deprive students of both agency and choice, conferences are the perfect vehicle for doing that.

Conferring with a Reader Who's Lost

In addition to promoting motivation and engagement, reading books of students' own choosing gives them a sense of ownership and control. But choice has its limits, especially if, as writer and educator Kevin Perks (2010) notes, it isn't coupled with a sense of purpose and competence. When it comes to meaning-based conferences, this means you may find students reading books of their own choosing with apparent engagement but who are, in fact, totally lost because they don't have enough competence—even when the book is at their level. And that's what I discovered with Meera, a fourth grader who was reading the Katie Kazoo, Switcheroo book *Open Wide*, by Nancy Krulik.

I began by asking her if there was anything she was working on as a reader, and she said she was trying to picture the story in her head as she read, which I could see the class had been working on from the charts in the room. Then I asked her to read from where she had left off, and she turned to a page three-quarters of the way through the book and read what I now ask you to read, drafting your own understanding.

> *"AAAAHHHHH!" Matthew screamed as a blast of icy cold water hit him in the eye.*
>
> *Matthew's scream shocked Katie. She jumped backward with surprise.*

> *When she did, she accidentally stepped on the lever that moved the dental*
> *chair up and down.*
>
>   *"WHOAAAA!" Matthew shouted as the chair shot up in the air.*
>
>   *Bam! He flew out of the chair and landed right on his rear end.*
>
>   *"I'm outta here!" Matthew screamed. He went for the door.*
>
>   *"Matthew, wait!" Emma cried out.*
>
>   *"Don't go!" Katie shouted. She leaped in front of the door to block his path.*
>
>   *Matthew tried ducking under her arm, but Katie stopped him.*
>
>   *Matthew turned and ran back to the dental chair. He grabbed the*
> *water pick. Then he shot a big stream of water across the room.*
>
>   *"Hey, stop that!" Katie shouted. (58)*

Meera read the passage fluently, and when she finished, I asked her to tell me what was going on here. "They're at the dentist," she said, "and the dentist isn't being very nice." As many students do, Meera used a pronoun rather than specifically identifying characters, and if you don't already, ask students who use unclear pronouns to clarify whom they're referring to. In this case, Meera said, "Katie, Matthew, and Emma," and before I could even ask what made her think that, she pointed to the illustration on the opposing page that showed two children, a girl with glasses and a boy who was shooting a water pick at a dentist.

As happened with Julio, my alarm bell went off, as Meera could have been another student who was relying too much on picture clues. But my comprehension alarm went off earlier, when she said the dentist wasn't being nice because, while a dentist appears in the picture, he's actually not mentioned in the text. So I asked her the question I'd asked Julio: "Is there anything in the words that make you know the dentist is there?"

At that point, Meera turned to the previous page, pointed to an exchange of dialogue in which the dentist was mentioned and said, "Here." And once again, please read this passage, holding up your draft to hers.

>   *"Ick," Katie remarked. "How gross."*
>
>   *Emma stared at her in surprise. "Dr. Sang! That's not nice," she hissed.*
>
>   *Katie blushed again. Emma was right. That had been kind of mean.*
>
> *But it just popped out. (57)*

On the one hand, these two excerpts present few problems at the inferential level. The dialogue's clearly tagged, most of the pronouns appear close to their antecedents, and all of the action is explicitly stated. But Dr. Sang hasn't done or said anything here; he's just addressed in a conversation Emma is having with Katie. And that gave me pause. Not only did Meera have a problem navigating dialogue, but she seemed to have missed something really important—that Katie had become the dentist. Meera was also an example of a student using a strategy in ways that weren't strategic because she had missed the critical textual clues that would have helped her align what she was visualizing with the words on the page.

Whenever you stumble on something this big with a student who is far along in a book, try to graciously draw the conference to a close and give yourself time to consider how to address what you've learned. You'll want to research the book, for instance, to see if what the student missed was stated explicitly or not, as that suggests different reading issues and different instructional paths. In this case, as I flipped through the book, I discovered that Katie's propensity for switcheroo-ing had been stated explicitly in the beginning, which meant Meera had problems not only with dialogue but with retaining—or perhaps comprehending—what the text had explicitly stated. And recognizing that, her teacher and I drew up an individualized action plan (see "Designing a Complex Plan of Action," on page 24), which included giving Meera some small-group time to practice negotiating dialogue and using a know/wonder chart to help her read more actively, hold onto what she read, and monitor her comprehension. And since we wondered if the element of magic might have tripped her up, we also decided to look for an accessible read-aloud involving magic, knowing that others might benefit from that, too.

This complex action plan addressed the problems this conference revealed, but I think there are additional implications for the teaching of reading from this conference. We need to spend at least as much time seeing what students are doing with the books they're reading as we do assessing their levels. And we have to go beyond just checking on fluency, word skills, or strategies and really research the meaning students are making. Had I stopped after assessing Meera's fluency, for instance, I would have never discovered how lost she was because she had no problems reading the words. A problem-based approach to conferences, however, allows us to go further and dig deeper to really understand meaning making—which should be the goal of all instruction.

WHY THIS WORK MATTERS

Many of you undoubtedly know the value of independent reading—and if you're fortunate, you work in a school where it's still alive and flourishing. But for those of you who may be fighting to hold onto something you know is precious, bring back what your school might have abandoned in its rush to meet the CCSS, or launch independent reading for the first time, it's worth remembering this: Year after year, the National Assessment of Educational Progress (NAEP) report, commonly known as the Nation's Report Card (National Center for Education Statistics 2013), has found that children who "read for fun" consistently outperform those who don't on standardized tests across all age groups and demographics.

Also, in addition to showing the connection between pleasure and learning, neuroscientists studying brain scans of readers have found that reading—especially reading fiction—makes us more empathetic, tolerant, compassionate, and able to appreciate different perspectives (Bergland 2014). That is, reading makes us more humane. And according to the National Endowment of Arts overview of reading in America, *To Read or Not to Read*, reading also "seems to awaken a person's social and civic sense [and it] correlates with almost every measurement of positive personal and social behavior" the NEA surveyed (2007, 6).

Unfortunately, the data from these reports also show that reading for pleasure has been declining in troubling ways, and those of us who work in classrooms know that schools are often the first—and sometimes only—place where students get to experience the pleasure of reading and learn, as playwright Bertolt Brecht wrote, that "thinking is one of the chief pleasures of the human race" (1980, 27). For all these reasons, we need to preserve independent reading in classrooms and use every moment we can wrest away from test prep and assessments to sit down beside children reading books and listen to what they say.

STEERING THE SHIP

MAKING RESEARCH-BASED TEACHING DECISIONS

IF YOU LEARN THIS . . .	YOU CAN DO THIS . . .
The student hasn't been able to figure out something at the literal or inferential level, which will directly impact her ability to think more deeply about the text	Help the student shore up her basic comprehension by setting her up to solve whatever problems she hasn't yet figured out
The student's basic comprehension is sound enough to engage in deeper thinking (if he's not already)	Invite the student to develop a line of inquiry from either problems or patterns he has noticed
The student's not engaged with what she's reading (which is often connected to a lack of choice)	Grab onto whatever the student is thinking or feeling and notice and name what she's doing to build her sense of agency; then help her develop a line of inquiry from that
The student seems completely lost in a supposedly just-right book or poses other puzzling problems	Give yourself more time to research and plan a course of action rather than decide what to teach in the moment

FIGURE 10.2 *Steering the Ship*

Coda
Emerging from *Dynamic Teaching* for Deeper Reading

The mind, once expanded to the dimensions
of larger ideas, never returns to its original size.
—Oliver Wendell Holmes

My daughter, who's now in her twenties, has always been my beach buddy. As often as I can over the summer, I pack up a Zipcar with beach towels, folding chairs, a big sun-bleached umbrella, lots of water, a good book, and fresh fruit—and, of course, plenty of sunscreen. Then I pick her up from her apartment and drive east out of Brooklyn, first following traffic, then the cries of seabirds, and, finally, the scent of salt in the air. We're the only ones in our family who are as happy as clams to spend the day on a towel, encrusted with salt and sand, getting up only for walks on the beach and periodic dips in the water, which even in summer is shockingly cold.

Neither of us does much actual swimming (we tend to save that for pools), but we love to go out and bob in the waves, with my daughter plunging mermaid-like into them just as they crest and curl, which I never do. When asked why, I've told her I don't want to get my hair wet, which is true but not the whole story. You see, I'm afraid—of what, I'm not sure. Riptides, the current, all those creepy-crawly things that live underwater. But my daughter doesn't buy it, and one day she called me out.

"C'mon, Mom," she said, "it's only water. You can't possibly be scared of that."

I paused a moment to remember her at five, refusing to get into the pool for swim lessons at our local YMCA, and at six, scrambling up my leg like a monkey scaling a tree when she thought a crab had pinched her toe while we explored a tide pool. And I remembered many times when she was younger when I did something that made me afraid—going from store to store in Paris to ask the shopkeepers if she could use their bathroom in my poor, pitiful French, agreeing to go with her on the Coney Island roller coaster with its old, wooden, rickety seats—simply because I didn't want her to see me afraid. And while I did at some point officially declare that my roller-coaster-riding days were over, that day at the beach I looked out at the waves heading toward me, picked one out, then took a depth breath just as it started to crest. Then I dove right into the dark, unknown core of it with my heart hammering in my chest, emerging moments later feeling empowered, exhilarated, and refreshed—and wondering why it took me so long to take the plunge in the first place.

I share this story because it's my hope you feel something akin to that as you emerge from this book: excited, reenergized, and eager to take this work into your classroom. Your students will inevitably benefit from it as readers, thinkers, and learners who are literally growing their brains' capacity to see big pictures, innovate, and solve problems, all of which is urgently needed in our complex times. But, I think, this work also does something for us as teachers: It creates opportunities for us to be big-picture thinkers, innovators, and problem solvers, too. And by not tying us down to a script or a lesson plan that claims students will meet outcomes that are hard, if not impossible, to reach in a single sitting, it allows us to reclaim the status of professionals in a world that too often sees us as the problem.

Of course, that does mean accepting the fact that learning and reading are exceedingly complex and shortcuts aren't the answer. But I'm reminded here of something else attributed to Oliver Wendell Holmes: "For the simplicity on this side of complexity, I wouldn't give you a fig. But for the simplicity on the other side of complexity, for that I would give you anything I have." While a problem-based approach to teaching reading is, indeed, complex, simplicity—versus simplification—does lie on the other side. There's the simplicity of seeing thinking as the basic act of noticing something and then making something—a question, an inference, an interpretation—out of what you have noticed, and the simplicity of using basic two- and three-column charts to help make that thinking process visible. There's the simplicity of having meaning be the purpose of all reading, and the simplicity of reconceiving text complexity around how much a reader has to figure out. There's also the simplicity of offering instruction and feedback to help students understand a handful of concepts—such as that writers purposely choose words and details to convey ideas and meaning, which is why readers need to closely attend to details and words—rather than teaching a gazillion minilessons that too often fail to take root. And finally, there's the simplicity of having all your reading instruction working toward the same end through the same simple means, through teaching methods that directly align with all that we know and believe about learning.

So go forth, get messy, have fun, and keep learning, expanding both your students' and your own minds. In the end, it's what keeps us alive.

Works Cited

Achieve, College Summit, National Association of Secondary Principals and National Association of Elementary School Principals. 2013. "Implementing the Common Core State Standards: The Role of the Elementary School Leader. http://www.achieve.org/files/RevisedElementaryActionBrief_Final_Feb.pdf

Alexander, Robin. 2000. *Culture and Pedagogy: International Comparisons in Primary Education.* Malden, MA: Blackwell.

Allen, Janet. 2007. *Inside Words: Tools for Teaching Academic Vocabulary, Grades 4–12.* Portland, ME: Stenhouse.

Bacon, Francis. 1605. *Valerius Terminus; of the Interpretation of Nature.*

———. {1625} 1986 . "Of Studies." *The Essays.* New York: Penguin Classics.

Barclay, Rachel. 2014. "Curiosity Changes the Brain to Boost Learning and Memory." *Healthline.* October 2. www.healthline.com/health-news/curiosity-boosts-learning-and-memory-100214#1.

Barnhouse, Dorothy, and Vicki Vinton. 2012. *What Readers Really Do: Teaching the Process of Meaning Making.* Portsmouth, NH: Heinemann.

Beck, Isabel, Margaret McKeown, and Linda Kucan. 2013. *Bringing Words to Life: Robust Vocabulary Instruction.* New York: Guilford.

Beers, Kylene, and Robert Probst. 2012. *Notice & Note: Strategies for Close Reading.* Portsmouth, NH: Heinemann.

———. 2016. *Reading Nonfiction: Notice & Note Stances, Signposts, and Strategies.* Portsmouth, NH: Heinemann.

Berger, Warren. 2014. *A More Beautiful Question: The Power of Inquiry to Spark Breakthrough Ideas.* New York: Bloomsbury.

Bergland, Christopher. 2014. "Can Reading a Fictional Story Make You More Empathetic?" *Psychology Today*, December 1. www.psychologytoday.com/blog/the-athletes-way/201412/can-reading-fictional-story-make-you-more-empathetic.

Bomer, Katherine. 2016. *The Journey Is Everything: Teaching Essays That Students Want to Write for People Who Want to Read Them.* Portsmouth, NH: Heinemann.

Brecht, Bertolt. 1980. *Life of Galileo.* New York: Penguin Books.

Bruner, Jerome. 1996. *The Culture of Education.* Cambridge, MA: Harvard University Press.

Cain, Sean, and Mike Laird. 2011. *The Fundamental Five: The Formula for Quality Instruction.* CreateSpace Independent Publishing Platform.

Coleman, David. 2011. "Bringing the Common Core to Life." Presentation for the New York State Education Department, Albany, New York, April 28.

Coleman, David, and Susan Pimental. 2011. "Publishers' Criteria for the Common Core State Standards in English Language Arts and Literacy, Grades 3–12." http://usny.nysed.gov /rttt/docs/publisherscriteria-literacy-grades3-12.pdf.

Covey, Stephen. 1989. *The 7 Habits of Highly Effective People.* New York: Simon and Schuster.

Clyburn, Gay. 2012. "Learning Opportunities: Productive Struggle, Explicit Connections and Deliberate Practice." *Carnegie Commons Blog,* February 9. www.carnegiefoundation .org/blog/learning-opportunities-productive-struggle-explicit-connections-and -deliberate-practice/.

Danielson, Charlotte. 2007. *Enhancing Professional Practice: A Framework for Teaching.* 2nd edition. Alexandria, VA: Association for Supervision and Curriculum Development.

———. 2011. *The Framework for Teaching: Evaluation Instrument.* Princeton, NJ: Danielson Group.

Dewey, John. 1916. *Democracy and Education.* New York: Macmillan.

———. 1938a. *Experience and Education.* New York: Touchstone.

———. 1938b. *Logic: The Theory of Inquiry.* New York: Henry Holt.

D'Mello, Sidney, Blair Lehman, Reinhard Pekrun, and Art Graesser. 2014. "Confusion Can Be Beneficial for Learning." *Learning and Instruction* 29 (February): 153–70.

Fisch, Karl, Scott McLeod, and Jeff Brenman. 2014 "Did You Know? Shift Happens." (Video). www.youtube.com/watch?v=PcZg51Il9no.

Fisher, Robert. 2007. "Creative Minds: Building Communities of Learning for the Creative Age." *Pantaneto Forum* 25 (January). www.pantaneto.co.uk/issue25/fisher.htm.

Foresman, Scott. 2013. "ReadyGEN K–5 Sampler, Grade 3, Unit 4." New York: Pearson. https://assets.pearsonschool.com/asset_mgr/current/201324/ReadyGEN_NYC _Final_lowres.pdf.

Forster, E. M. 2008. "Fifth Anniversary of the Third Programme." In *The BBC Talks of E. M. Forster, 1929–1960: A Selected Edition,* edited by Mary Lago, Linda K. Hughes, and Elizabeth MacLeod Walls, 410–19. Columbia, MO: University of Missouri Press.

Fountas, Irene C., and Gay Su Pinnell. 2015. "Instructional Level Expectations for Reading." Portsmouth, NH: Heinemann. www.heinemann.com/fountasandpinnell/handouts /InstructionalLevelExpectationsForReading.pdf.

Freire, Paulo. 1998. *Pedagogy of Freedom: Ethics, Democracy and Civic Courage.* Lanham, MD: Rowman and Littlefield.

Gawande, Atul. 2011. "Personal Best." *The New Yorker,* October 3. www.newyorker.com /magazine/2011/10/03/personal-best.

Green, Elizabeth. 2014. *Building a Better Teacher: How Teaching Works (and How to Teach It to Everyone).* New York: W. W. Norton.

Guthrie, John T. 1996. "Educational Contexts for Engagement in Literacy." *The Reading Teacher* 49(6): 432–445.

Guthrie, John T., A. Laurel, W. Hoa, Allan Wigfield, Stephen M. Tonks, Nicole M. Humenick, and Erin Littles. 2007. "Reading Motivation and Reading Comprehension Growth in the Later Elementary Years." *Contemporary Educational Psychology* 32 (3): 282–313.

Hale, Shannon. 2008. "The Moral of the—Wait, What's a Moral?" *Squeetus Blog*, October 3. http://oinks.squeetus.com/2008/10/the-moral-of-th.html.

Hattie, John. 2012. *Visible Learning for Teachers: Maximizing Impact on Learning.* New York: Routledge.

Hawking, Stephen. 2000. "'Unified Theory' Is Getting Closer, Hawking Predicts." *San Jose Mercury News*, January 23.

Hinton, Christina, Kurt Fischer, and Catherine Glennon. 2012. "Mind, Brain, and Education." *Students at the Center Series.* Washington, DC: Jobs for the Future. http://www .studentsatthecenter.org/sites/scl.dl-dev.com/files/Mind%20Brain%20Education.pdf

Hitchings, Henry. 2013. "Those Irritating Verbs-as-Nouns." *The New York Times*, March 30. http://opinionator.blogs.nytimes.com/2013/03/30/those-irritating-verbs-as-nouns/.

Johnston, Peter. 2004. *Choice Words: How Our Language Affects Children's Learning.* Portland, ME: Stenhouse.

———. 2012. *Opening Minds: Using Language to Change Lives.* Portland, ME: Stenhouse.

Jong, Erica. 2007. *What Do Women Want? Essays by Erica Jong.* New York: TarcherPerigree.

Kain, Patricia. 1998. "How to Do a Close Reading." Cambridge, MA: Writing Center at Harvard University. http://writingcenter.fas.harvard.edu/pages/how-do-close-reading.

Keene, Ellin O. 2015. "What Price Beauty? A Call for Aesthetic Education." In *The Teacher You Want to Be: Essays About Children, Learning, and Teaching*, edited by Ellin O. Keene and Matt Glover. Portsmouth, NH: Heinemann.

Keene, Ellin, and Susan Zimmerman. 1997. *Mosaic of Thought.* Portsmouth, NH: Heinemann.

Kohn, Alfie. 2015. "A Dozen Essential Guidelines for Educators." In *Schooling Beyond Measure: And Other Unorthodox Essays About Education.* Portsmouth, NH: Heinemann.

Kolowich, Steve. 2014. "Confuse Students to Help Them Learn." *The Chronicle of Higher Education*, August 14. http://chronicle.com/article/Confuse-Students-to-Help -Them/148385/.

Lehman, Christopher. 2013. "Blog-a-Thon Post 7: Most Fun #CloseReading Post Ever Because Students Are Hilarious and Filled with Rage." *Christopher Lehman* (blog), September 23. https://christopherlehman.wordpress.com/2013/09/23/blog-a-thon-post-7-most -fun-closereading-post-ever-because-students-are-hilarious-and-filled-with-rage/.

Lemov, Doug. 2010. *Teach Like a Champion: 49 Techniques That Put Students on the Path to College.* San Francisco: John Wiley.

Lewis, C. S. 1961. *An Experiment in Criticism*. Cambridge: Cambridge University Press.

Lowry, Lois. n.d. "A Message from the Author." RandomHouse.com. www.randomhouse.com
/teachers/guides/give.html.

Maats, Hunter, and Katie O'Brien. 2015. "Hands-Off Teaching Cultivates Metacognition."
Edutopia, April 21. www.edutopia.org/blog/hands-off-teaching-cultivates
-metacognition-hunter-maats-katie-obrien.

McGinley, William, and Robert J. Tierney. 1988. *Reading and Writing as Ways of Knowing and
Learning*. Technical Report no. 413. Champaign, IL: Center for the Study of Reading,
University of Illinois at Urbana–Champaign. www.ideals.illinois.edu/bitstream
/handle/2142/17772/ctrstreadtechrepv01988i00423_opt.pdf?sequence=1.

McNeil, Michele. 2013. "Rifts Deepen Over Direction of Ed. Policy in U.S." *Education Week*,
May 7. www.edweek.org/ew/articles/2013/05/08/30debate_ep.h32.html.

Merry, Tim. 2015. "Planning vs Preparation." *Change Ahead* (blog), January 28. www.timmerry
.com/blog/planning-vs-preparation.

National Center for Education Statistics. 2013. *The Nation's Report Card: Trends in Academic
Progress, Reading 1971–2012, Mathematics 1973–2012*. Washington, DC: Institute of
Education Sciences, U.S. Department of Education. http://nces.ed.gov/nationsreport
card/subject/publications/main2012/pdf/2013456.pdf.

National Endowment of the Arts. 2007. *To Read or Not to Read: A Question of National Conse-
quence*. Research Report no. 47. Washington, DC: National Endowment for the Arts.
www.arts.gov/sites/default/files/ToRead.pdf.

Nietzsche, Friedrich. 1996. *On the Genealogy of Morals*. Translated by Douglas Smith. Oxford:
Oxford University Press.

Newkirk, Tom. 1984. "Looking for Trouble: A Way to Unmask Our Readings." College English
46 (8): 756–66.

———. 2012. "The Text Itself: Some Thoughts on the Common Core Standards for English
Language Arts." *Heinemann Journal*. www.heinemann.com/pd/journal/TheTextItself
_Newkirk_Essay_S12.pdf.

Oatley, Keith. 2014. "How Reading Transforms Us." *The New York Times Sunday Review*,
December 21: 10.

Obama, Barack. 2015. "President Obama and Marilynne Robinson: A Conversation—II." *The
New York Review of Books*, November 19. www.nybooks.com/articles/2015/11/19
/president-obama-marilynne-robinson-conversation-2/.

O'Connor, Flannery. 1961. *Mystery and Manners: Occasional Prose*. New York: Farrar, Straus,
and Giroux.

Paul, Annie Murphy. 2012. "Why Floundering Is Good." *Time Magazine*, April 25. http://ideas
.time.com/2012/04/25/why-floundering-is-good/.

———. 2013. "How the Power of Interest Drives Learning." *Mind/Shift*, November 4. http://ww2.kqed.org/mindshift/2013/11/04/how-the-power-of-interest-drives-learning/.

Pearson, P. David. 2011. "Toward the Next Generation of Comprehension Instruction: A Coda." In *Comprehension Going Forward: Where We Are/What's Next*. Portsmouth, NH: Heinemann.

Peck, M. Scott. 1993. *Further on the Road Less Traveled: The Unending Journey Toward Spiritual Growth*. New York: Simon and Schuster.

Perkins, David. 1986. "Thinking Frames." *Educational Leadership* (May): 4–10. www.ascd.org/ASCD/pdf/journals/ed_lead/el_198605_perkins.pdf.

———. 2009. *Making Learning Whole: How Seven Principles of Teaching Can Transform Education*. San Francisco: Jossey-Bass.

Perks, Kevin. 2010. "Crafting Effective Choices to Motivate Students." *Adolescent Literacy in Perspective* (March/April): 2–3.

Peterson, Ralph, and Maryann Eeds. 1999. *Grand Conversations*. New York: Scholastic.

Petroski, Henry. 2003. "The Evolution of the Grocery Bag." *American Scholar* 72 (4): 99–111.

Piggott, Jennifer. 2011. "Rich Tasks and Contexts." NRICH. http://nrich.maths.org/5662.

Pink, Daniel. 2006. *A Whole New Mind: Why Right-Brainers Will Rule the Future*. New York: Penguin Group.

Ray, Katie Wood. 2006. *Study Driven: A Framework for Planning Units of Study in the Writing Workshop*. Portsmouth, NH: Heinemann.

Ritchhart, Ron. 2015. *Creating Cultures of Thinking: The 8 Forces We Must Master to Truly Transform Our Schools*. San Francisco: Jossey-Bass.

Ritchhart, Ron, Mark Church, and Karin Morrison. 2011. *Making Thinking Visible: How to Promote Engagement, Understanding and Independence for All Learners*. San Francisco: Jossey-Bass.

Roth, Michael S. 2014. "Young Minds in Critical Condition." *The New York Times Sunday Review*, May 11: 5.

Sanders, T. Irene. n.d. "From Forecasting to Foresight: A Complex Systems View of the Future." Washington, DC: Washington Center for Complexity and Public Policy. www.complexsys.org/downloads/essenceofforesight.pdf.

———. 2003. "What Is Complexity?" Washington, DC: Washington Center for Complexity and Public Policy. www.complexsys.org/downloads/whatiscomplexity.pdf.

Santelises, Sonja, and Joan Dabrowksi. 2015. *Checking In: Do Classroom Assignments Reflect Today's Higher Standards?* Equity in Motion series. Washington, DC: Education Trust. http://edtrust.org/wp-content/uploads/2014/09/CheckingIn_TheEducationTrust_Sept20152.pdf.

Sartre, Jean Paul. 1949. *What Is Literature?* New York: Philosophical Library.

Saunders, George. 2005. "The New Mecca." *GQ*, October 31. www.gq.com/story/george
-saunders-on-dubai.

Shanahan, Timothy. 2013. "Why Discussions of Close Reading Sound Like Nails Scratching
on a Chalkboard." *Shanahan on Literacy* (blog), March 24. www.shanahanonliteracy
.com/2013/03/why-discussions-of-close-reading-sounds_2091.html.

———. 2016. "Should I Set Reading Purposes for My Students?" *Shanahan on Literacy* (blog),
April 24. www.shanahanonliteracy.com/2016/04/should-i-set-reading-purposes-for
-my.html.

Solnit, Rebecca. 2013. *The Faraway Nearby.* New York: Viking Penguin.

Sontag, Susan. 1995. "The Art of Fiction No. 143." Interview by Edward Hirsch. *The Paris
Review* 137 (Winter). www.theparisreview.org/interviews/1505/the-art-of-fiction-no
-143-susan-sontag.

Sousa, David A. 2011. *How the Brain Learns.* Thousand Oaks, CA: Corwin.

Stefanou, Candice, Kathleen Perencevich, Matthew DiCintio, and Julianne Turner. 2004.
"Supporting Autonomy in the Classroom: Ways Teachers Encourage Student Decision
Making and Ownership." *Educational Psychologist* 39 (2): 97–110.

Sternberg, Robert J., and Wendy M. Williams. 1996. *How to Develop Student Creativity.*
Alexandria, VA: Association for Supervision and Curriculum Development.

Thompson, Terry. 2010. "Are You Scaffolding or Rescuing?" Choice Literacy. www.choice
literacy.com/articles-detail-view.php?id=735.

Tierney, John. 2013. "The Coming Revolution in Public Education." *The Atlantic*, April 25.

Wagner, Tony, and Ted Dintersmith. 2015. *Most Likely to Succeed: Preparing Our Kids for the
Innovation Era.* New York: Scribner.

White, Zoë Ryder. 2015. "Joy, Choice, and Authenticity: A Conversation with Simone
Dinnerstein, Jeremy Greensmith, and Adrian Greensmith." In *The Teacher You Want
to Be: Essays About Children, Learning, and Teaching*, edited by Matt Glover and
Ellin Oliver Keene, 108–23. Portsmouth, NH: Heinemann.

Wiggins, Grant. 2015. "On Transfer as the Goal in Literacy." *Granted, and . . .* (blog), April 20.
https://grantwiggins.wordpress.com/2015/04/20/on-transfer-as-the-goal-in-literacy
-7th-in-a-series/.

Wiliam, Dylan. 2011. *Embedded Formative Assessment.* Bloomington, IN: Solution Tree.

———. 2014. "Is the Feedback You're Giving Students Helping or Hindering?" *Dylan Wiliam
Center Blog*, November 29. www.dylanwiliamcenter.com/is-the-feedback-you-are
-giving-students-helping-or-hindering/.

Williams, Joseph J., and Tania Lombrozo. 2010. "The Role of Explanation in Discovery and
Generalization: Evidence from Category Learning." *Cognitive Science* 34: 776–806.

Willingham, Daniel. 2007. "Critical Thinking: Why Is It So Hard to Teach?" *American Educator* (Summer): 8–19.

Willis, Judy. 2014. "The Neuroscience Behind Stress and Learning." *Edutopia*, July 18. www.edutopia.org/blog/neuroscience-behind-stress-and-learning-judy-willis.

Yates, Daisy. 2014. "Curiosity Prepares the Brain for Better Learning." *Scientific American*, October 2. www.scientificamerican.com/article/curiosity-prepares-the-brain-for -better-learning/.

Youth Communication. 1998. *"The Price of War."* In *Things Get Hectic: Teens Write About Violence That Surrounds Them*, edited by Philip Kay, Andrea Estepa, and Al Desetta, 261–62. New York: Touchstone.